The European Council

Gatekeeper of the European Community

Mary Troy Johnston

Westview Press
BOULDER • SAN FRANCISCO • OXFORD

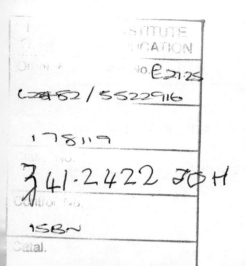
This Westview softcover edition is printed on acid-free paper and bound in library-quality, coated covers that carry the highest rating of the National Association of State Textbook Administrators, in consultation with the Association of American Publishers and the Book Manufacturers' Institute.

Copyright © 1994 by Westview Press, Inc.

Published in 1994 in the United States of America by Westview Press, Inc., 5500 Central Avenue, Boulder, Colorado 80301-2877, and in the United Kingdom by Westview Press, 36 Lonsdale Road, Summertown, Oxford OX2 7EW

Library of Congress Cataloging-in-Publication Data
Johnston, Mary Troy.
  The European Council : Gatekeeper of the European Community / by
  Mary Troy Johnston.
    p. cm.
  Includes index.
  ISBN 0-8133-8505-9
  1. European Economic Community.   European Council.   2. European
federation.   I. Title.
JN15.J64   1994
321'.04'094—dc20   93-29167
                                                                          CIP

Printed and bound in the United States of America

The paper used in this publication meets the requirements
of the American National Standard for Permanence of Paper
for Printed Library Materials Z39.48-1984.

10   9   8   7   6   5   4   3   2   1

The European Council

Contents

Preface		vi
List of Acronyms		ix
Introduction		xv
1	Summitry and Legitimacy	1
2	Politics and Axle Weights	20
3	Bureaucrats, Eurocrats, and National Politicians	54
4	The Delors Plan and Technical Decisionmaking	75
5	The Train of History	100
6	When Politicians Become Eurocrats and Eurocrats Become Politicians	129
	Appendix: European Council Meetings	148
Bibliography		151
Index		164

Preface

U.S. scholars responded to the first decade of the European Economic Community, as it was then called, with fascination that yielded volumes of advanced theories on the processes of supranational integration. During the 1970s, the Community's decisionmaking crisis disappointed observers and seemed to require little scholarly attention in the United States. At the time I began researching the European Council in 1987, the academic community here reawakened to a European Community (EC) transformed especially in the complexity of its institutional dynamics. The expectations of previous decades regarding EC institutional patterns of behavior were no longer sufficient. The need for new and revised theories was widely stated. I was convinced that the need was as great for careful empirical evaluation to inform theory building, the main consideration that influenced my research.

This work represents my contribution to developing a new understanding of the EC, an understanding already well-advanced by the excellent recent works of U.S. scholars. Among European scholars, some devoted several decades to this subject and others drew from their own experience in service to the EC to add to our knowledge. On my particular subject, I was fortunate to be able to rely on the solid documentation of Simon Bulmer's and Wolfgang Wessels' *The European Council: Decision-Making in European Politics* (1987). I am grateful to the authors for establishing beyond a doubt the significance of this institution. Jan Werts' published legal dissertation, *The European Council* (1992), is outstanding for its scope and research. Regrettably, it only came to my attention after my manuscript was complete.

The analysis I offer here reflects a markedly positive view of the European Council and was influenced by the time frame during which I conducted my research. I arrived in Brussels for the first interviews in 1987. The EC institutions were involved in the preliminary negotiations necessary to prepare the Copenhagen European Council of December 1987. The "Delors Plan," the subject of Chapter Four was the sole agenda item at Copenhagen. Especially interesting for my purposes was the technical complexity of the Delors Plan. In the past it was generally understood that heads of government should not be asked to deal with technicalities because they lacked the expertise as well as the time to adequately comprehend and decide such issues. Its success with the Delors Plan suggested that the European Council had greater decisionmaking capacity than previously understood. Additional interviews I conducted in London in 1991, as officials prepared the Maastricht European Council, reinforced this conclusion.

I am grateful for the extremely kind receptions I received in Brussels and in London. Frequently my requests for interviews in Brussels were met with the response that I would be meeting a member country's official in charge of European Council preparations. A question I intended to explore in Brussels was the role of the "Antici," an official who serves as a liaison between national politicians and national delegations of officials during European Council meetings. In Brussels I discovered that the interviewees "in charge of European Council preparations" were Anticis, and I enjoyed the special pleasure of meeting the majority of the Antici group. Consistently, interviewees from the member governments, the Commission, the Council secretariat and the European Parliament generously provided information and assistance.

Financing for the trip to Brussels and income for a year of dissertation research and writing was provided by the Selley Foundation at Tulane University, New Orleans, La., established by Paul and Elizabeth Selley in 1987. I am deeply indebted to the Selleys for their insight into what is required in terms of original research and concentrated effort to produce a quality study. The generosity of Loyola University, New Orleans, La., supplied a travel grant that made possible the research in London in 1991.

During the dissertation stage of this project, it was my great fortune at Tulane to have Dr. William B. Gwyn as my major professor, advisor, and dear friend. I benefited immensely from his mastery of research skills and expertise in cross-national comparisons in Western Europe and institutional behavior. He supported me in all of my pursuits, including my pursuing an academic career while also building a family. At Tulane, Dr. James D. Cochrane and Dr. Henry L. Mason shared their considerable expertise in "regional integration" with me. In addition to those mentioned above, I am grateful to Dr. James F. Davidson for encouraging my scholarly development. As for friendships cemented during this period, Dr. Elba De Lugo and I braved graduate school together.

In 1988 I accepted a teaching position at Loyola University in the department of political science. The members of this department could not have been more supportive and helpful. For advice about computers and elite interviewing, I am grateful to Dr. Conrad Raabe. For their attention to the manuscript, I owe special appreciation to our department chairperson, Dr. Phil Dynia, and members Dr. Stan Makielski and Dr. Eric Gorham. Phil demonstrated over and over again his commitment to my success. Stan gave almost daily assistance that included editing the entire manuscript, his sweeping intellect and personal goodness always in evidence. Only if I continued his tradition of dedicated service to students and colleagues would Stan find satisfaction in repayment of his contribution. My student Michael Starke enthusiastically assisted me with research. Loyola colleagues Dr. William Barnett, Dr. Chris Lingle, and Dr. Bernard Cook graciously read all or parts of the manuscript and added their particular expertise, as did the Italian Consul in New Orleans, Dr. Fabrizio Mazza.

For document production I wholeheartedly appreciate the efforts of Jenny Rubick. If not for Jenny, my work would have been extended many months and made much harder for the lack of comic relief. At Westview Press, Alison Auch was most considerate and competent as the assistant acquisitions editor. The law firm of Sullivan, Stolier and Daigle of New Orleans, was exceedingly kind to provide computer services. Aware of the valuable contributions of so many, I alone am responsible for the final product and all of the conclusions and information within.

I become more grateful to my parents each day as I experience parenting, but am now especially mindful of their concern for my education. Martha Vessell remarkably kept things running smoothly at home. I thank her for the smiling faces on my two children whenever I walked through the door and to the children, Troy and Brigitte, for rewarding me so. My late father-in-law provided the best company in the world during both interview trips abroad. His encouragement was sorely missed as I completed the book.

Despite the efforts of all those I have mentioned and my own efforts, this book could never have been accomplished without the unwavering confidence, delightful sense of humor, and sacrifice of his own time by my husband, Chris, a model partner in a two-career family. I thank him for the secure home front from which I launched my academic career and dedicate this book to him.

Mary Troy Johnston

Acronyms

CAP   **Common Agricultural Policy**

One of the major commitments of the Treaty of Rome, the CAP was France's strategy to ensure agricultural self-sufficiency. Under the CAP, decisionmakers agree common prices for categories of EC agriculture, trade policies in farm products and other related issues, with the effect that the Community is now responsible for the majority of member countries' legislation in this sector.

COREPER   **Committee of Permanent Representatives**

Member countries' permanent representatives, also called Ambassadors, reside in Brussels. They are responsible for following Community negotiations and reporting back to national governments. As COREPER they meet in advance of foreign ministers to conduct preliminary negotiations and make decisions on issues that can be resolved at the official level. The 1965 Merger Treaty formally recognized the existence of COREPER.

CSCE   **Conference on Security and Co-operation in Europe**

To improve relations in Cold War Europe, the CSCE process of dialogue and consultation began in 1972. An important result of this process, the Helsinki Final Act of 1975 was most significant for its human rights contents. With the end of the Cold War, further institutionalization of the CSCE increased its importance as a regional multi-purpose organization. Its fifty-two current members include European countries, Canada, the United States, and the new states of the former Soviet Union.

EBRD   **European Bank for Reconstruction and Development**

Founded in 1990, the EBRD assists the democratic transition and conversion to market economies in the countries of Eastern and Central Europe, with special emphasis on developing private enterprise. The United States, Canada, Japan, and the EC countries are major shareholders. Mr. Jacques Attali of France is the bank's first president.

ECSC   **European Coal and Steel Community**

Founded by the Paris Treaty of 1951, the ECSC created a common market in coal and steel. The brainchild of Jean Monnet, the ECSC became the model for more experiments in European integration, especially in its supranational institutions. The six members of the ECSC, Belgium, Netherlands, Luxembourg, Italy, France, and Germany, went on to found Euratom in 1958 and the EEC in 1959. All three communities merged under one set of institutions in 1967.

ECU   **European Currency Unit**

EC currencies, weighted according to GDP and trade volume, supply the value of the ECU. Originating with the EMS, the ECU is an accounting unit for all of the financial operations of the Community. Its use now extends to transactions between EC central banks and has recently spread to a number of banks in Eastern and Central Europe.

EFTA   **European Free Trade Association**

Established in 1960 under British influence as a counter-organization to the EEC, EFTA did not have the supranational-political ambitions of its rival but was likewise committed to free trade among its members. Britain, Denmark, and Portugal left EFTA to join the EEC. Four current members of EFTA, Austria, Sweden, Finland, and Norway, have applied to join the EC, as it was later called. Remaining members are Switzerland, Liechtenstein, Norway, and Iceland. A special relationship between EFTA and the EC exists in the "European Economic Area," this agreement concluded in 1992.

EMS　　　　　**European Monetary System**

On the initiative of German Chancellor Helmut Schmidt and French President Giscard d'Estaing, the EMS was launched in 1979 as a consultative process designed to promote stable exchange rates in the EC. The main operational mechanism for accomplishing monetary stability was the ERM. While a member of the EMS, Britain controversially refrained from joining the ERM until 1990 and subsequently suspended its ERM membership, along with Italy, during the currency crisis of September 1992.

EMU　　　　　**European Economic and Monetary Union**

Aspirations for EMU date to the early 1970s and moved to the Community's center stage with the 1988 committee to study monetary union headed by Commission President Jacques Delors. Subsequently, the Intergovernmental Conference on Economic and Monetary Union met throughout 1991 to make proposals to be included in a new treaty amending the Community's constitutional documents Provisions on EMU found their way into the Maastricht Treaty of December 1991, and committed to three stages of monetary union. The final stage, Stage III, envisioned the introduction of a single currency and the establishment of an EC central bank, with the condition that participating countries had to have achieved "economic convergence" based on strict economic performance criteria.

EPC   **European Political Cooperation**

EC cooperation in foreign policy making, EPC began as a process of informal consultations in the early 1970s. EPC has now evolved a complex institutional structure and extended its scope to security issues. Consensus-based and entirely dependent on national decisionmakers, EPC does not yet have the supranational features of EC decisionmaking but is an important Community activity.

ERM   **Exchange Rate Mechanism**

Financial authorities of EC member countries, central bankers, and representatives from Finance Ministries consult with each other through the ERM. They determine the values of national currencies in ECUs, permissible ranges of currency fluctuations, revaluations, and devaluations, and have the capacity to take stabilization measures in the currency markets.

Euratom   **European Atomic Energy Community**

One of the early experiments in European integration, Euratom was founded in 1958 to encourage nuclear research and development and enable European countries to have a nuclear role. After Euratom's merger with the EEC and ECSC, Community institutions now concern themselves with issues such as reactor safety and support for nuclear industries.

GATT   **General Agreement on Tariffs and Trade**

An international organization founded in 1948, the GATT is committed to global trade liberalization. Highly technical trade agreements are produced through major negotiations, seven of which have taken place, including the Uruguay Round begun in 1986. As of 1992, 105 countries had acceded to the GATT.

G-7   **The Group of Seven**

An informal organization which concerns itself mainly
with global economic issues, the G-7 includes Canada,
Japan, the United States, Germany, Italy, France, and
Britain. Since 1974 it has met once a year at the
highest political level, in summits of heads of
government advised by their financial authorities.
Trade and monetary policies mainly form the basis of
their discussions.

IGC   **Intergovernmental Conference**

A Community tradition, intergovernmental conferences,
so-called because of their consensual and non-binding
qualities, take place to contribute to drafting major
treaties. Two intergovernmental conferences, one on
Political Union and one on European Economic and
Monetary Union, met throughout 1991 to prepare
proposals eventually included in the Maastricht
Treaty on European Union of December 1991.

NATO   **North Atlantic Treaty Organization**

The North Atlantic Treaty, signed in 1949, led to the
organizational development of the defense alliance
that conducted Western Europe's military policy during
the Cold War. Unprecedented in the sophistication of
military cooperation, NATO's integrated command
continued to be relevant in the post-Cold War era.
Presently, NATO is redefining its role both militarily
and politically. NATO members are Belgium, Canada,
Denmark, France, Germany, Greece, Italy, Luxembourg,
Netherlands, Norway, Portugal, Turkey, Britain, and
the United States.

PoCo   **Political Committee**

A main structure of the Community's EPC process, PoCo
is formed of a political director from each member
country's Foreign Ministry. Political directors are
constantly in contact with each other and meet to

prepare preliminary texts on issues of foreign policy and security in advance of a meeting of the Community's foreign ministers.

SEA **Single European Act**

Also known as the Single Act, the SEA amended the constitutional documents of the Community in 1987. Credited with revitalizing the Community, the Single Act made institutional reforms, committed the member governments to completing the internal market, known as project 1992, and extended the scope of the Community in research and development, the environment, and, more controversially, on social issues.

UN **United Nations**

Founded by the United Nations Charter in 1945, the UN was designed not only to respond collectively to threats to peace but to foster the socio-economic conditions for peace. Failing in its collective security mission until recently, the UN developed specialized agencies, regional commissions for economic development, and other bodies with the overall objective of relieving human misery and promoting human rights. As of October 1992, the UN had 179 members.

WEU **Western European Union**

Founded by the Brussels Treaty of 1948, this moribund organization was revived during the mid-1980s by the members of the EC interested in more cooperation on security issues. An upgraded WEU was presented as a development to strengthen the European pillar of NATO. Current members are Belgium, France, Germany, Greece, Italy, Luxembourg, Netherlands, Portugal, Spain, and Britain. Headquarters of the organization have been moved from London to Brussels. The precise relationship between the EC and the WEU is still undetermined.

Introduction

Almost seventeen years after the institutions of the Treaty of Rome set up operations as the European Economic Community, a little noticed event occurred. In December 1974, heads of government announced their intentions to meet regularly on Community affairs and called themselves the European Council. At Maastricht, The Netherlands, in December 1991, the same body made history, unveiling a treaty for the Political Union of Europe. Public doubts over the Maastricht plans to add more federal elements to the EC heightened the Council role to an even greater extent. Attempting to recover Community legitimacy in December 1992, the Edinburgh Summit responded to citizens' concerns. The Community's highest politicians made decisions about setting more realistic EC financing objectives during the economic downturn. They considered as well decentralizing and democratizing EC decision-making while better informing the public about Community activities and processes.

Already the utmost authority on difficult sovereignty issues, constitutional matters, financing, enlargement, foreign policy and other political subjects, heads of government now expand their role into new territory. Clearly, they see themselves as the most important link between the Community and national constituents, recently accepting more responsibility for socializing citizens in the values and culture of the Community.

Now almost two decades old and essential to the present-day Community, the European Council, despite its standing as an extra-Treaty institution, has undergone remarkable institutionalization. However, questions about its legitimacy and proper function in relation to previously existing EC institutions still crop up.

This work considers the extent to which the Council has become institutionalized and its impact on the Community. To what extent has it established predictable patterns of behavior (*i.e.*, processes of functioning)? Has it demonstrated adaptability, multiplying its functions and, as a result, its relevance to the Community? Does it function well or badly and in a manner supportive of or detrimental to integration?

This study focuses on institutionalization in a variety of ways. Chapter One presents the history of the transformation of the summit into the European Council. In addition, it fits this development into the international and national political contexts of the time and various perspectives on integration. Chapter Two considers the patterns of interaction between the European Council and the so-called "normal" institutions that originated in the Treaty of Rome. This interaction is especially important as integrationists suspected developments of an extra-Treaty nature of diminishing supranationalism. Thus, whether the European Council is an integrative or disintegrative innovation is the main question this chapter initiates and one subsequent chapters continue to pursue. Chapter Three describes the meetings of heads of government and the usefulness of the organized negotiating arenas and informal contacts these provide for decisionmaking and consultation. Chapter Four's emphasis on decisionmaking shifts the focus to the functions of this institution. Both complex and politically challenging negotiations and comparable in terms of issue content, the British budget dispute (1980-1984) and the Delors Plan (1987-1988) demonstrate the evolution of European Council decisionmaking. Chapter Five considers the political, organizational, and legal preparations for the increased involvement of heads of government in a more influential EC international and regional role. The considerable limits that impose themselves on this expanding function also receive attention. Chapter Six at last considers the significance of the European Council in the EC institutional scheme and whether it has favorably enhanced the stability, policy competences, and capacities of the EC system.

At this point, brief descriptions of the central institutions of the EC system may be helpful to the reader. Among the Treaty institutions, the Council of Ministers has the main responsibility for decision-making. It is actually multiple councils of ministers. Among the "technical councils," there exists the economic and finance Council (Ecofin), so-called because either economics or finance ministers from member governments participate. Other specialized councils include fisheries, environment, agriculture, research, transportation, and industry. National ministers who possess the appropriate portfolios attend these meetings. Convening most frequently, usually several times a month (whereas less significant councils may meet only once every several months), is the council of foreign ministers. Also called the general affairs council and the foreign affairs council, it is authoritative not only because of the prestigious position of foreign ministers in their governments but also owing to special functions it has evolved. The title of "general affairs" suggests its responsibility for coordinating the work of lesser councils and also for making decisions when, usually for political reasons, they cannot be made below. "Foreign affairs" suggests the competence this council attained in European political cooperation (EPC), the separate decisional process for foreign policy and, more recently, security matters. Eventually it seems EPC may expand its focus in security matters, in which case the participation of defense ministers could conceivably be required. With the exception of EPC, the Council of Ministers may make a decision only when it has a proposal of the Commission before it. Permanent Representatives of the member governments in Brussels are responsible for preliminary negotiations in advance of council meetings. In support of ministerial decisionmaking, the Committee of Permanent Representatives (COREPER) is the top of a dense layer of national officials, which also comprises over a hundred working groups of experts meeting on both permanent and ad hoc bases. Like the European Council, COREPER initially evolved as an extra-Treaty invention.

As for the Commission, France, Germany, Italy, Britain, and Spain each send two persons to this seventeen-member college, whereas smaller member countries each send one. National governments put forth their choices of Commissioners, which the European Council almost always ratifies. According to the mandate of the Treaty, Commissioners represent the Community and refuse to be agents of national interests. Modeling the role of national ministers in relation to their departments, individual commissioners preside over directorates-general (DGs), the bureaucracy that generates proposals and supervises policy implementation. As for implementation, the Commission largely depends on member states' more abundant resources and ability to micro-manage. The Commission seems to be misunderstood by the public as powerful only in its role as a bureaucracy. In reality its political powers are considerable and growing. The major Treaty-based supranational and political powers of the Commission include the exclusive right of policy initiation in Community matters and enforcement of EC treaties. In the latter instance, the Commission may initiate proceedings at the European Court of Justice against a member government suspected of failing to carry out its Treaty obligations.

Previously formally limited to the role of observer in EPC, the Commission, as a result of Maastricht, will submit proposals along with member governments in this sector. In anticipation of Maastricht's ratification and the Community's expanded international responsibilities, the 1993 reorganization of the Commission divided the former external relations DG into two new DGs, one for foreign and security matters and the other for external economic affairs. A further indication of its increasing international clout, the Commission has since 1972 enjoyed a mandate to negotiate for the entire Community in GATT.

Despite possessing important budget powers and the ability to dismiss the Commission, the European Parliament was long restricted to only a consultative role in decisionmaking. Once heads of government consented to direct elections for the European Parliament (the first elections held in 1979), parliament's claim that it was the most democratic of the Community institutions carried new weight. Elections, therefore, justified new powers of decision which came with the Single Act in 1987. As a result, parliament became a participant in an amendment procedure which applies to select issues. Maastricht extended parliament's scrutiny to the main issues of EPC. After the 1994 European elections, there will be 49 additional members of the European Parliament (MEPs), bringing the new total to 567, to accommodate a unified Germany and other countries' requests for additional seats.

Realizing that the Treaty of Rome represented a compromise between intergovernmentalism and supranationalism, integrationists looked to the Community's evolution to fulfill their goals. If the Community evolved favorably, according to integrationists, the Commission would become a European administrative and political executive accountable to a fully functional, democratically elected European Parliament. The influence of national decisionmakers in the Council would have receded. These expectations, already disappointed, met the arrival of the European Council.

1

Summitry and Legitimacy

The European Council emerged as the *de facto* highest level decisionmaker in the European Community (EC) without a legal foundation for this role. An extra-Treaty innovation, the European Council was created by the people who would comprise it. At the Paris Summit of December 1974, EC heads of government announced the existence of the new body in which they would participate along with their foreign ministers and two representatives of the Commission. The European Council intended to meet routinely and consider EC affairs and political cooperation.[1] French President Giscard d'Estaing stated to the press at the Paris Summit's close, "The European Summit is dead, long live the European Council" and thus contributed the name.[2] Previously, a name had not been agreed precedenting the unplanned manner in which the European Council has developed.

Indeed, the precise functions of the European Council are still not established in the important texts comprising the legal identity of the Community. The Single European Act (SEA), henceforth the Single Act, did not delineate the role of the European Council when it amended the Treaty of Rome in 1987. However brief the mention of the European Council in the Single Act, that it was included assures its continuing existence. Significantly, the Single Act's text on the European Council is separated from that on EC institutions established by the Treaty of Rome. The distinction between the European Council and the original EC institutions, which underlines the former's dubious institutional status, formally survives although blurred in practice.

The institutional arrangements provided by the Treaty of Rome were novel and are, so far, inimitable. The Treaty of Rome's supranationalism towers over the feebler intergovernmental designs of other international and regional organizations. Because the European Council was not present at the Community's creation, it was bound to wage an uphill struggle for legitimacy. To institutional purists, the European Council did not deserve to exist because it was not in the Treaty of Rome. To members of potentially rival institutions, it would upset a delicate institutional balance by shifting influence away from the supranational institutions, the Commission and the European Parliament. In turn, the already influential intergovernmental side, the Council of Ministers' structure, would be strengthened.[3]

So much concern for protecting the content and spirit of Treaty arrangements flows from federalism's influence in the development of the Community. Federalism emphasizes an essential relationship between constitutional design and integration, the equivalent of a belief that integration can be constitutionally mandated. Thus, periodically the EC carries out institutional reforms to bring about more integration. The extra-Treaty nature of the European Council conflicts with federalism's more legalistic tradition of institutional development and deprives this institution of integrative credentials.

The controversy over treaty tampering began with de Gaulle's proposal of summitry and continues to affect perceptions of the European Council. This chapter reviews the history of summits, as meeting of Community heads of government were first called. The original factors leading to the creation of the European Council and the earliest conceptions of the role of heads of government in the EC are considered below.

Summitry: Internal and External Implications

Meetings of EC heads of government date from the Paris Summit of February 10-11, 1961. Not only was the setting of this first summit Paris, but its purpose was to explore French President de Gaulle's special project for political cooperation. From this occasion onward, summitry would have a close association with the French and, in particular, French presidents personally interested in summitry's advantages for EEC member countries.[4] Three French presidents in succession would initiate calls for summits during the 1960s and early 1970s. After Pompidou failed in a similar attempt, his successor, Giscard d'Estaing would ultimately succeed in almost singlehandedly founding the European Council.

From the beginning of the 1960s until de Gaulle retired from the presidency in 1969, the French had a notorious reputation for being anti-integrationist, which has only been rivaled recently by the British under Mrs. Thatcher.[5] If de Gaulle had benignly proposed summitry, other member countries would have questioned his motives. Because de Gaulle proposed summitry as a vehicle for circumventing the institutional arrangements of the Treaty of Rome, member countries, especially the Benelux countries, were strongly opposed.

The purpose of the first meeting of the EEC heads of government in Paris in 1961 was to discuss de Gaulle's ideas on political union. Economic integration had been launched within the EEC context, but agreeing an acceptable framework for political cooperation remained problematic. In 1954 the Gaullists had helped defeat the proposal for a European Defense Community, and its accompanying plan for a European Political Union, in the French National Assembly. This defeat postponed indefinitely the ambition to bring "high politics" within the domain of the supranational institutions. De Gaulle's strategy was to dispense with the EEC framework altogether and create a separate intergovernmental framework in which to house political cooperation. In his plan for the political union, de Gaulle desired routine summits of heads of government from the member states, an institutional feature unknown to the EEC.

Jean Dondelinger, author of the first study of the European Council, considers why heads of government are absent from the EEC framework.[6] He observes that the Treaty of Paris establishing the European Coal and Steel Community (ECSC) and, to a lesser extent, the EEC's Treaty of Rome, presupposed a "certain effacement of the member states before the Community institutions."[7] The founders might have reasoned that these institutions could have more difficulty establishing their authority if they had to do so in direct dealings with heads of government.

Certainly, the example set by de Gaulle gave credibility to those who believed that heads of government would tend to intimidate fledgling institutions and undermine their authority. De Gaulle's "confederal" view of the Community held that EEC institutions exercised authority only as the result of a revocable grant from the member countries; this grant did not extend to subjects which affected the vital interests of the member countries. Indeed, de Gaulle interpreted his duties under the Fifth Republic constitution as personally acting for France in vital foreign policy matters. This is how the claim of the president's constitutional "reserved domain" in foreign policy came to be made by de Gaulle's successors and explains his personal predilection for summitry in connection with political union.

At their first summit in Paris, EEC heads of government agreed to explore the question of finding a framework for political cooperation.[8] They charged a committee with the task of drafting proposals for a political union and instructed it to report back to the heads of government. This committee was known as the Fouchet Committee after its chairman Christian Fouchet. Another summit in Bonn, July 18, 1961, held for the purpose of reviewing the proposals of the Fouchet Committee, did not meet with success. Important differences surfaced among the EEC member countries which made it impossible to operationalize political cooperation until approximately a decade had passed.

The Benelux countries and Italy did not want the EEC reduced to a sideshow by the creation of a completely separate political union. Loyal to the supranational integration being pursued in the EEC framework, these countries supported expanding its policy competences and strengthening its institutions. They also suspected that the French and Germans would have too much power in the proposed political union. The organizational and procedural arrangements of the EEC seemed to offer the best protection for small country interests. The Benelux countries and Italy continue to take similar positions at significant junctures in the Community's development, naturally falling behind proposals amplifying its supranational character. Furthermore, these countries are prone to suspect Franco-German cooperation of being exclusionist or marginalizing less politically powerful member countries.

With the differences over the political union, a rift opened ominously between the four integrationist members and de Gaulle, who favored intergovernmental cooperation. The embittered atmosphere made the member countries susceptible to further arguments, such as that over British entry and the "empty chair crisis." Especially the latter was related to the intergovernmental-supranational division in the Community. France's refusal to participate in the Community institutions for six months was precipitated by de Gaulle's objection to the supranational content of a Commission proposal. This proposal linked implementing the Common Agricultural Policy (CAP) to awarding new budgetary powers to the European Parliament, an institution favored by integrationists. As the Treaty of Rome committed the member countries to effecting the CAP, France maintained that the Commission proposal was devious in setting conditions on fulfilling what were after all Treaty obligations. The French were only brought back into the Community by the other member countries' acceptance of the Luxembourg Compromise in January 1966. The Luxembourg Compromise provided that a member country could declare a vital national interest at stake in the Council of Ministers and insist on discussion continuing until a consensus was found. Its practical effect was that majority voting did not become the practice of the Council of Ministers in 1966, as it should have according to the Treaty of Rome. Integrationists condemned the Luxembourg Compromise as a critical derailment in Community development that permitted the predominance of intergovernmentalism in the functioning of the

Community throughout the 1970s, until the Single Act renewed majority voting in specific sectors.

Profound differences in member countries' conceptions of European integration produced ill feelings and stalemates on essential issues in the 1960s. EEC heads of government did not meet again for more than six years after their unproductive summit in Bonn in 1961. When they met in May 1967, their purpose was to celebrate the tenth anniversary of the finalization of the Treaty of Rome. At this summit, heads of government were still conscious of the need to agree a means of political cooperation. Choosing words cautiously, they consented "to study the possibility of gradually tightening their political links through methods and procedures relevant to experience and circumstances."[9] Resentment over de Gaulle's power plays did not dissipate easily. The impasse persisted as other member countries and the Commission refused to satisfy France's policy concerns.

Pompidou followed de Gaulle in the French Presidency in 1969 and was personally interested in fashioning a new French EC policy.[10] He announced his desire to meet other Community political leaders during the presidential election. Once Pompidou was president, the French took the initiative in arranging a summit. Pre-summit preparations included Pompidou's consulting with German Chancellor Kurt Kiesinger in Bonn in September 1969.[11] France's initiating summitry and then looking to Germany for confirmation had also preceded the first summit in Paris in 1961.[12]

The summit at The Hague, December 1969, maintained continuity with past summits by including political cooperation in the agenda. In several respects, it provided a precedent for future summits and European Councils. The heads of government were as much concerned with the internal as the external dimension of the Community, if not more so. Furthermore, their political agreements removed stumbling blocks that had delayed decisionmaking on important issues.

The summit agenda was exhaustive owing to the multiple linkages participants intended to pursue. The French theme for the summit was the Community's "completion," "deepening," and "widening," in that order of priority.[13] Completion signified attending to unfinished tasks, to which the Treaty of Rome obligated member countries. Deepening referred to expanding the policy scope of the Community. Widening indicated clearing Community membership for Britain and other members of the European Free Trade Association (EFTA), the organization Britain defensively launched when it chose, initially, not to join the EEC.

Above all, France sought completion. The aim was to permanently ground the CAP, from which she already handsomely benefitted, and, thus, make sure it would survive intact in an enlarged Community. Considering that the CAP was the costliest of Community policies and potentially not of much benefit to the British, France's strategy was well within reason. The informal agreement the summit produced on giving the EC its "own resources," as envisaged by the Treaty, was the same as the agreement on stable financing for the CAP. Even the summit's support for European Economic and Monetary Union (EMU) under deepening was related to French concerns over the continuation of the CAP. In the lead-up to The Hague, 24 October 1969, Germany had to revalue its currency, which complicated both technically and politically the EC's common pricing of agricultural goods. With the idea of establishing mechanisms to avoid such disruptions to the Common Market and exert more control over regional currency fluctuations, heads of government instructed the Council of Ministers to produce a plan for EMU in 1970.

After The Hague summit, President Pompidou reported on radio and television his satisfaction with France's obtaining

> ... an undertaking from its partners that definitive financial arrangements would be approved within a few weeks, thus ensuring the continuity of the common agricultural market and giving hope to French farmers.[14]

Predictably, the Council of Ministers made the decisions on implementing the Community's own resources in its last session in 1969.

For his part, Pompidou consented at The Hague to new budgetary powers for the European Parliament, giving a token to integrationists. In addition, he dropped the French veto on British entry. The summit communiqué gave "the Community" future responsibility for negotiating the entry of new members, which implied a new power for the Commission as well as the inappropriateness of unilateral decisions on membership.

Integrationists did not fare as well in the summit's work on political cooperation. Setting the deadline of July 1970 to have proposals in hand, heads of government requested the Foreign Ministers "to study the best way of achieving progress in the matter of political unification, within the context of enlargement."[15] Hence, negotiations on political cooperation would parallel those on enlargement, also set to begin in 1970. Anti-federalist Britain would have the opportunity to influence the design of the Community's foreign policy capacity, which, of course, was also in the interest of France. In order to have Britain in the Community, smaller, more integrationist-minded member countries decided the sacrifice was well worth making, as indicated by the following statement of Netherlands Foreign Minister Joseph Luns the month preceding the summit:

> For several years now the Netherlands has considered that should Great Britain join the Common Market it would be necessary to accept in Europe political co-operation more or less reflecting the views outlined in the second Fouchet plan.16

A French-type arrangement for political cooperation was eventually implemented in that it excluded the Commission and provided for no supranational means of decisionmaking. Basically, it entailed EC foreign ministers meeting to sound out each others' opinions and concert foreign policy positions only if everyone agreed. Integrationists were alarmed by this "first step toward setting up machinery specifically excluding the Treaties of Rome from its terms of reference and having no procedure for decisionmaking based on a majority basis."17 Nonetheless, member governments recognized summitry's potential usefulness to Community decisionmaking and the EC's international standing.

Despite previous successes, the path was not smooth to the next summit in Paris, October 1972. U.S. President Nixon in August 1971 announced that dollars could no longer be redeemed for gold and ended the post-War international monetary system. In doing this, the United States absolutely refused any longer to take the major responsibility for international monetary management. Given the new situation of "monetary interdependence," an international solution to this crisis would have been optimal.18 Monetary interdependence had arisen with the increase of international money flows and their potential to distort the effects of national economic policies.

In general, interdependence presents governments with challenges that cannot be answered within their traditional means: that of controlling the impact of external events on the effects of national policies. In the past the national context used to be almost sufficient for policy-making. With external influences now so thoroughly permeating national environments, governments cannot restrict themselves to the national context and hope to insure the intended outcome of their policies. Spero clarifies this point specifically as it applies to the monetary authority of governments:

> The desire for economic control has been a major characteristic of postwar government, and a major tool for that control has been monetary management. Interdependence, however, undermines national monetary tools.19

Monetary issues were a major irritant in West-West relations during the latter years of the 1960s and first years of the 1970s. Some of the positions of the players are worth reviewing here considering that echoes of these arguments and sentiments still ring loudly. Europeans resented a precarious dollar's role as the lead currency in the international economy since these countries had amassed dollars as their principal reserve currency. They were anxious because of U.S. inflation and the erosion of gold reserves in relation to dollars in circulation.[20] A crisis of confidence in the U.S. economy threatened the dollar and especially European economies since they were strongly invested in the dollar. De Gaulle, as early as 1965, adopted a definite response to the problems of the dollar, that of converting France's dollars into gold. Under de Gaulle, France established its activist, aggressive, and nationalistic foreign economic policy style. This style contrasted with the German "diffidence" and British "default" (to U.S. leadership) in international economic matters so aptly characterized by Hayward and Leruez.[21] Therefore, it is no surprise that other European countries did not follow France by cashing in their dollars but, instead, hoped for internal economic reforms in the United States to reduce inflation.[22]

Divisions in West-West relations over exchange rate policy partially resulted from the success of integration. To function to the advantage of all of its members a common market required a stable exchange rate environment. Thus, integration of the EC market meant that maintaining exchange rate stability was a much higher priority of EC governments, especially the French government, than when their economies were autonomous. The U.S. trade deficit and European trade surpluses put upward pressures on European currencies. The United States insisted that Europeans take the measures necessary to bring about a readjustment, including trimming surpluses and revaluing their currencies against the dollar. For their part, Europeans argued for a depreciation of the dollar and domestic efforts to improve the U.S. trading position.

The recovery of European and Japanese economies during the 1960s and their increased participation in an international economy previously dominated by the United States meant that international economic relations needed to be rebalanced. Strong feelings existed on both the European and U.S. sides. The Europeans felt that the United States had unfairly shifted its burden of economic adjustment to them. The United States, neither admitting its own diminished economic status nor the new strength of European economies, continued to insist on the perquisites afforded by its former status. The costs of providing Europe with the nuclear umbrella and forces translated into a sense of entitlement on the part of the United States. Europeans were expected to demonstrate their appreciation by making economic allowances for the United States. The U.S. inability to reconstruct a lasting international monetary regime has been explained in the following striking terms: "... the United States did not have sufficient power to compel others to accept a regime in which only it would have monetary autonomy."[23]

The lines of a U.S. versus a European approach to the problems of the international economy were emerging, enough so that Britain recognized more clearly its interests in Europe:

> The dollar crisis [August 1971] led those in charge of the City's strategy to rethink London's place in the international financial world. Europe, they became convinced, provided the direction for the City's flight forward: London would find a new role as the "financial growth pole" for Europe.[24]

President Pompidou's reaction to the international monetary crisis was to urge the holding of an EC summit in August 1971, but he was unable to convince all of the member countries of its necessity. He acted out of concern that U.S. actions would disrupt plans for EMU. French ambitions for EMU were to strengthen EEC influence on U.S. economic policy decisions with repercussions for Europe and to make the EEC a zone of currency stability. The Germans did not yet share the French preference for this regional solution as indicated by their decision to float the German currency the previous May, this policy opposed by the French.[25]

At the beginning of 1972 the member countries became more amenable to holding a summit. Old disputes resurfaced in the planning of the Paris Summit. The Germans reopened the issue of giving political cooperation a secretariat, and to complicate matters further, the French wanted the secretariat based in Paris. The Benelux countries raised the objection, voiced during discussions of the Fouchet proposals, that the secretariat would be outside EC institutional arrangements and could diminish the authority of the Commission. Preparations presented so many difficulties that Pompidou suggested possibly canceling the summit if differences were not sorted out. As it proved too controversial, the issue of the secretariat was removed from the prospective summit agenda. Clearly, the supranational-intergovernmental division in the Community was still alive but had been subordinated to restoring confidence in the process of European integration. In his opening speech at the Paris Summit of October 1972 Pompidou reminded the others of the "preliminary agreement" to postpone Treaty reform so as not to waste time with constitutional arguments.[26]

   The purpose of the summit was to chart the course of a revitalized and enlarged Community. Even though Britain, Denmark, and Ireland would not formally accede to the Community until the first day of the new year, their heads of government participated in this planning session for the future. The smaller member countries had long awaited British membership. Keen to pry loose the French and German grip on the Community and have other democratic traditions to compete with French presidentialism, they expected Britain to be their champion. In Paris British Prime Minister Edward Heath actively initiated new policy directions for the Community. Furthermore, his approach to the General Agreement on Tariffs and Trade (GATT) demonstrated that he was loyal to Britain's Community relationship over its "special relationship" with the United States. Heath supported the Community's having the responsibility to negotiate on behalf of the member countries in the upcoming GATT round of trade liberalization. More controversially, Heath encouraged the summit to set a deadline for the commencement of the GATT discussions and took the position that the removal of non-tariff barriers be included on the agenda, both of which were against U.S. interests. The summit decided in favor of Heath, with the exception of insisting the United States adhere to a starting date. On this point, Germany proved to be "the more sympathetic partner to the United States," convincing the others not to add to the pressures President Nixon was already experiencing with a "protectionist" Congress.[27]

   The summit produced multiple and far-reaching commitments. Member governments looked forward to turning "the whole complex of the relations of member states into a European Union," before the beginning of the next decade.[28] The summit neither provided a clear conception of unification nor accepted the definition offered by the Commission, which compared the European Union to a government with decisionmaking power and accountability to a directly elected parliament.[29] The "catchall" agenda demonstrated summitry's completely unrestricted province as well as the lack of focus of the Community at this time. It included institutional questions, implementing the EMU and upgrading political cooperation. Furthermore it proposed to extend Community activities into new areas such as regional and social policy, developing relations with the Third World, and science and technology. Regularizing summitry and holding general elections for the European Parliament were both on the agenda but neither succeeded. Despite the genuinely European mood of the participants and the summit's positive symbolism, immediate results were disappointingly few. However, these early objectives definitely served as orienting concepts and guidelines for action in the grand scheme of the Community. This summit's contribution was that it "functioned as a kind of constitutional convention," even though several decades were needed to enact the provisions.[30]

A flurry of ministerial meetings followed the summit. Finance and foreign affairs ministers convened to come up with a detailed anti-inflation and economic recovery program. While the Commission anticipated developing policy "over employment, living and working conditions and worker representation in the function of companies," as a result of the summit pronouncements on social policy, social affairs ministers formed another Council of Ministers. For the most part, all of their work came to naught. The decade dedicated to European Union turned out to be the least productive in the life of the Community.[31]

Impressed with the Paris Summit, Jean Monnet personally began to lobby EC heads of government and other highly placed politicians he knew in an effort to convince them to take political responsibility for the affairs of Europe. For Monnet, Europe's "pre-federal" stage of development translated into its need for greater political authority. A "Provisional European Government" of EC heads of government would be a useful transitional structure.[32]

By the end of 1973 high oil prices had damaged European economies by fueling inflation. After Israel's gains in the October War, Arab states were even more determined to use oil as a weapon to remind the industrialized countries of what interests were at stake in choosing sides in the Middle East. The next summit occurred earlier than anticipated, again on the initiative of President Pompidou. The French president still strived to permanently establish summitry in the Community in the interest of influencing international events. As Pompidou had desired summitry to enhance EC member countries' bargaining power with the United States during the international monetary crisis, his reflex during the oil crisis was the same. EC member countries were more dependent on oil from the Middle East and had more flexibility in their policies toward this region. Therefore, summitry could potentially produce a distinct EC policy response to the oil crisis.

The member countries agreed to hold another summit in Copenhagen in December 1973. In accord with the preferences of the small member countries, the summit participants included for the first time the EC foreign ministers. Having first gained admission to the previous summit in Paris, the Commission president was also present in Copenhagen.[33] The composition of this summit reflected a concern to maintain continuity with the Community institutions, although Pompidou's first preference had been a "fireside chat" restricted to heads of government.[34] The Copenhagen meeting of heads of government was curious because of the unexpected presence of an Arab delegation at the meeting. The member countries had not elaborated beforehand a unified position on the Middle East and the oil crisis, which formed the central focus at Copenhagen. This lack of consensus is not surprising in view of the persistent failure throughout the 1970s to adopt a common position on issues related to the Middle East.[35] It is doubtful whether realistically the member countries should have been expected to present a united front on the oil crisis and Middle East conflict. The gravity of the situation, the entanglements of EC member countries with the United States, and the immatureness of the state of European integration, including the newness of the machinery for political cooperation, made it improbable that EC member countries could have shaped an effective policy response to Middle Eastern events given so little time. Thus, the presence of the Arab observers was unfortunate in so far as a muddled and non-committal response was all the summit had to offer them.

The summit also had to attend to some ongoing business as a result of commitments entered into at the previous summit. For example, the implementation of EMU had been fraught with difficulties, and negotiations on setting up a regional fund had come to a standstill. These issues, like many others in the next years, were complicated by the economic downturn experienced by the member countries and, consequently, their domestic preoccupations. The communiqué issued by the member countries at the end of the summit reflected a concern that progress be made on a variety of issues, but consisted of loose commitments instead of a clear plan of action. The outcome of Copenhagen was ambivalent. Although it failed to offer a clear and determined strategy for solving the serious problems at hand, nonetheless it produced some positive results. The experience of Copenhagen confirmed that member countries "still regarded the EC as an appropriate level for problem-solving" while demonstrating that future summits should be better organized.[36] On the actual future of summitry, at Copenhagen the member countries came closer to accepting summitry as a permanent feature of the EC. The communiqué held that heads of government would meet depending on "circumstances" and when needed "to provide a stimulus or to lay down further guidelines for the construction of a united Europe" and "whenever the international situation so requires."[37]

Much change had taken place to make summitry seem a useful and less threatening innovation since it had been proposed by de Gaulle. As the international environment increasingly impinged on domestic environments during the 1970s, summits became a vehicle for heads of government to become more involved in a foreign affairs role. The foreign policy orientation of heads of government evolved in an effort to manage interdependence.[38] Pompidou's tendency to use summitry as a response to international crises demonstrated an attempt to broaden and use more effectively the domestic warehouse of policy tools.

Pompidou was not alone in feeling the pull of international events. In his memoirs, former British Prime Minister Harold Wilson recalls the internationalization of his role. He records the numerous meetings he attended, between March 1974 and April 1976, that consisted exclusively or predominantly of heads of government. His calculations put the number at fifteen which meant on the average a meeting of this sort every seven weeks.[39]

As part of a general pattern, summitry was more acceptable in the EC context. It appeared less the attempt to subject Community institutions to national control and, especially, to French presidential control. That summitry had become more commonplace further added to its acceptability. De Gaulle's elevated conception of summitry had offended integrationists, involved as they were in the opposite enterprise of trying to elevate the Community institutions.

EC summitry was better prepared to influence international economic relations than other examples of summitry. The EC was well-advanced in setting up policy mechanisms and in establishing the habit of cooperation among its members. Increased appreciation of the EC's appropriateness to international management led heads of government to consider more seriously the role they should take in this organization. Aside from the external dimension, the EC had its own needs that perhaps could be answered by summitry.

As the 1970s progressed, observers watched the deepening of a decisionmaking crisis in the Community. The crisis had become so severe by the mid-1970s that the Community was suffering not only from "butter and beef mountains" but also from a "proposal mountain."[40] The Council of Ministers seemed incapable of taking decisions on a growing backlog of proposals. The increasing complexity of the Council had presented problems of coordination as well. Multiple Councils and the rising involvement of groups of officials through the Committee of Permanent Representatives (COREPER) had led to fragmented decisionmaking. Dondelinger aptly described the result: "The Council had become an institution which spent most of its time negotiating with itself."[41] This institutional weakness was also seen in the Commission. As Commission proposals failed to succeed in the Council, the temptation was to present proposals with a greater chance of success. The Commission was increasingly criticized for giving into the interests of member governments in preparing and amending its proposals and suffered from a lack of influence with the Council.

As early as 1973 Monnet recognized the seriousness of the Community's decisionmaking problems. He assessed the cause of this situation as a combination of the Community institutions' lacking political authority and a procedural failure, in that majority voting had not been implemented in the Council to facilitate decisionmaking. On a more positive note, Monnet observed that the political leaders in the member countries were all "European by conviction or persuasion" as long as their European involvement did not interfere with their own power.[42] Weighing all these factors, Monnet concluded that the involvement of heads of government was needed to unblock decisionmaking.

In 1974 personnel changes in most of the governments of the EC member countries created another factor favorable to regularizing summitry. In the six original member countries, the men who rose to the highest office shared the common experience of having participated in the Council of Ministers.[43] French President Giscard d'Estaing, among the new leaders with practical EC experience, followed his predecessors in encouraging the development of summitry. EC heads of government met briefly in Paris in September 1974 where the subjects broached were wide-ranging as usual. According to Harold Wilson's account, their main subject was "European political union" followed by a discussion on "the growing unemployment problem and related issues of inflation, oil prices and national balances of payments."[44] The coincidence of international and domestic concerns is demonstrated vividly in the subjects covered at this meeting. Also significant at this meeting was that each head of government pledged himself ready to become personally engaged in advancing European cooperation. The atmosphere was propitious for putting summitry on a regular basis even though important details remained to be agreed. The heads of government planned to proceed with a December summit where, among other subjects, the future of summitry would be decided. Letters were sent to the French president in the intervening months on the remaining points. So as to avoid the disorganization of the previous summit in Copenhagen, advance preparations for this summit were intensified.

At the Paris Summit of December 1974, a package deal emerged to accommodate the member countries' concerns over summitry. The Benelux countries, still worried that summitry would detract from the supranational elements of the Community, received several concessions.[45] The most important concession was an agreement that direct elections to the European Parliament would commence in 1978 or afterward, this delay a compromise in itself. Supporters of direct elections aimed to give the Community democratic legitimacy of its own and make the European Parliament a counterweight to member country politicians. Not prone to support the supranational evolution of the Community, Denmark and Britain reserved final decision on this item.

Summitry should not be seen as taking the place of institutional changes preferred by integrationists that also offered advantages for EC decisionmaking. Member countries stated their intention to use more majority voting and give a larger legislative role to the European Parliament. Over a decade later in 1987 the Single Act painstakingly and restrictively delivered on both promises. At any rate in Paris the appearance had been given of a roughly equal exchange between intergovernmental and supranational measures.

Included in the Paris communiqué was the assurance that EC foreign ministers would be present at meetings alongside heads of government and "would act as initiators and co-ordinators."[46] Added assurance was that, in the European Council, the Commission would continue to carry out the functions assigned to it in the legal texts. The communiqué prepared the way for the European Council to take decisions on EC affairs by stating that it could convene "whenever necessary, in the Council of the Communities."[47] The Treaty of Rome required only that government ministers comprise the Council. Heads of government, after all, are the highest government ministers. Therefore, the European Council presumed that it could become legal by forming itself into a Council of Ministers. An objection to this logic is that, technically, the French President is not a head of government. Nonetheless, the suggestion was that in the event the European Council took a decision in a domain belonging to the Council of Ministers, it would submit to Treaty provisions. Undoubtedly, the EC heads of government anticipated an unwelcome reception for the European Council. By linking it to the existing Treaty structure, they sought to present it as a development in full accord with the Treaty of Rome and allay criticism.

Instead of viewing the European Council as "constitutionally" illegitimate in the beginning, it is more correct to view it as having partial legitimacy. For various reasons, it possessed more legitimacy for its foreign affairs role than it did for a Community decisionmaking role. Whether as the result of their constitutional responsibilities or their political positions, most EC heads of government are ultimately responsible for foreign affairs for their governments. The clearest exception is in the Netherlands where the constitution gives the Dutch foreign minister this authority. Effective foreign policy action by the EC could only benefit from the participation of heads of government, especially considering its major ambition to influence the United States. Furthermore, since political cooperation was an added competence, and it had even seemed possible the EC might be prevented from having any association whatsoever with political cooperation, the Treaty institutions did not have a clear mandate in this sector. In its foreign affairs role, the

European Council could be seen as filling a void and possessing the requisite authority to do so.

Its role in internal matters, however, has been more difficult to justify. As the communiqué anticipated, the European Council has fulfilled a decisionmaking role in the Community. In this, it has not subscribed to the rules and procedures which govern Council decisionmaking. Even though the communiqué had devised a way for the European Council to behave as a proper Treaty institution, it has opted to remain an extra-Treaty and extra-legal innovation. In essence, the European Council defines its own boundaries. The freedom of its role has prompted a continuing controversy.

In summary, the European Council appealed to the nationalistic impulse to make the EC an international power player while giving rise to fears that it would upset the Community's delicate progression toward federalism. No matter how confused its credentials, the European Council has an established position in the EC institutional structure and exerts a significant influence on EC policy content and scope, which the following chapters explore.

Notes

1.   Political cooperation is the EC terminology used for describing the policy mechanisms and aspirations for foreign policy and security cooperation.
2.   As quoted in Annette Morgan, *From Summit to Council: Evolution in the EEC* (London: Chatham House: PEP, 1976), p. 5.
3.   The Council of Ministers' system consists of multiple Councils of Ministers. It has evolved to comprehend meetings of many types of government ministers, environment ministers, transport ministers, economic and finance ministers, and others constituting the category of the Technical Councils. Overarching the Technical Councils is the Council of Foreign Ministers, also known as the General Affairs Council. It is the most authoritative Council of Ministers and the coordinator of the Council system. In the early days of the Community, the foreign ministers took most of the decisions, the only other ministers meeting in the EC context being the finance ministers. The proliferation of the Councils is not the only factor adding to the complexity of the Council of Ministers. Beneath the Council of Ministers, an extra-Treaty body, the Committee of Permanent Representatives (COREPER), became increasingly important throughout the 1960s. Composed of national civil servants stationed in Brussels, COREPER assists the Council of Ministers in sorting out the technical details of Community proposals. Its existence was formally recognized by the Merger Treaty of 1965. Presently, there are two bodies of COREPER which will be discussed in Chapter 2, and a myriad of working groups, permanent and ad hoc, are attached to COREPER.
4.   The European Economic Community (EEC) was the term of reference for the Community until the late-1960s when the Merger Treaty, effective in 1967,

established one Council and one Commission for the EEC, Euratom, and the European Coal and Steel Community (ECSC), heretofore institutionally separate. Furthermore, it became more and more apparent that the scope of the Community had extended beyond economics, indicated by the new reference to it as the European Community (EC). The British popular press and British politicians persisted into the early 1980s in calling it the Common Market to indicate its lack of political significance.

5. What de Gaulle and Mrs. Thatcher shared in common was a lack of attachment to the kind of integration being pursued in the EC, which stresses the continuous build-up of the powers of EC institutions. In his conviction that a strong Europe was necessary to deal with the United States, de Gaulle was a "European" where Mrs. Thatcher was not.

6. Jean Dondelinger's unpublished paper, "Le Conseil Européen," 20 November 1975, is available in the library of the Secretariat of the Council of Ministers, Brussels.

7. Dondelinger, "Les Origines du Conseil Européen: Historique et Motivations," paper presented to Colloque sur "le Conseil européen," Louvain-la-Neuve, 6-7 October 1977, p. 6. (Translated from French by the author).

8. The descriptions of summits up to the Paris Summit of 1974 rely heavily on the already cited work of Morgan and on the work of Simon Bulmer and Wolfang Wessels, *The European Council: Decision-Making in European Politics* (London: The Macmillan Press Limited, 1987), p. 28.

9. Morgan, *From Summit to Council*, p. 11.

10. By this date, the term European Community (EC) had become appropriate. See endnote 4.

11. *Ibid.*, p. 12.

12. Bulmer and Wessels, *The European Council*, p. 28.

13. Former Commissioner Robert Lemaignen maintained that "since [the Commission] has been put into force, this effective mechanism has been attacked in a more or less underhand way by the Governments." He mistrusted the summit objectives of heads of government. "Completion (*achievement),*" he mused, "is a word with two meanings: you can *achever* (finish off) an enemy." As quoted in *Bulletin of the EC*, 1 (1970), p. 122.

14. *Bulletin of the EC*, 2 (1970), p. 141.

15. "Communiqué of The Hague Summit," *Bulletin of the EC*, 1 (1970), pp. 11-15. The chronology of the summit's communiqué seems to reflect the ordering of priorities stated by the French.

16. As quoted in *Bulletin of the EC*, 1 (1970), p. 121.

17. Morgan, *From Summit to Council*, p. 14.

18. Joan Spero identifies the elements of "monetary interdependence" as the "internationalization of banking and production (via multinational coporations) and the rise of a Eurocurrency market." See *The Politics of International Economic Relations*, 3rd ed. (New York: St. Martin's Press, Inc., 1985), pp. 48-49.

19. *Ibid.*, p. 50.

20.   See Stephen George's description of the international context of the late 1960s through the early 1970s in *An Awkward Partner: Britain in the European Community* (New York: Oxford University Press, 1990), pp. 42-46.

21.   Jack Hayward and Jacques Leruez, "Nationalism and the economy," in *French and British Foreign Policies in Transition; The Challenge of Adjustment*, eds., Françoise de la Serre, Jacques Leruez and Helen Wallace (New York: Berg Publishers, 1990), p. 68.

22.   I am grateful to Dr. Chris Lingle for pointing out that the most recent arguments between European countries and the United States have concerned the U.S. budget deficit and the impact of relatively high U.S. real interest rates upon foreign exchange rates.

23.   Robert O. Keohane, *International Institutions and State Power* (Boulder, Co.: Westview Press, 1989), p. 92.

24.   Henk Overbeek, *Global Capitalism and Britain's Decline* (Amsterdam, 1988), as quoted in George, *An Awkward Partner*, p. 61.

25.   George, *An Awkward Partner*, p. 55.

26.   *Bulletin of the EC*, 11 (1972), p. 14.

27.   This brief description of the politics of the GATT negotiations in the early Community is owing to George, *An Awkward Partner* , pp. 57-58.

28.   *Bulletin of the EC*, 11 (1972), p. 63.

29.   *Ibid.*

30.   Ross B. Talbot, *The European Community's Regional Fund* (Oxford, 1977), p. 197, as quoted in George, *An Awkward Partner*, p. 57. European Councils continue to be significant to the Community's constitutional development.

31.   Morgan, *From Summit to Council*, p. 16.

32.   Jean Monnet, *Memoirs* (London: Collins, 1978), pp. 503-09.

33.   The Commission was excluded from the first afternoon's discussions on the future of political cooperation.

34.   Bulmer and Wessels, *The European Council*, p. 33.

35.   Despite the emphasis on forming a common energy policy in the 1970s, the member countries were not able to come to agreement on this issue. The immediate need for a common energy policy has declined with conservation measures, restoration of oil supplies, the discovery of new and more reliable sources (*i.e.*, North Sea oil) and eventual worldwide overproduction. Nonetheless, the member countries have made significant advances in shaping a common foreign policy towards the Middle East beginning with the Venice Declaration announced by the European Council in June 1980.

36.   Bulmer and Wessels, *The European Council*, p. 35.

37.   "Communiqué of the Copenhagen Summit," *Bulletin of the EC*, 12 (1973), p 9.

38.   See Bulmer and Wessel's discussion of interdependence as a stimulus to heads of government to operate on an international level in their search for solutions to domestic problems and the particular utility of the EC for solving problems associated with interdependence, *The European Council*, pp. 24-25. See also former British Prime Minister Harold Wilson's discussion of how his own

role became internationalized in *The Governance of Britain*, (London: Weidenfeld and Nicolson and Michael Joseph, 1976) pp. 119-21.

39. Wilson, *The Governance of Britain*, pp. 119-20.

40. Roland Bieber and Michael Palmer, "Power at the top - the EC Council in theory and practice," *World Today*, August 1975, p. 311.

41. Dondelinger, "Les Origines du Conseil Européen," p.14. (Translated from French by the author).

42. Monnet, *Memoirs*, p. 502

43. Dondelinger, "Les Origines du Conseil Européen," p. 14.

44. Wilson, *The Governance of Britain*, pp. 122-23.

45. This description follows Bulmer's and Wessels' discussion of this package deal, *The European Council*, pp. 43-45.

46. *Bulletin of the EC*, 12 (1974), p. 7.

47. *Ibid*.

2

Politics and Axle Weights

The process of decision that culminates in a European Council entails action on multiple EC levels, input from twelve national administrations and numerous informal official and political contacts. The complexity of this decisionmaking process requires that negotiations on European Council matters begin months in advance. The European Council meets for only a day and a half, two times a year in regular session. With the accession of new members, it takes longer to get around the table to hear all of the views of member governments. That a *tour de table* will take approximately two hours restricts the agenda and permits only limited discussion on particular issues.[1]

Careful preliminary preparations and negotiations take place to facilitate the work of the European Council. Ideally, they clear the field of decisions that officials and ministers can take to enable heads of government to concentrate on the central issues. By the time the European Council meets issues should be at the ripening point. Remaining differences should be narrowed to the point where heads of government have only a few political choices to decide. The European Council should have before it proposals that identify possible areas of compromise and guide negotiations. If preliminary negotiations are enough advanced, European Councils will begin with discussions of draft conclusions prepared by officials.

If officials can simplify and condense an issue to the point it fits on a notecard, this is all the better for heads of government who do not have time to be full-time students of EC affairs. When officials do not succeed in sorting out peripheral issues, heads of government tend to feel their time is wasted and that they are doing the job of their officials. Often lacking the thorough knowledge belonging to officials and ministers used to dealing with EC matters, heads of government are usually anxious to avoid technically complex issues.[2] In doubt about the merit or national implications of proposals, heads of government may be tempted to postpone agreement until more evidence exists for a proposal.

Decisionmaking delays in the European Council are especially to be avoided. European Councils negotiate, predominantly, complex and intricately constructed packages that link multiple categories of issues. If the European Council fails to achieve a package deal, the specialized Councils (*e.g.*, the Agricultural Council, the Budget Council, etc.) will inherit the outstanding issues. They must try to resolve the issues that fall under their portfolio before heads of government meet again. In the specialized councils, member countries may continue to insist on particular issue linkages with the effect that progress on individual issues in the package may not be possible until the next European Council. Decisionmaking in other Community institutions, although dependent on the results of a European Council, is not completely dependent. After all, European Councils treat select issues. Even though these issues are significant and often interconnected, they amount to only a portion of the Community's responsibilities. Disagreements in the European Council will make progress on related issues difficult, but decisionmaking and administrative action in other areas will proceed as usual. This was seen as the Community continued to function fairly normally despite Mrs. Thatcher's opposing specific issues in the European Council.

Because European Councils are so newsworthy, journalists will present the results in exaggerated terms. Therefore, decisionmaking failures in the European Council may lead to overblown public perceptions of a Community in crisis. The failure of successive European Councils to resolve the British budget dispute in the early 1980s drew negative press coverage. The images projected were a European Council haggling over petty issues and a stagnating Community.[3] Therefore, it is preferable that the haggling takes place a notch or two below the European Council where negotiations are not exposed to so much publicity.

The conscientiousness of decisionmakers and officials in preparing a European Council suggests they realize its symbolic importance. The European public is more likely to identify with the European Council as the Community's political executive than the rival for this role, the Commission. The electoral accountability of heads of government, even if only through parliaments, assures links with the European public. The Commission suffers from being perceived, incorrectly, as nothing more than a supranational bureaucracy. It has to contend with the criticism that attends all bureaucracies. With the 1989 rebellions against the centralizing bureaucracies of Communist states, the Commission is even more vulnerable in this regard. It must be even more careful not to look ambitious to turn the Community into a superstate over which it hopes to preside. The political dimensions of the Commission's more diversified role and the legitimation of this role by the Community's legal texts are not easily understood and readily accepted by the public. Whereas the Commission's legitimacy is legally based, the European Council's is politically based, which makes the latter a more affective, not to mention a more powerful symbol. As the European Council is better able to generate public expectations about Europe than other Community institutions, officials are intent on seeing that European Councils are public relations successes.

The Technical-Political Overlap of European Council Issues

Despite the extensive preparations directed toward removing technical barriers to agreement, the European Council frequently deals with incredibly complex issues on which national positions are still very far apart. Part of this is owing to the technical-political overlap of many of the issues that reach the European Council. It must be remembered that if an issue is purely technical, it is resolved long before it reaches the European Council.

The European Council in Athens, December 1983, devoted a lot of effort to setting up a system of milk quotas to curb surpluses in dairy products, a subject that has a purely technical appearance and would normally be the responsibility of agricultural ministers. Obviously, however, milk quotas touched on delicate political sensitivities, namely those of the Irish who faced pressures from dairy farmers opposed to production ceilings. The British had their own political stake in the matter, Mrs. Thatcher having promised the British parliament to put mechanisms in place to control agricultural spending. Like many agricultural questions, budgetary questions involve difficult allocative choices, which might push them to the level of heads of government. At the same time, they are quantitatively complicated enough to require the input of experts in decisionmaking.

Pre-summit preparations are not always successful in paving the way for agreement at the European Council level. In that the issues considered by the European Council are the ones that cause the most political problems for member countries, negotiations on these issues are inherently difficult at any level. Sometimes, technical obstacles cannot be cleared away until central conflicts are resolved by political authorities either at the ministerial level or by the heads of government themselves. In an attempt to circumvent possible roadblocks, European Councils are generally intensely prepared events. On occasion preparations have been so far-reaching that it has been possible to introduce early into a session of the European Council a draft text of conclusions to provide the basis of discussion. Such was the case in Milan in June 1985.[4] Whether advance preparations actually deliver the promise of a successful European Council, they are seen as necessary to relieve the burden on heads of government and, if possible, to prevent failure in the Council's meetings.

The Threat to "Normal" EC Decisionmaking

As important as easing the job of heads of government are the opportunities for decisionmaking that pre-summit bargaining provides other EC actors. Without these early negotiations, their fears of loss of authority to the European Council would be entirely fulfilled. The "debate" that grew up around the creation of the European Council expressed concern that the addition of a new structure would disturb the normal functions of the original Treaty institutions.[5]

Early concerns centered on the Commission. It appeared that the Commission's right of initiation, guaranteed by the Treaty of Rome, was in jeopardy because the European Council was under no legal obligation to act on a Commission proposal. Hallstein had referred to the Commission's right of proposal as its "motor function,"[6] and integrationists value this Commission function for its supranational quality. It was feared that the European Council would take over the motor function and the Commission's influence would decline in the shadow of the European Council. Supporters of the Commission and the Commission itself were not without foundation for their worries. The Commission had not been included immediately as a participant in the summits that preceded the establishment of the European Council. When the European Council came into being, Commission proposals were already being blocked in the Council of Ministers, which was to become the frustrating pattern of the 1970s. A Commission that could not muster authority with the Council of Minsters could hardly expect to muster authority with the European Council.

The effects of the advent of the European Council on the European Parliament, another of the institutions favored by integrationists, could not be as detrimental. The European Parliament simply did not have as much to lose to the European Council, as the Commission did. Its role at the time was mainly consultative, and even this minimal role was not fully developed as the Council of Ministers did not always appreciate nor seek out the advice of the European Parliament. The European Parliament was not, as of then, a directly elected body. Indeed, the heads of government gave their consent to direct elections in the bargain that produced the European Council. The first election of members of the European Parliament (MEPs) was not held until 1979, approximately five years after the European Council started meeting. Direct elections were a concession to integrationists, but the European Parliament remained deprived of important powers. Integrationists' main objection to the European Council was that it represented developing the intergovernmental side of the Community over the supranational side. If institutional reform continued to emphasize the intergovernmental side, integrationists' ambitions of a fully functional European Parliament would never be realized.

Finally, another of the insecurities surrounding the European Council was that it would undermine the decisionmaking authority of the Council of Ministers. This concern was voiced more loudly as the European Council progressively assumed, in times of indecision in the Council of Ministers, a decisionmaking role in EC matters. The criticism was that the European Council prolonged the EC decisionmaking process by yet another stage, duplicating decisionmaking and causing delays in the Councils. The concern seemed especially justifiable when decisions stagnated in the European Council, as happened frequently in the past.

The discussion that follows will treat in detail the role of EC institutions in the process of preparing a European Council in order to establish the linkages that exist between the European Council and other EC institutions. Preparations for a European Council do not display the full extent to which EC institutions have had to adjust their roles to accommodate the European Council. Nonetheless, the extent of involvement of EC institutions in European Council preparations has a bearing on the way one views the Council: whether it can be seen as continuation of Community business on another level or whether it attempts to operate above and beyond the original Treaty institutions.

The Role of the Presidency and the Council Secretariat

The planning and staging of a European Council belongs to the presidency-in-office, which rotates among member countries every six months. The main reflection of the entire term of the presidency, the European Council, is either a crowning event or an exercise in frustration. At the beginning of the term, the president of the Council of Ministers, the foreign minister from the country holding the presidency, traditionally presents to the European Parliament the outlines of the program to be acted on by the EC institutions. This program must include subjects that have not been brought to conclusion during the previous presidency and subjects of continuing interest to member governments. For instance, the completion of the internal market spanned many presidencies, requiring their coordination and cooperation. In the event a previous European Council has failed to reach conclusions, the incoming presidency has to resume the negotiations on the same subjects to prepare the way for agreement in the interim or at the next European Council. In effect, incomplete dossiers are passed from one presidency to the next. Besides having thrust on it certain subjects for handling, the presidency can also handpick a few subjects and encourage their progress. A presidency likes to steer its own course and would prefer not to inherit problems that promise to consume all of its energies. The European Council, scheduled near the end of the six-month term, is the last chance for the presidency to wrap up business and push its program to a successful conclusion. In organizing the subject matter for a European Council, few Presidencies are able to begin with a clean slate.

For example, after the failure of the Copenhagen European Council of December 1987, the German Presidency inherited negotiations on the Delors Plan in the first half of 1988. In Copenhagen Chancellor Kohl supported the Dutch call for an extra European Council to be held during the German Presidency. Undoubtedly, an element in Kohl's calculations was that he did not want the entire German Presidency devoted to the Delors Plan.[7] As it turned out, the Germans wrapped up the negotiations on the Delors Plan during the extraordinary Brussels European Council in February. Then, they turned to matters connected to the internal market and other pet projects, pushing these to conclusion at the Hanover European Council of June 1988.

Ideally, each country would like to use its presidency to direct the policy emphasis of the Community to areas of its choosing with the European Council serving to advertise its successful steering of the Community. In its management capacity, a presidency schedules the meetings of working groups, the Committee of Permanent Representatives (COREPER) and all of the Councils. To put pressure on participants to make decisions and to indicate it is serious about making progress in negotiations, it may also call unscheduled meetings of these bodies. Furthermore, the presidency establishes the agenda of meetings. A representative of the presidency is always in the chair. Having the chair gives the presidency the advantage of structuring discussion by introducing chosen topics and to some extent controlling input from the participants. A former permanent representative privy to the inside workings of the Council of Ministers' meetings termed it "almost impossible" to get the Council to yield decisions which go against the desires of the presidency.[8] With all these means at its disposal, the presidency can target certain issue areas for concentration and attempt to make sure they are thoroughly prepared in the months preceding a European Council. These are also the means for neglecting issues the presidency does not want on the European Council agenda.

The secretariat of the Council of Ministers (henceforth the council secretariat) assists the presidency in tasks related to the European Council. In terms of authority, the council secretariat is under the direction of the presidency and obliged to do what the presidency asks of it. The council secretariat is similar to the Commission in that both institutions are regarded as community-minded, their personnel committed to serving Community interests above national interests. Because the council secretariat is a stable institution, unlike the presidency which rotates to a different country every six months, its cumulative experience can make it a valued consultant to the presidency.

The conduct of a presidency is a monumental task. It requires attention to a morass of organizational detail if the work of all of the Council bodies is to be processed in a timely and coordinated fashion. The Council of Ministers has evolved into an incredibly complex structure in which issues are processed through multiple horizontal and vertical channels. Simultaneous negotiations have to be geared to yield results before the commencement of the next layer of decision. Therefore, scheduling of Council and Council-related meetings is an immense task in itself since it has to predict progress in negotiations and react to negative developments. In addition, a presidency in its capacity of chairing all meetings must have precise knowledge of EC procedures and issue areas, an understanding of the motives behind countries' bargaining positions and large quantities of political finesse. The council secretariat is qualified to come to the aid of the presidency as a technical assistant, legal specialist, factual informer or political advisor.

True to nature, the council secretariat is most involved in administrative duties such as preparing papers at the request of the presidency or sorting out organizational details, including room selection, timetables, and translation for meetings. In carrying out the managerial and technical tasks, the council secretariat can also have an effect on political outcomes. By participating in agenda organization, the council secretariat can help the presidency decide on a strategic arrangement of subjects. In briefs prepared for the presidency for the conduct of meetings, the council secretariat identifies possible compromises. As the drafter of presidency compromise proposals and final agreements, it can provide nuanced tilts of wording if so desired by the presidency.

As of 1993 the present Secretary-General of the Council of Ministers Niels Ersbøll, known for his activism in Council affairs, attempts to exert influence whenever there is an opening for his participation. A former

Danish permanent representative, he is astute in his knowledge of Council procedures and practiced in the art of Community negotiation. In meetings of the General Affairs Council, the Council composed of foreign ministers, the secretary-general is seated next to the president of the Council, which presents an opportunity for their close interaction. The secretary-general does not chair meetings, as does his counterpart in NATO, but his presence during crucial discussions may be used for influence. For example, the secretary-general of the Council was asked to attend high-level strategy sessions in Paris during planning for the Fontainebleau European Council of June 1984.[9] The extent of his emphasis on European Council matters can be gauged from the fact that four members of his staff devote all of their time to this subject.[10]

Countries holding the presidency will be more or less open to the advice of council secretariat officials. When the Germans have held the presidency, they have been known to collaborate extensively with the council secretariat.[11]

Negotiations on the Official Level

Preparations for a European Council take place on an official level in COREPER II, the body of COREPER attended by permanent representatives, otherwise known as ambassadors. If extra specialization is required to cope with complex subjects, informal working groups may be set up on an ad hoc basis to assist COREPER II. The participants will be national civil servants or, for convenience, officials from member countries' permanent representations. Two working groups, one on structural funds and another on budget management, were formed by COREPER II to consider the most technical aspects of the Delors Plan.[12]

Returning to COREPER II, it is distinct from COREPER I in that the latter body is attended by deputy permanent representatives and deals with the Community's more technical issues. Deputy permanent representatives tend to have a specialist background. For example, the British deputy permanent representative is always drawn from the Department of Trade and Industry.

The permanent representatives of COREPER II (henceforth COREPER) tend to be drawn from member countries' foreign ministries, where in most countries the general goals of EC policies are established.[13] The foreign ministry background means that permanent representatives have developed working relationships with foreign ministry officials and have been acclimated to national attitudes concerning EC affairs. Each country has its own way of circulating officials so that they become anchored in a network that links the national capital to Brussels, and so that Brussels officials do not become too detached from the national mindset on EC policy issues. The foreign office connection is necessary for permanent representatives because, after all, it is COREPER II that prepares the meetings of the General Affairs Council (*i.e.* foreign ministers), the next level of decisionmaking before the European Council.

Preparations for a European Council take place from the beginning to the end of a presidency. The General Affairs Council normally meets once a month, and it is left to the presidency to decide what meetings will be completely or partially devoted to the substance of a European Council. During the negotiations for the Delors Plan before the Copenhagen European Council of December 1987, the foreign ministers used close to the entirety of their meetings in September, October, and November discussing the plan, and they met in conclave several days before the European Council in a last-ditch bargaining effort.[14] A "conclave," an informal meeting of foreign ministers, makes every attempt to narrow differences on problematic issues that threaten to doom the upcoming European Council to failure. The holding of conclaves has come into increasing practice. The foreign ministers were extremely preoccupied with the Delors Plan, but European Council business does not always consume so much of their attention. Normally the subject matter of the European Council will be brought up over the course of several meetings of the General Affairs Council with the foreign ministers focusing more attention on it as the meeting date approaches. Member governments, wary of giving up too many concessions early in the game, frequently will only reveal their real negotiating positions close to the European Council.

Each General Affairs Council is organized by COREPER which may take care of preparations during its weekly meeting. If the negotiations promise to be difficult, the presidency may call additional meetings of COREPER. COREPER is preceded by yet another meeting of officials, called "anticis," whose responsibility it is to follow every step of the preparation of the European Council. The Antici Group originated during the 1975 Italian Presidency. The Italian permanent representative, whose last name was Antici, created the group to coordinate the details of European Council preparation. Each member country has an antici, usually a middle ranking foreign ministry official. The Commission and the secretary-general of the Council are also represented by anticis, bringing the membership of the Antici Group to fourteen. It has become commonplace for a country to bring an extra antici on board while it holds the presidency. The antici arrives in Brussels approximately a year in advance of a presidency to receive his training.

The Antici Group is completely informal, and discussion within the group tends to be free ranging. The Antici Group meets the day before COREPER to tie down its agenda. The antici meeting also presents the presidency with the opportunity to indicate the precise points it would like to have settled in the upcoming COREPER meeting. At the same time, it presents member countries with a chance to signal in advance their positions or to indicate if there is movement or change in a previous position. The antici meeting is not prolonged because issues are not negotiated there. It facilitates the flow of information between the presidency, the council secretariat, the Commission and the member governments.

Within COREPER the following day, each permanent representative sits with an antici on one side and an expert on the subject under consideration on the other side. The permanent representative is the spokesman for his country's negotiating position, and both the expert and antici are present in an advisory capacity. The antici may be asked to place a call to the home government from time to time to ask for instructions or to report on developments in COREPER. On points of discussion that countries deem to be of special national consequence, permanent representatives will be closely instructed on what points to concede and where to hold firm to a bargaining position. Some subjects arouse such fierce national opposition that it would be futile to hope for a settlement in COREPER. Such problematic issues are referred to the political level, to the foreign ministers' meeting or in some cases, they are not broached until the meeting of the European Council. In COREPER discussions center on the supposedly negotiable issues.

How much negotiating room do permanent representatives have on issues involving fewer political stakes? That permanent representatives are assisted by two national representatives, the expert and antici, is an indication that national interests are well protected and that concessions are not made in the course of negotiations without thorough examination. The hands of all permanent representatives are tied to some extent, depending on the significance of an issue for a country but also having to do with each country's administrative practice for coordinating negotiating positions between the capital and Brussels.

To illustrate the latter point, the Italian permanent representative is more casually linked to the national administration than his counterpart in Britain. In Brussels the British are known for receiving precise instructions on each point of negotiations whereas instructions from Rome tend to be more fluid and leave more room for discretion on the part of the Italian permanent representative. The Italian permanent representative tends to propose policy angles to national officials in Rome and does not normally receive instructions that contravene the view of the Permanent Representation. A report of the House of Lords' Select Committee on the European Communities confirms that the Italian Permanent Representation is influential and states that this is also true for the Luxembourg Permanent Representation.[15]

In the British case, coordination of EC negotiating positions seems to be more systematic, and the national administration is more likely to call the shots in negotiations. The British permanent representative returns to London at least one time per week, on Fridays, for a regularly scheduled meeting with Whitehall officials in order to consult and prepare positions on matters expected to unfold in the Community institutions the following week. Other times, he might be called to London for consultation on a higher political level. Sir Michael Butler, the British permanent representative in Brussels from 1979 until 1985, states that as a result of these routine visits, he always knew "exactly what ministers and officials in London were thinking."[16]

Contrasted with the British example, contacts between officials of the Italian Permanent Representation and Rome occur more spontaneously, as the need arises. An identity of views between the capital and Permanent Representation does not have to be established in advance for all of the points of the upcoming negotiations. The Italians depend on what was described by one interviewee as an existing climate of "close personal and intellectual links" between Brussels and Rome officials, officials who know each other from past working experiences, as protection enough for Italian interests in Community negotiations.[17]

Against the background of the different ways in which the British and Italians coordinate their EC positions, it is interesting to note that the British have earned the reputation of being *non-communautaire* whereas the Italians are generally thought of as *communautaire*. At least part of the British reputation is owing to what is seen as their stubborn defense of national interests within Community institutions. The British are hardly alone in the defense of national interests, but they may be more meticulous in the definition of their interests and in setting the requirements for compromise on a point.

Bargaining within COREPER, therefore, has to accommodate national standards ranging from the very precise to those more loosely defined. The agents of their national governments, permanent representatives, must seek solutions acceptable to their governments. Otherwise, decisions risk being overturned and renegotiated at the next level. COREPER, however, is not completely a national instrument. Permanent representatives, immersed in the work of the Community and aware of other countries' political preferences and constraints from their frequent negotiations with each other, can adopt a larger frame of reference than their own countries' needs. They at least can understand the requirements of satisfying twelve national interests and the additional interest of the Community, as represented by the Commission. Without putting into jeopardy national loyalties, permanent representatives are uniquely placed to communicate to their home governments the concessions necessary to create movement in a negotiation or to suggest an alternative strategy that will find greater favor with participants. In other words, the communication between Brussels and the capital is a two-way flow and does not necessarily have to create national obstacles to Community solutions.[18]

Negotiations on the Political Level

COREPER is an instrument, which if it works well, lessens the burden on foreign ministers. Conclusions of COREPER must be acceptable to Foreign Minsters to become effective. If a negotiation is successfully concluded within COREPER, it is referred to the General Affairs Council where, barring any further objections, it receives a nod. Even if COREPER has done its work well, it does not have the political clout to crack the toughest issues, which become the subject matter of the General Affairs Council.

COREPER is not the only institution that feeds issues to the General Affairs Council. Until now, no mention has been made of the "Technical Councils." Technical Councils is a term for the meetings of government ministers, other than foreign ministers, who also act in a Community capacity. Among the Technical Councils are the Agricultural Council, the Transport Council, the Environmental Council, etc., each of these a Council of Ministers in its area of specialization. The Farm Council meets several times a month, given the large involvement of the Community in this sector, whereas other Technical Councils may meet as infrequently as one time in a three-month period.

If the handling of so-called technical issues raises high-level political concerns, the Technical Councils are sometimes drawn into the bargaining process unfolding around a European Council. If one of the Technical Councils is unable to resolve an issue because of its serious political content, the issue may ultimately be referred to the General Affairs Council, responsible for general coordination of the work of the Council of Ministers' system. Failing resolution in the General Affairs Council, the issue may go all the way to the European Council. In past years this was frequently the case with agricultural issues because satisfactory solutions for curbing agricultural spending were elusive. In November 1987, agricultural ministers held six meetings in ten days to work out compromises on the agricultural components of the Delors Plan before the Copenhagen European Council in early December.[19]

Since the entire package hinged largely on effective control of agricultural spending, an agreement on agriculture needed to be pre-cooked so that the heads of government could move to the larger package. Both agricultural ministers and foreign ministers failed in their task, with agriculture remaining an unresolved element of the package when the European Council met. The heads of government also failed to find the answers causing the impasse at Copenhagen. The work of the Technical Councils is sometimes crucial to the outcome of a European Council and vice-versa. Decisions not taken at European Councils sometimes have the effect of halting the work of the Technical Councils.[20] The association of the Technical Councils with the work of the European Council shows the degree to which the European Council is enmeshed in the Community institutional structure.

Whether it is an impasse in the Technical Councils, bargaining that has dead-ended in COREPER, or key issues the Commission and presidency have set aside for high-level political attention, the foreign ministers have the misfortune of inheriting the most difficult issues. Even though foreign ministers are well-placed in their respective governments and each has considerable authority, individual foreign ministers may also be limited in their range of compromise. They may be acting on instructions agreed with a Prime Minister, who has a strong interest in the subjects before the General Affairs Council and is constitutionally and politically the unquestioned Head of Government. Former British Foreign Secretary Sir Geoffrey Howe although an authoritative figure in his own right, was constantly frustrated that Mrs. Thatcher did not rely more on his judgment. Such was also the case with the former British Chancellor of the Exchequer Sir Nigel Lawson. Both men tried in vain for several years to convince Mrs. Thatcher to agree to British participation in the exchange rate mechanism of the European Monetary System (EMS). Under the threat of resignation by her foreign minister and the pressure of the momentum building up around economic and monetary union, Mrs. Thatcher at last consented to put sterling in the exchange rate mechanism at the Madrid European Council of June 1989. This was a large step for Mrs. Thatcher, but for the other member countries, who were by then considering the possibilities of a European central bank and a common currency, the gesture had lost its significance. Prime ministerial dominance over Cabinet has not been practiced to the same extent by Mrs. Thatcher's successor, Prime Minister John Major.

In the same way his counterpart in Britain has to answer to his prime minister, the Danish foreign minister has to be mindful of positions agreed within the Folketing Market Relations Committee (MRC). In Denmark the tradition of parliamentary control over EC matters has been firmly established. Indeed, the role of the MRC is commonly referred to as "giving the ministers a mandate for their negotiations," although the mandate may leave the responsible minister some negotiating room.[21]

Even though foreign ministers on the EC level have the ability to overrule other types of ministers, within their own domestic governments they are not always superior to other ministers. In Germany the constitutional arrangements give ministers leeway in their respective policy sectors. The German foreign minister is especially constrained in his actions on the EC level when the national position has to be coordinated among several ministries since he has no power to make policy decisions in sectors other than his own.[22] At times, the intervention of the German Chancellor is needed, which is in itself a sensitive task, because German ministers refuse the give and take required to make a position negotiable within the General Affairs Council.

Besides constitutional factors that determine the structures of national governments and affect the authority of foreign ministers in the EC context, political situations also have an impact on the conduct of foreign ministers. The majority of EC foreign ministers are members of coalition governments. As a result, they are obliged to take into consideration the needs of the coalition partner or partners in carrying out their responsibilities in the General Affairs Council. Political factors such as government stability, anticipation of national elections and the individual prestige of the foreign minister within his government have to be considered by all foreign ministers, whether they represent a governing coalition or single party governments.

All of the work of the foreign ministers is not done in the structured setting of the General Affairs Council. A standard feature of foreign ministers' reunions is that negotiations proceed on several levels. Disagreements can be smoothed over and deals clinched during bilateral consultations to the side of Council meetings. The luncheon preceding a meeting of the General Affairs Council also presents bargaining opportunities. Those present at lunch are almost all foreign ministers and Commissioners with the exception of note-takers and a few interpreters to assist the ones not comfortable conducting business in French or English. Forthright discussion and deal-making are inevitably a part of these luncheons. Because officials are not present to be alerted to the fine points of discussion, misunderstandings can arise later. Therefore, an agreement exists that anything concluded informally over lunch will be confirmed afterwards in the formal Council meeting.[23] The formal meetings of foreign ministers devoted to European Council matters are prepared by the Antici Group in much the same way

COREPER meetings are prepared. In their formal meetings, foreign ministers are assisted by their permanent representatives, anticis and a national delegation comprised of expert staff. If the presidency feels that discussion can be improved by a climate of confidence, attendance can be further restricted, although the anticis and permanent representatives are almost always present. The anticis are sometimes said to be invisible to satisfy presidency requirements.[24] If the presidency is determined to have a negotiation concluded, it can prolong the meeting hoping to weaken the defense of national positions. Sir Christopher Tugendhat, former vice-president of the Commission, records a meeting of foreign ministers in which Sir Geoffrey Howe had to muster his strength to defend a point in the British budget dispute for most of nine consecutive hours.[25] Another tactic used by the presidency to break an impasse is to disband the formal meeting and to hold "confessionals" in its place. During confessionals, the president of the Council of Foreign Ministers and the Commissioner in attendance sound out each national delegation individually, inching forward to compromise through protracted negotiations.

The presidency will schedule a conclave several days before a European Council if, as is often the case, extra bargaining effort is required to advance negotiations. The conclave is an informal reunion of foreign ministers with their permanent representatives and anticis. It offers an opportunity for foreign ministers to review the presidency's agenda for the European Council and for all of the participants — the Commission, the presidency, and the member governments — to indicate what their positions will be at the European Council. It is the last chance to probe problematic issues. If differences remain, they will spill over into the European Council. The success or failure of the European Council can usually be predicted based on whether advance preparations have been able to spur significant movement on the central questions.

The Commission's Interactions with the Presidency and Member Governments

From start to finish of preparations for a European Council, the presidency and the Commission are thrust into a working relationship.[26] The degree of interdependence between the Commission and the presidency varies according to the country that holds the presidency, the issues being confronted, and the strength of the Commission.

If the presidency and the Commission share an identity of views on the subject matter at hand, cooperation is naturally facilitated. Larger countries can afford to be more independent of the Commission. They have an easier time building supporting coalitions for their own initiatives. They can tap the abundant expertise in their home administrations to create their own proposals or to provide statistical support for a position. Therefore, the key assets of the Commission, the ability to mastermind bargains in the EC framework, and expert knowledge of the EC issue areas may not count for as much with larger countries. Smaller countries holding the presidency lack informational and technical resources and an ability, comparable to that of the major powers, to influence other member governments. Therefore, they may desire the services of the Commission and even an alliance with the Commission in difficult negotiations to supplement their influence.

Also entering into the relationship between the presidency and the Commission is the presidency's committment to seeing the Commission carry out its Treaty role. Countries differ in their attachment to the supranational role of the Commission, that of an authoritative and Community-minded initiator of proposals and neutral arbiter in EC negotiations. Some countries more quickly accede legitimacy to the Commission in its representation of the Community interest. Others are more likely to view the Commission as a power player, not so different from the Twelve, in the process of self-aggrandizement. Countries' perceptions are affected by the competence of particular Commissions and their attachment to personalities in the Commission, although these perceptions may be influenced by the way a country views supranationalism.

Mrs. Thatcher's personal difficulties with Commission President Jacques Delors toward the end of her tenure were notorious. She supported Delors' reappointment as Commission President for a second term in 1988, even though she could have sided with other influential leaders who seriously considered a change in this position. Mrs. Thatcher evidently expected Delors to return the favor and certainly not to boldly challenge her Community views. The former British prime minister felt personally betrayed by Delors' address to the British Trade Union Congress (TUC) in September 1988, in which he advocated the development of EC social policy. Not only was his audience her political opposition, but she had also publicly stated her disagreement with the policy. The Labour Party was able to use the TUC's receptiveness to Delors (seemingly heightened for the occasion) to announce its new course as the party of Europe. Otherwise, the event would have gone unnoticed. From Mrs. Thatcher's point of view, Delors, with no right to interfere in British internal politics in the first place, had launched a political attack on her. Their relationship was irreparable after this conflict.

Even though personalities came to play an increasing role in Mrs. Thatcher's disagreements with the Commission, tension always existed in the relationship. Mrs. Thatcher's commitment to defending British sovereignty naturally put them at odds. Differences also occurred on the basis of particular issues. For instance, at the Dublin European Council of December 1984, Mrs. Thatcher criticized the Commission for proposing to spend too much money on the Mediterranean region and thereby raising the expectations of the Greeks.[27] In the final analysis, the British have had difficulty acclimating to Community institutions even though it now seems they are about to achieve a better *modus vivendi*.[28]

Whether a country is "friendly" to the Commission does not have to affect the working relationship between the Commission and that country when it holds the presidency. Their respective positions on issues are of utmost importance in uniting or dividing the Commission and the presidency. A presidency may also consider it politically expedient to ally with the Commission considering that both parties have a better chance of accomplishing their goals if they are working in tandem.

If a Commission, united in purpose, presents a program that takes advantage of timely and pressing issues and capitalizes on the key concerns of member governments and their publics, it becomes a force to be contended with. Once the Commission, through the ingenuity of its proposals, takes control of the European Council agenda, it moves into a central negotiating position. Faced with a fully functional Commission, the presidency has to admit the full participation of the Commission.

The role of the Commission in the European Council process is similar to its role in the Treaty-based decisional process. The Commission is, by Treaty authority, the sole proposer in the Councils, even though informal channels of influencing proposals are available to all participants in the normal EC decisionmaking process. It is true the Commission faces more competition in agenda-formation from the presidency and member governments at the European Council level. They are not only able to submit their own proposals but will want to influence issues as important as those before the European Council. The presidency, as the filter for all communications relating to a European Council and preparer of the agenda, can stifle the development of submissions it does not support. Obviously, a head of government insistent on bringing a subject before the European Council cannot be stopped from stating his or her case in the meeting. The Commission, nonetheless, is in a strong position.

Part of the Commission's strength derives from its role in implementing European Council decisions. If European Council decisions are to be put into legal form, which often needs to be done, they must be enacted by the Council of Ministers in accordance with Treaty rules. The Council of Ministers has to have a Commission proposal before it to take a legally binding decision. The Commission's hand is further strengthened because the Council of Ministers needs unanimous agreement to alter a formal Commission proposal. Unanimity is not easy to obtain because the Commission can usually find a supporter among the member countries. If the Commission is not the sole proposer in the European Council, it resumes its status of privileged initiator while business is being tidied up in the aftermath of a European Council. The Commission would be hard-pressed to refuse to submit a proposal on a point agreed by twelve member governments, but the Commission gains a bargaining edge by being in a position to unravel a meticulously woven agreement.

As a result, the Commission is intimately involved in European Council matters. Most of the preparatory work for European Councils is done on the basis of Commission papers, albeit they are supplemented by presidency papers and, more infrequently, by texts from member governments on points of special interest to them.[29] The Commission was the author of the Delors Plan, the main item of European Councils in 1987 and the first part of 1988, although compromises on its individual parts were concluded on the basis of presidency compromise proposals and as the result of bargains between members governments. The Delors Plan is significant in that it is an example of the Commission's capturing the center of European Council policy-making, as it did more recently with European Economic and Monetary Union (EMU).

Although the Commission has been able to safeguard its role, it has had to share its influence with the presidency. The presidency not only proposes alongside the Commission, but it is also an agent of compromise alongside the Commission. The presidency and the Commission are responsible for juggling the components of package deals and weighing the trade-offs and concessions necessary to bring negotiations to a successful conclusion, not only in the European Council but in the preliminary bargaining in COREPER and the Councils. It is not surprising that the presidency and the Commission are the vehicles of compromise. Each has a large stake in seeing that the European Council takes decisions, the presidency wanting to claim the fruit of its efforts and the Commission needing decisions so that its program will not be blocked. If they pool their weight, they are in a better position to nudge participants in a chosen direction whereas if they are divided on a point, they must contend with each other in addition to dissatisfied member governments in order to arrive at the point of compromise.

The Commission is in the best position when it has the active support of the presidency for its program and when its room for maneuver is not hampered by the European Parliament.[30]

The European Parliament's Interactions with the Commission and Council of Ministers

Although the European Parliament is the EC actor farthest removed from European Council affairs and has tended to be resentful of its small ability to influence developments, it is not without means of seeing that its point of view is taken into account when European Council issues are negotiated.[31] Member governments may be able to turn a blind eye to the European Parliament, but the Commission has to be more responsive to the European Parliament, or at least perceived that way. Commission accountability to the European Parliament is evident in Treaty arrangements. Expectations that greater accountability should evolve still thrive, especially in the European Parliament. The Treaty gave the European Parliament the power to dismiss the Commission if it is dissatisfied with the latter's conduct. However, the European Parliament has no power to appoint a Commission more to its liking. Because the vote of censure against the Commission is a blunted sword, it is threatened from time to time but has never been carried out.[32] Appointment of the Commission is the prerogative of the European Council, although this almost always amounts to ratification of member country nominations.[33] Therefore, the Commission, only in theory, is responsible to the European Parliament.

The Commission follows the path of accomodation with the European Parliament. Certainly, the Commission wants to avoid criticism that it is trying to escape the democratic control of the European Parliament. It is equally important that the two most supranational institutions must not be seen to be in conflict. Therefore, the Commission has personnel responsible for following the proceedings of the European Parliament and stays in close communication with its partner in supranationalism. Effort is devoted to trying to concert the views of the two bodies, and, frequently, they follow the same lines. De Bassompierre calls the Commission an "ally of the European Parliament in its permanent confrontation with the Council...."[34] Thus, the European Parliament can be slightly comforted that it has a friend in the Commission during COREPER and Council meetings, but definite limits to this friendship exist. The Commission is likely to disappoint the European Parliament when positions are compromised for the sake of getting an agreement. Consequently, the Commission is pulled between its need for decisions and its desire to avoid the criticism of the European Parliament.

In the end, the European Parliament is only very indirectly linked to the horse-trading that goes on before a European Council. In trying to influence European Council matters, it faces practical difficulties. "A parliament cannot negotiate" is the way in which the European Parliament's disadvantage in the European Council process was explained by a Brussels official.[35] Admitting the normal problems of coordination, member governments and the Commission have the advantage over the European Parliament of being able to be flexible in negotiations. Unlike the European Parliament, each has representatives with enough authority to initiate shifts in negotiating positions to facilitate compromises and to respond to changes in other participants' negotiating strategies. It goes without saying that a parliament is, by nature, an unwieldy body. Its strength is not efficiency but representativeness.

The European Parliament has correctly felt that it has been at a disadvantage in relation to European Council business. Formal channels for informing the European Parliament about European Councils have been slow to develop. Since 1981 the European Parliament has received a post-European Council briefing delivered in person by the president of the European Council, a concession long in coming. Because the European Council does not publish an official agenda, the European Parliament is not always aware of the issues that will be taken up by the heads of government.[36] The European Parliament occasionally draws out information about an upcoming European Council when Commissioners and representatives of the Council of Ministers appear for question time. Too much emphasis should not be placed on this means of gathering information. Question time in the European Parliament has not developed into a rigorous exercise for putting checks on power holders. It is not well-attended by MEPs, and the questions are not always hard-hitting. Question time is effective in Britain where it developed as a tradition and because of the adversarial nature of competition between Government and Opposition. Superimposed on the very different conditions in the European Parliament, it has not been effective. An MEP went as far to say that oral questioning in European Parliament tends to be a "non-starter" whereas written questions will sometimes produce interesting replies.[37]

The European Parliament is further disadvantaged because the preparatory work of the European Council is not done on the basis of formal Commission proposals but on Commission papers and documents from other sources not legally requiring the consultation of the European Parliament. With the Commission's considerable success in recapturing the right of initiation vis-à-vis the European Council, most notably with the Delors Plan and EMU, the European Parliament's opportunities have increased. The committees of the European Parliament were able to prepare reports relating to aspects of the Delors Plan. The European Parliament in plenary session held debates and passed resolutions on the contents of the plan. The resolutions of the European Parliament are included in the foreign ministers' briefs, although it is not known how frequently they are consulted in Council of Ministers' meetings. The British Presidency, in the first half of 1986, initiated the practice of selecting a resolution of the European Parliament during Council of Ministers' meetings and using it as the basis of a debate which lasted several minutes, indicating that in prior times parliamentary resolutions had gone mostly unnoticed.[38] The European Parliament has reason to fear that its debates fall on deaf ears and that its paper work is pushed to the side, but this has been true not only for European Council matters but for other Community business as well.[39]

Unlike the Commission, fortified by its exclusive right of proposal in the Council of Ministers, the European Parliament has lacked the means to insure its views are taken into account when the normal EC decisionmaking process and European Council process overlap. The one exception has been in the budgetary area where the European Parliament has considerable powers and has been able to make trouble for the European Council, and for that matter for the Commission, when it has felt its views have been disregarded.[40] As a result of the Single Act, agreed by the European Council, the European Parliament gained some new tools to increase its influence with Community institutions.[41] The European Parliament now has the possibility, even though circumscribed, to suggest amendments to Commission proposals. On internal market issues on which there is majority voting, those identified by the Single Act, the European Parliament can propose amendments during the now required Second Reading. The suggested amendments will succeed if they are first approved by the Commission and if they are not unanimously rejected by the Council of Ministers. This is known as the "cooperation procedure." During the first sixteen months of the procedure Parliament succeeded with about one-half of its proposed amendments.[42]

A definite result of this power is the intensification of the interaction between the European Parliament and the Commission. The Commission's diplomacy toward the European Parliament will be severely tested as it is faced with having to reject or approve the European Parliament's proposed amendments. So far, the Commission has cultivated its relationship with the European Parliament. Delors and other Commissioners, active in parts of the Delors Plan, met with leaders of the Political Groups in the European Parliament after the Brussels European Council of February 1988, to discuss implementing legislation that would be necessary after the agreement in Brussels. The meeting was supposed to provide a precedent for similar consultation after future European Councils.[43]

The European Parliament may be able to translate its new opportunities into more influence with the European Council. That the president of the European Parliament is now invited to address European Councils is symbolic acceptance that the European Parliament is a player in the European Council process. As the European Parliament has always had to wage a forceful and ingenious struggle for higher status, it is unlikely that it will see a dramatic transformation of its position.

The European Council: An Integrative or Disintegrative Innovation?

During the 1980s scholars tended to be concerned that the European Council's impact on the Community was disintegrative. As evidence of the disintegrative potential of the European Council, integrationists focused on, what seemed, the machinations of heads of government to gain more national control over EC decisionmaking by either circumventing the normal EC process or tinkering with institutional norms.

Bonvicini and Regelsberger documented two cases of unorthodox preparations for European Councils as demonstration of the dangers that lay in wait for the normal EC process.[44] Athens, December 1983, was a case in which a special preparation, decided on at the previous European Council in June, was implemented. A "Single Group of Preparation" was composed of permanent representatives, the EC link, and national officials who were in most cases assistants to foreign ministers. It was charged with preparing the meetings of so-called Jumbo Councils. These Jumbo Councils, also experimental in nature, were joint meetings of foreign and finance ministers and, in addition, other relevant ministers depending on the subjects under consideration.

The extraordinary preparations for Athens differed from strict community practice but were not necessarily intended to favor intergovernmentalism over supranationalism. At least, the regular EC institutional actors were present even if they were merged into groups improvised for the occasion. The preparations for Athens represented a reorganization of institutional groupings and not so much a neglect of EC institutional involvement. After Athens, the regular use of Jumbo Councils was rejected not so much for institutional purism but because they were deemed to be inefficient, involving at a minimum twenty-four participants. Now one finds only the exceptional use of Jumbo Councils. Commission President Jacques Delors requested that finance and agricultural ministers meet in a Jumbo session two weeks before the European Council in Brussels, June 1987. Delors, even though pro-integration, takes a practical approach to institutional innovation.[45]

Even more threatening would be a case where the regular EC institutional actors were largely left out of European Council preparations. The Fontainebleau European Council of June 1984, is provided as an example of this tendency.[46] By the time of Fontainebleau, the British budget dispute had reached crisis proportions. President Mitterrand took it upon himself to personally engineer the success of Fontainebleau. As a result, a larger amount than usual of the preparatory work was managed from the capital of the presidency, in this case Paris, which served as a filter for dossiers. Bilateral diplomacy on official and political levels with the main parties to the dispute were crucial to preparations. Lesser play was given to the usual actors, COREPER, the Council of Minister and the Commission.

In isolation, Fontainebleau indicates the ability of an influential member country, through manipulation of the presidency, to take control of European Council preparations and limit the participation of EC institutions. If Fontainebleau is taken together with all of the preceding European Councils that over five years contributed to the final compromise, it will be seen that EC institutions played a large, if not exhaustive role, in the overall process. The Brussels European Council of March 1984, directly preceded Fontainebleau and was on the verge of compromise. A figure for British compensation was almost agreed in Brussels so that most of the preparatory work had been accomplished before Fontainebleau. The British budget dispute had boiled down to a Franco-British dispute with the Germans hesitating over who would pay the costs of the final agreement. The issue had been so narrowed that it lent itself to behind-the-scenes diplomacy. In fact, Fontainebleau was unusual to the extent it was unprepared. Not only was the main issue ripe for decision, but the first direct elections to the European Parliament took place in the same month and presented a distraction.[47]

On the whole, the institutional preparations for a European Council have not represented a radical departure from the traditional processing of EC issues. The European Council has utilized existing EC decisionmaking machinery and has not created competing structures. As long as issues require complex bargaining involving the interests of a number of member governments, EC institutions provide the only structured bargaining arena. In addition, the Commission is the only player with the credentials to represent the Community point-of-view, and, for this, the presidency is no substitute. Because of the needs fulfilled by EC institutions, the European Council has not maintained a separate existence. It has been appended onto the existing EC structure as the highest level decisionmaker above the General Affairs Council with minimal alterations in the roles of other EC institutions.

Invariably, the creation of a new institution, especially one that automatically brings with it the political standing and celebrity of the European Council, will require adjustment on the part of existing institutions. From the discussion of the Commission's role in preparations for a European Council, it can be seen that the Commission no longer plays a role identical to that prescribed in the Treaty of Rome. It has had to share its agenda-setting responsibility with the presidency and other member governments in European Council matters. It has also had to share its mediating role with the presidency. The Commission's role has undergone a parallel evolution in the normal EC process.

Through the European Council, the Commission has gained opportunities for influence and face-to-face contacts with heads of government. That the Commission's role has been defensible and that the Commission has earned a place among heads of government points to the resilience of the Commission and its secure basis in the Treaty of Rome. The Commission has not been coopted by the European Council as the price for gaining acceptance by the heads of government. On the contrary, the Delors Commissions have been notably aggressive in their pursuit of Community interests. The Delors Commissions have also been adept at consolidating support for initiatives in the European Parliament and among member governments, an enlarged Community presenting more opportunities for coalition-building. In sum, the Commission appears to be capitalizing on its level of influence in European Council affairs.

The presidency is another actor that derives influence from its involvement in the European Council process. The ability to organize the details of European Council preparations, to determine policy priorities and to influence the final shape of compromises all work together to give the presidency significant influence on the course of a European Council. Nonetheless, the presidency faces certain limitations on its control. A severe limitation is that the term of the presidency lasts only six months. If the presidency has inherited previously unresolved disputes, it may not have time to pursue its own priorities. The shortness of the term and the fact that in a Community of Twelve, a country has the opportunity to hold the presidency once every six years, with changeovers in government and administrative personnel normally occurring during this time, mean that countries are not all that experienced in conducting a presidency. Therefore, the presidency usually relies on the permanent institutions in Brussels, the Commission and the council secretariat, for coaching on how to manage European Council business. Another limitation is inherent to the office of the presidency, obligated to work for Community solutions instead of in a self-serving manner. The presidency is best able to use its influence when it does not have a special stake in a negotiation whereas if it is a party to a dispute, its room for maneuver is reduced. Despite these limitations, the presidency has been enhanced by its European Council responsibilities.

On the opposite end of the spectrum, the European Parliament has been seen as a "loser" in relation to the European Council.[48] The European Parliament has a weaker basis in the Treaty of Rome than the Commission, but it has even been denied its Treaty role of consultation in negotiations preceding a European Council. The situation has the potential of improving with the Single Act and Maastricht, although it is still too early to make predictions. When the Commission is performing a role of importance in relation to the European Council, the European Parliament is in a more advantageous position because of its influence with the Commission. Nonetheless, the European Parliament remains frustrated in its efforts to exert influence on national politicians whether they are in the Council of Ministers or the European Council.

Like the European Parliament, the Council of Ministers, especially the General Affairs Council, has been judged a loser in its relations to the European Council. In an analysis that followed on the heels of the British budget dispute, because of the deepening role of the European Council in EC decisionmaking in budgetary and agricultural sectors, the Council of Ministers was likened to a secretariat of the European Council.[49] Observers were concerned with the "court of appeal" function of the European Council that seemed to reduce the authority of the Council of Ministers. What was meant by this court of appeal function was that the European Council involved itself in issues that given the normal functioning of the Community would have been settled at lower decisional levels. The objection was that the European Council presented the temptation for decisionmaking to be postponed to yet another level, causing decisional inefficiency and the dysfunction of the Council of Ministers.

In reality, it was because the Council of Ministers had not taken decisions that the heads of government intervened. Given the highly political nature of the issues the Community was faced with, there was a certain inevitability about the European Council's having to solve them. The situation existed that the Council of Ministers did not possess the authority to settle issues that widely, and sometimes bitterly, divided the member governments. Therefore, the European Council stepped in to fill a gap in authority and supplement the process in the Council of Ministers.

Throughout the British budget dispute, the French were especially insistent that the European Council should not do the work of agricultural and finance ministers, that it should not be transformed into a Technical Council. To press their point, the French refused to address a problem concerning sheepmeat at the European Council level.[50] The experience of the European Council has shown that a neat division does not exist between technical and political issues. As Carole Webb observes:

> Firstly, one government's technical issue is very often another's test of its commitment to the interests of an important domestic group or to an important national priority. Averaging out the axle weights of lorries to a Community norm might appear to the Commission to be an essentially technical procedure, to the British it implies an assault on its rural environment, to the French it puts at stake the interests of its leading lorry producer.[51]

The technical content of an issue does not make it politically neutral and, consequently, susceptible to resolution by specialists. If an issue deeply divides heads of government, likely it divides their ministers and officials with EC responsibilities.

It is significant that with the highly complex Delors Plan, the heads of government recycled some of the issues leftover from the British budget dispute. Yet, with the Delors Plan, the same objections were not voiced about leaving these subjects for decision by heads of government. One reason was that these subjects, the control of agricultural spending and rearranging budgetary priorities, had become politically significant to all of the member countries. Britain was no longer isolated in its concerns. Another reason is that the need for the European Council to involve itself in Community decisionmaking has become more generally accepted, not to mention that the habit is well-formed.

With the European Council, the lines of authority of the EC are closer to those of national governments, where prime ministers are not denied direct participation in the policy process. In the absence of the European Council, prime ministers would, undoubtedly, try to exercise their authority through government ministers in the Council of Ministers instead of retreating from EC politics altogether.

Has the existence of the European Council altered the authority of the Council of Ministers? The European Council has had a mixed impact on the Council of Ministers. For instance, the Agricultural Council was, to some extent, brought under control by European Council decisions on

46

the Delors Plan. This should not be seen as a negative effect of the European Council. Throughout the years, the Agricultural Council eluded the control of the General Affairs Council with its consistently overly generous pricing decisions. Foreign ministers have not had the political clout to tamper with decisions of the Agricultural Council, even though these decisions were not always in the broad Community interest.[52] As a result, it fell to the European Council to intervene in this policy area and take the measures heads of government could tolerate politically.

The Budget Council has also felt the impact of the European Council. During the British budget dispute and also with the Delors Plan, the European Council has significantly affected budgetary policy. The Budget Council had to delay decisions on the 1988 Community budget until the Delors Plan had been concluded. Consequently, the EC was put under the stress of starting the new year without an approved budget. European Council intervention in the budgetary process can be faulted with causing delays, but it has also had positive effects. The European Council can be credited with increasing the resources of the Community as part of the deal ending the British budget dispute and, again, in conjunction with the Delors Plan. Whereas the most extensive inroads of the European Council have been made in the agricultural and budgetary sectors, other policy sectors, such as the environment, have been mostly untouched by the heads of government. Consequently, some of the Technical Councils have been largely unaffected by the activities of the European Council.

As for the foreign ministers, the discussion of their role in European Council preparations shows that they have ample opportunity to take decisions before a European Council. Indeed, it is preferable for them to take decisions to ease the burden of the European Council. Furthermore, the European Council does not become involved in all of the current business of the General Affairs Council but only the problematic areas. For example, the foreign ministers negotiated the accession of Spain and Portugal and routinely conclude trade agreements with little interference from the European Council.[53] If a European Council is months away, it may exact a minimum amount of attention from the foreign ministers, and figure as only one agenda item among many others at the monthly meeting of the General Affairs Council.

A substantial limit to the extent to which heads of government can act in place of other Councils is the brevity and infrequency of European Council meetings whereas according to 1992 estimates, about eighty Council sessions take place annually.[54] The workload of the Council of Ministers is so abundant and vastly differentiated that it has to be parcelled out, as indicated by the proliferation of working groups, presently numbering more than a hundred, servicing the Council of Ministers. Although the European Council has the ability to reign in certain policy sectors and decisively orient policies in those sectors, it cannot realistically substitute for the Council of Ministers or even give cursory attention to all of the issue areas it encompasses.

So far, the evidence suggests that the European Council has not been a harbinger of institutional disruption. It is normal that an institutional newcomer will raise concern about the potential effects on the institutional balance and will cause insecurity in the older institutions. Much like the European Council, COREPER is an institution that gradually developed in response to the needs of the Council of Ministers. It did not have a formal existence until the Merger Treaty of April 8, 1965. COREPER was greeted with some of the skepticism that accompanied the establishment of the European Council. A permanent representative whose term spanned the first twenty years of COREPER's life described the adverse reactions of the Treaty institutions to COREPER. The European Parliament saw in COREPER "a dangerous animal and a potential threat to the powers of the Commission."[55] The Commission was discomforted by the arrival of COREPER on the institutional landscape and attempted "to ignore it whenever possible."[56] With the passage of time, COREPER's status in the Community is undisputed, so much so that commentators have worried about the effects of the European Council on COREPER.[57]

In answering the question of whether the European Council can be seen as an integrative or disintegrative innovation, the European Council has filled an institutional niche without dislodging the Treaty institutions. It is almost possible to conclude that there are enough similarities so as not to make a difference between European Council decisionmaking and normal EC decisionmaking. The European Council has entered a more mature phase in which it has been harnessed more effectively to the work of the Community. Brussels officials exercise more control over the agenda of the European Council. Because an issue is blocked does not necessarily mean that it will be referred to the highest political level for decision.[58] The European Council is restricting itself to issues of political importance for which it has the most capacity. The Treaty institutions, with the exception of European Parliament, perform important functions in preparing European Councils. The European Council is most vulnerable to criticism in its effects on European Parliament, although it has improved the status of European Parliament through agreement to direct elections and new powers of decision.

The importance of a European Council is that it serves as an impetus for decisions at lower levels so that the European Council will not be overburdened by decisionmaking responsibilities and result in failure.

Even though preparations for a European Council often are not conclusive, they represent an intensification of the EC decisionmaking process at all levels. In this view, the European Council has succeeded in motorizing the EC, not by replacing the Commission "motor," but by bringing political force to bear on a necessarily tedious decisionmaking process. At least twice a year the EC machine runs at high gear under the mounting pressure of a European Council.

Notes

1.   Interview by the author with an official from a Permanent Representation in Brussels, 11 November 1987.
2.   Mrs. Thatcher was exceptional in that she relished negotiating the details of issues at the European Council level. By most accounts Mrs. Thatcher arrived at European Councils having mastered her briefs and ready to deal on the basis of figures, if necessary. Her grasp of the minutiae of EC subjects may be one reason she received such a favorable solution to the British budget dispute.
3.   John Wyles, "Summit Setbacks Hide Real Progress," *Europe, Magazine of the European Community*, May-June 1984, p. 27.
4.   Interview by the author at a Permanent Representation in Brussels, 6 November 1987.
5.   Bulmer and Wessels consider the impact of the European Council on the EC institutional balance throughout their work. See especially Chapter 6, *The European Council*, pp. 103-31.
6.   Walter Hallstein, *United Europe: Challenge and Opportunity* (Cambridge: Harvard University Press, 1962), p. 21.
7.   Rumors were already in the air in Brussels, November 1987, that the Germans might need a second European Council during their Presidency to accomplish all they desired. In the course of two interviews by the author, 10 November 1987, one at a Permanent Representation and one at the Commission, the possibility of an extraordinary European Council was mentioned. It still remained to be seen whether the European Council in Copenhagen, December 1987, would formally agree to an extraordinary meeting there.
8.   Sir Michael Butler, *Europe: More than a Continent* (London: William Heinemann Limited, 1986), p. 26.
9.   Stephen Holt and Jean-Marc Hoscheit, "The European Council and Domestic Policy-Making," paper presented to Kerkrade Colloquium on the European Council, 26-27 October 1984, p. 28.
10.   Gianni Bonvicini and Elfriede Regelsberger, "The Organizational and Political Implications of the Establishment of the European Council on Both European Community and EPC Decision Making," paper presented to Kerkrade Colloquium on the European Council, 26-27 October 1984, p. 17.
11.   Helen Wallace, "The Presidency of the EC: Tasks and Evolution," in O'Nuallain and Hoscheit, eds., *The Presidency of the European Council of Ministers*, p. 16.

12.   Interview by the author at a Permanent Representation in Brussels, 13 November 1987.

13.   At the time of the European Coal and Steel Community (ECSC), Economics Ministries tended to take charge of Community affairs in their countries. The increased (and increasing) political significance of the EC, originally the EEC, required greater participation by Foreign Ministries in Community matters. From the earliest days of the EEC, Foreign Ministers met more frequently in the Council of Ministers than other types of government ministers. Responsibilities originally performed by Economics Ministries, for instance, coordination of internal governmental positions, have passed to Foreign Ministries in most countries. Simon Bulmer and William Paterson specify the different tasks performed by the German Economics and Foreign Ministries in relation to EC affairs. See *The Federal Republic of Germany and the European Community* (London: Allen and Unwin, 1987), pp. 31-35. As early as 1973, Helen Wallace observed three roles that Foreign Ministries generally performed in relation to the EC: "the diplomatic representational one; that of giving political coherence to their government's positions in the internal policy-making of the communities; and, lastly, that of helping to shape a Community identity." See Wallace, *National Governments and the European Community* (London: Chatham House/PEP, 1973), p. 40, as quoted in Bulmer and Paterson, *Ibid.*, p. 33. Bulmer and Paterson, p. 33, include a fourth role of Foreign Ministries: the involvement in European Political Cooperation (EPC). Chapter 5 of this study is concerned with EPC.

14.   Interview by the author at a Permanent Representation in Brussels, 10 November 1987.

15.   "European Union," Fourteenth Report from the House of Lords' Select Committee on the European Communities, Session 1985-86, Her Majesty's Stationery Office, H L 226, p. 82. This report presents an impressive analysis of the national structures for defining member countries' positions in COREPER and the Council of Ministers.

16.   Butler, *Europe: More than a Continent*, pp. 114-16, describes the extensive contacts the British Permanent Representative has with London officials and politicians.

17.   Interview by the author at a Permanent Representation in Brussels, 13 November 1987.

18.   The Co-ordinating Commission (Cocor) was the antecedent of COREPER in the ECSC. Haas attributed several positive features to this commission, comprised of civil servants from the member states: "The members [of this commission] have grown to know one another well; negotiations tend to become less and less formal; increasingly a process is initiated of seeking the best compromise in terms of a common technical solution to a given economic problem." Such attributes lead Haas to see Cocor, and other lesser Council bodies, in terms of "a novel community-type organ as against the traditional principle of a diplomatic conference." See *The Uniting of Europe*, p. 491.

19.   Tim Dickson and Quentin Peel, "European Community farm crisis talks collapse in disarray," *Financial Times*, 27 November 1987, p. 26. See also Richard Owen, "Brussels budget hopes fade," *The Times*, 27 November 1987, p. 10.

20.   During the European Council in Luxembourg, April 1980, the Agricultural Ministers met simultaneously on the request of French President Giscard d'Estaing. See *Bulletin of the EC*, 4 (1980), p. 8. This unusual situation came about because the British had maintained a veto on farm prices in the Agricultural Council until they received satisfaction on their budgetary complaints. If the Luxembourg European Council could reach agreement on the budget issue, then, the agricultural ministers would be able to go ahead with their pricing decisions. Failure at Luxembourg meant further postponement of the work of the Farm Council. A breakthrough on the contentious issue was finally achieved at a foreign ministers' meeting in May, relieving the deadlocked situation in the Farm Council.

21.   Karsten Hagel-Sørensen and Hjalte Rasmussen, "The Danish Administration and Its Interaction with the Community Administration," *Common Market Law Review*, 22 (1985), p. 282.

22.   Autonomous management of their respective policy areas is "jealously guarded" by German ministers, according to Renate Mayntz, "Executive Leadership in Germany: Dispersion of Power or 'Kanzlerdemokratie'?" in *Presidents and Prime Ministers*, eds., Richard Rose and Ezra N. Suleiman (Washington, D.C.: American Enterprise Institute for Public Policy Research, 1980), p. 143. This is owing to a combination of constitutional rules and coalition government in Germany. The former German Finance Minister Gerhard Stoltenberg, tried to reassert control over monetary policy after the German Foreign Minister Hans-Dietrich Genscher, in the capacity of President of the Council of Ministers, had pushed for further development of the EMS. The German public seemed unhappy that Stoltenberg had permitted Genscher a say in monetary policy. Stoltenberg isssued a statement the press interpreted as a "shot across the bows" of Genscher. See David Marsh, "Stoltenberg calls for EC to end all capital controls," *Financial Times*, 18 March 1988, p. 2. Other member countries with coalition governments would tend to experience similar situations in which government ministers guard their policy sectors.

23.   For descriptions of these luncheons, see Butler, *Europe: More than a Continent*, pp. 75-77 and Christopher Tugendhat, *Making Sense of Europe* (Harmondsworth, Middlesex, England: Penguin Books Limited, 1986), pp. 158-59.

24.   Interview by the author at a Permanent Representation in Brussels, 6 November 1987.

25.   Tugendhat, *Making Sense of Europe*, pp. 157-58.

26.   The last comprehensive work on the Commission was David L. Coombes, *Politics and Bureaucracy in the European Community; A Portrait of the Commission of the E.E.C.* (Beverly Hills, Ca.: Sage Publications, 1970). More recent

research is needed on this institution since its importance has increased in recent years under the competent leadership of Jacques Delors and with its new powers in the Single Act and Maastricht. The Presidency has received more recent scholarly attention. See Colm O'Nuallain in collaboration with Jean-Marc Hoscheit, eds., *The Presidency of the European Council of Ministers; Impacts and Implications for National Governments* (London: Croom Helm, 1985); Guy de Bassompierre, *Changing the Guard: An Insider's View of the EC Presidency* (New York: Praeger, 1988); Emil Joseph Kirchner, *Decision-making in the European Community: The Council Presidency and European Integration* (Manchester, UK: Manchester University Press, 1992).

27. See Ian Murray, "Papandreou demand puts damper on EEC summit," *The Times*, 5 December 1984, p. 1.

28. Michael Welsh, a British MEP, discusses British neglect of the views of the Commission and European Parliament during its Presidency in 1986. As a result, Britain had difficulty getting initiatives through the Social Affairs Council. According to Welsh, "The British refusal to accept or understand the role of Community institutions did indeed cause deep distrust of British motives." See "Labour Market Policy in the European Community: The British Presidency of 1986," RIIA Discussion Paper No. 4 (London: Royal Institute of International Affairs, Chatham House, 1988), pp. 19-20. With Mrs. Thatcher's replacement, Britain's relations with EC institutions are improving.

29. Bonvicini and Regelsberger, "The Organizational and Political Implications." See the appendix for a table of Commission submissions to the European Council from June 1977 to June 1984.

30. Interview by the author at the Commission in Brussels, 10 November 1987.

31. Sources on the European Parliament include the following: Robert Goehlert, *The European Parliament: A Bibliography* (Monticello, Il.: Vance Bibliographies, 1982); Juliet Lodge, "The European Parliament," in Lodge, ed. *The European Community; Bibliographical Excursions* which includes an excellent bibliography on the European Parliament; Emil Joseph Kirchner, *The European Parliament: Performance and Prospects* (Aldershot, Hampshire, England: Gower, 1984); John Fitzmaurice, *The European Parliament* (Aldershot, Hampshire, England: Gower, 1985); Fitzmaurice, "An Analysis of the European Community's cooperation procedure," *Journal of Common Market Studies*, 26 (June 1988), pp. 389-400.

32. Motions of censure against the Commission have been tabled at least four times in Parliament, in December 1972, June 1976, December 1976, and March 1977. In half of these cases, the motions were subsequently withdrawn. In the other half of these cases, the motions were defeated by a vote of Parliament. "The European Parliament; its powers," booklet published by the Secretariat of the European Parliament Directorate-General for Information and Public Relations, Publications and Briefings Division, January 1983, p. 22.

33. Germany, France, Italy, Britain, and Spain each have two nationals on the Commission and the remaining countries have one national.

34.   De Bassompierre, *Changing the Guard*, p. 17.

35.   Interview by the author at the Commission in Brussels, 10 November 1987.

36.   Bulmer and Wessels, *The European Council*, p. 114.

37.   Interview by the author with an MEP at Tulane University in New Orleans, Louisiana, 1 March 1988.

38.   Interview by the author at a Permanent Representation in Brussels, 9 November 1987.

39.   De Bassompierre states, "But up to now, the Council [of Ministers] has all too often taken only very limited notice of Parliament's opinion." See *Changing the Guard*, p. 16.

40.   Parliamentary activism in the budgetary realm has touched on issues with which the European Council is concerned. The European Parliament, under its budgetary powers, was able to raise expenditure on the Regional Fund in 1978. The European Council had previously set a ceiling on Regional Fund expenditure, which was lower than the increase won by Parliament. In this instance, the European Parliament was determined not to admit budgetary authority to the European Council. In the early 1980s, before a permanent solution to the British budget problem was worked out, ad hoc rebates were given to Britain. These rebates had to pass the European Parliament, which objected to this solution as being inadequate. It maintained that ad hoc rebates skirted the more important responsibilities of reforming the CAP and developing and allocating more resources to other Community policies. On this basis, the European Parliament successfully blocked Britain's 1983 rebate. The rebate was not unblocked until after a settlement on the British budget dispute was reached at the Fontainebleau European Council, June 1984. More recently, the European Parliament and the Commission initiated proceedings at the European Court of Justice against the Council of Ministers because it had failed to present a draft budget by the required date of 5 October 1987. This threat put pressure on the European Council to take decisions on the Delors Plan in Copenhagen, December 1987, to clear the way for a budget agreement. As it turned out, the decisions were not taken at Copenhagen, and an extraordinary European Council in Brussels, February 1988, was needed to conclude the Delors Plan.

41.   Tim Dickson, "Brussels starts to take Strasbourg more seriously," *Financial Times*, 18 January 1988, p. 4.

42.   *The Europa World Year Book* 1992, v. 1 (London: Europa Publications Limited), p. 147.

43.   Interview by the author with an MEP at Tulane University in New Orleans, Louisiana, 1 March 1988.

44.   Bonvicini and Regelsberger, "Organizational and Political Implications," pp. 7-9.

45.   Peel, "EC spending talks collapse," *Financial Times*, 16 June 1987, p. 1. The idea that finance and agricultural ministers hold a Jumbo meeting at the same time as the European Council met in Brussels, June 1987, was also floated.

See Peel, "Martens launches bid to avert EC summit crisis," *Financial Times,* 22 June 1987, p. 1.

46. Bonvicini and Regelsberger, "Organizational and Political Implications," pp. 8-9.

47. Butler, *Europe: More than a Continent,* pp. 81, 104.

48. Bulmer and Wessels, *The European Council,* p. 114.

49. Bonvicini and Regelsberger, "Organizational and Political Implications," p. 14.

50. *Ibid.,* p. 15.

51. Carole Webb, "Introduction: Variations on a Theoretical Theme," in H. Wallace, W. Wallace and C. Webb, eds., *Policy-Making in the European Community,* 2d ed. (Chichester: John Wiley and Sons Ltd., 1983), p. 17.

52. An instance in which even the German Chancellor Schmidt found it difficult to overturn a decision made by the German farm minister in the EC Agricultural Council is recounted in the next chapter. Tugendhat records an instance in October 1984 when the finance ministers had come close to reaching an agreement on budgetary discipline as a part of CAP reform. The farm ministers were also meeting and caught wind of the other ministers' impending agreement. The French Farm Minister Michel Rocard voiced a strong negative reaction against the actions of the finance ministers to which his own ministerial colleague in the Farm Council had consented. The next day the foreign ministers rejected the tentative agreement of the finance ministers. See Tugendhat, *Making Sense of Europe,* p. 161.

53. Bulmer and Wessels, *The European Council,* p. 105.

54. *The Europa World Year Book* 1992, p. 147.

55. *Bulletin of the EC,* 10 (1980), p. 25.

56. *Ibid.*

57. Bonvicini and Regelsberger, "Organizational and Political Implications," pp. 18-20.

58. During the month before the European Council in Copenhagen, December, 1987, the Council of Ministers had failed to agree acceptable levels of radioactivity in food products. When asked whether this issue, if it remained unresolved, would go to the European Council, a Commission official replied that the upcoming European Council would only deal with the Delors Plan. Interview by the author at the Commission in Brussels, 17 November 1987.

3

Bureaucrats, Eurocrats, and National Politicians

In its infancy, the European Council existed as a forum for dialogue among heads of government who realized the need to be in direct contact with each other. However, as the Council has matured, it has assumed a more central and important role in European Council decisionmaking. The previous chapter demonstrated how adaptations to the decisionmaking role have been made by the intensive preparations of EC institutions and national governments to participate in the European Council process.

The meetings themselves have been affected by the more active role of heads of government in formulating EC policy, making today's European Council a multi-purpose forum. It is able equally to facilitate private and relaxed dialogue among heads of government and to manage technically sophisticated and wide-ranging policy negotiations. Considering the formal sessions of the European Council and related informal exchanges, this chapter focuses on the diverse activity inside and on the periphery of a European Council necessary to understand the range of the potential contributions of this institution.

Formal Sessions of the European Council

Some commentators might object to the use of the term "formal" in relation to the actual sessions of the European Council as the founders, President Giscard d'Estaing and Chancellor Schmidt, intended it as an informal meeting. Yet, the present-day European Council has developed far beyond the cozy fireside atmosphere of the first gatherings. In terms of preliminary organization, number of participants, available bureaucratic assistance, intensity of focus, and structure of discussion, the European Council of today stands in striking contrast to its more simple origins.

Decisionmakers and Support Staff

The first summit meetings aimed to create an intimate environment, so organizers restricted attendance as much as possible. To facilitate the constrained participation of heads of government, President Giscard d'Estaing and Chancellor Schmidt insisted that officials should not be looking over their shoulders.[1]

Originally, even foreign ministers were not privy to summit meetings. This condition provided special problems for the Dutch, whose prime minister has no constitutional authority in the realm of foreign affairs — a subject that inevitably comes up among heads of government.[2] Neither did this condition satisfy countries concerned about properly representing coalition governments. Excluding the foreign minister was especially inappropriate for a coalition in which the prime minister and foreign minister came from different parties. Occasionally, in European coalitions, the foreign minister not only represents the minor coalition party in government but enjoys the additional status of chairing his party. Denmark's foreign minister since 1982, Uffe Ellemann-Jensen, is also head of the Liberal Party. In this case, the foreign minister is clearly not the subordinate of the prime minister.

Certain prime ministers had good reasons then for requiring the presence of their foreign ministers in the European Council and they were able to prevail on this point. As a result of their participation in the Council of Ministers, foreign ministers were more knowledgeable than most heads of government about EC procedures and issues. In addition, they provided the much needed link to normal EC machinery and, therefore, assurance to those concerned about the extra-Treaty nature of the European Council.

National delegations of officials however did not gain permanent seats in the room with heads of government, even though some countries pressed for their inclusion. A different practice does exist in the Council of Ministers where a team of officials present in an advisory capacity are seated behind each foreign minister.

With the most recent Community enlargement, twenty-six persons participate in a European Council. Two seats are reserved for each country and the Commission. The Commission seats are occupied by President of the Commission Jacques Delors and his senior vice-president, Lorenzo Natali, during the Commission term, 1984-1988. Member country seats are traditionally filled by prime ministers assisted by their foreign ministers. France is always the exception because its president is the only head of state that participates in a European Council. During cohabitation (1986-1988), political opponents held the French Premiership and Presidency and created an awkward situation for French representation in the European Council. As the result of cohabitation, the French foreign minister, previously included in European Councils, lost his seat to the Premier.[3] Whenever the advice of the foreign minister was needed, one of the French seats had to be vacated in order to make a place for him. In this way, the convention of two seats per member country was preserved. With the end of cohabitation, the foreign minister regained his place in European Councils. Seats are not shared except on very rare occasions. For instance, with complex discussions on agricultural matters the Commission president has been known to request the assistance of his agricultural commissioner in the European Council, in which case, the latter occupied the vice-president's seat.[4]

In addition to European Council participants, a group of officials are positioned in the room and perform functions mostly unrelated to policy. Of these officials, several are responsible for notetaking. The Secretariat of the Council of Ministers supplies one of the notetakers (usually its own Antici performs this service), as does the presidency. The secretary-general of the Commission is also present. When Emile Noël held this position, he kept a personal record of the meetings. Other high officials responsible for observing European Council proceedings are the secretary-general of the Council of Ministers and a secretary for EPC. They are admitted to better supervise the preparation by their secretariats of the texts that derive from discussions in the European Council. These texts are produced at the end of the meetings. Additional officials are needed to oversee translation, a complicated task in that nine languages are used in the European Council as in the rest of the work of the Community.

The presidency, in addition to its notetaker, requires the assistance of other persons. These include the permanent representative and a high official close to the prime minister, in Germany, the chief of the Chancellery, and equivalent offices in other countries. Only the officials attached to the presidency play an advisory role, this warranted by the politically sensitive and technically challenging nature of chairing a European Council.[5] The prime minister, as president of the European Council, cannot be expected to possess on his own the level of preparedness required for chairing the meeting. A domestic problem or even the prime minister's normal workload could easily distract from preparations. A president is hard-pressed to know in detail all of the member countries' negotiating positions and the potential elements of a comprehensive compromise.

Officials figure more prominently in a European Council than in the past, not only inside the actual meeting but on its periphery. The Antici Group waits in a nearby room and the remaining members of the national delegations position themselves in rooms in the building where the European Council is in session. The presidency usually limits the size of each national delegation keeping in mind available space. It usually permits close to twenty persons in each national delegation. Large countries supplement their entourage with between ten and twenty persons who serve as support staff and are not seated with national delegations.

Cost is also a factor in determining how many officials are permitted to attend. A press report put Britain's expenses at over eight thousand pounds for hotel accommodations for its delegation and support staff at the Venice European Council of June 1980. That sum covered lodging for the forty-four people in the British party, eighteen of these comprising support staff. The cost is less if the European Council is held in a place where countries can use their own embassy facilities. Even given cost considerations, national delegations are not easily limited because heads of governments and foreign ministers feel they need expert advice and given the natural attraction that an international event has for officials.

The composition of national delegations will depend on the scope and priority of the agenda. Negotiations on the Delors Package at the Brussels European Council of June 1987, were deemed to be of such importance to Germany that three state secretaries, the highest ranking officials in their ministries, were part of this national delegation.[6] Government ministers, with the obvious exception of foreign ministers, and specialist commissioners usually do not choose to attend European Councils. Unable to be present in the meeting, they would tend to be idle while the European Council was in session.

Each national delegation normally includes personal advisors to the prime minister and foreign minister and other personnel on their staffs, an official responsible for press relations, specialists from affected ministries, the permanent representative, and possibly specialists attached to the Permanent Representation. Aside from the Foreign Ministry which always has officials present at European Councils, Agriculture and Finance are the ministries most often represented.

As can be easily seen, national delegations are not monoliths. All national delegations contain a mix of departmental interests. Many contain a mix of party interests. It needs to be recalled that countries with single-party executives are in the minority in the Community. In the more frequent case of a coalition government, the prime minister and foreign minister, normally from different parties, will each have followers sympathetic with their political objectives in the national delegation.

If tensions exist in a member country's executive, they likely carry over into the national delegation. Consider, for instance, the fact that President Mitterrand and Premier Chirac vied with each other over the composition of the French delegation to The Hague European Council of June 1986. This was the first European Council to be held after legislative elections the previous March had produced the situation of cohabitation. With difficulty, Chirac had managed to be included in the seven-nation economic summit in Tokyo, May 1986. At the time of The Hague meeting, Mitterrand still resisted Chirac's participation in international summits while Chirac insisted on it. Leading up to The Hague, negotiations between Matignon and the Elysée, the respective camps of the premier and president, took place as to how many officials identified with Chirac would be included in the national delegation. Ultimately, it was decided that Chirac would be accompanied by his diplomatic advisor, his official in charge of European affairs, and a personal press spokesman. Whether or not to include Chirac's press spokesman was a serious complication in negotiations. The Elysée conceded only after a week passed on the condition that Mitterrand's official for press relations would be solely responsible for expressing the views of the entire French delegation.[7] Thus, Mitterrand saw to it that uniform French positions be presented to the public and, more importantly, that these remain under his control. The rivalry between Mitterrand and Chirac was probably more intense than that in countries where coalition government is the norm.

Despite the extensive efforts to reconcile internal positions during preliminary preparations, further internal alignment may need to take place at the European Council. Events in the European Council may cause member countries to have to reevaluate previous positions. German leaders were well aware that they might have to take decisions at the Brussels European Council of June 1987, for which details had not been anticipated in prior consultations. Therefore, relevant ministers who had stayed behind in Germany had to be on call throughout the weekend of the European Council.[8] Ministers provided telephone numbers where they could be reached, and these were kept conveniently at hand during the European Council. Such high-level consultation is not often needed. The political and departmental representativeness of national delegations are usually adequate for purposes of consultation and supplying technical advice.

While the European Council is in session, members of national delegations naturally want to be informed about what is said in the European Council. Consequently, a surprisingly primitive system of passing information along to the delegations has developed. Approximately every twenty to thirty minutes, the notetakers in the European Council give their notes to the Antici of the presidency. He proceeds during the next quarter of an hour to orally summarize these notes for the Antici Group. Anticis rapidly scribble their own versions of the summary and are responsible for informing their colleagues in the national delegations.[9] By the time the news of the European Council reaches the national delegations, approximately thirty minutes have been used up. Furthermore, the accounts of the original dialogue given to national delegations have undergone, in most instances, three translations.

This curious reporting system is potentially haphazard, in that it entails the risk that the true version gets lost either in translation or by being circulated through so many hands. No official minutes exist to serve as proof of the original dialogue. The minutes of the presidency notetaker only supply an informal record. It seems intended that there is a certain amount of uncertainty about what was actually said in the European Council. That those present are the only ones who actually know what transpired is beneficial to the participants in a European Council. Exchanges can be very direct since they will never appear on record. Heads of government and foreign ministers, if necessary, can safely issue denials of press reports concerning happenings in the European Council. The means of informing national delegations allows a wide enough margin of error that European Council participants do not feel threatened by the circulation of information. Meanwhile, because many sources exist for leaks, the inside story of the European Council is accessible enough to outside observers.

A negative aspect of not having official minutes is that misunderstandings inevitably occur when the Council of Ministers decides what implementing legislation is needed to follow-up a European Council.[10] In the Council of Ministers, a country does not tend to stray too far from the principles stated in the European Council. That would give the same license to other countries while destroying essential trust. Nonetheless, questions of interpretation crop up, memories are sometimes tested, and points are further argued. An official interviewed referred to the conclusions of European Councils as agreements that are not really agreements.[11] Another spoke, for the point of illustration, of the German finance minister's trying, in subsequent negotiations in the Council of Ministers, to cut sums promised by German leaders in the European Council.[12] How much European Council minutes would facilitate the implementing process is unclear. Resorting to a variety of negotiating techniques to improve a country's bargaining position is a fact of life of EC decisionmaking. Furthermore, if someone is determined to argue the intent of a statement made in the European Council, he may not be deterred by a written record. The fact remains that the questionable legal status of European Council decisions gives license to disagreements when the Council of Ministers decides the details of implementation.

In favor of not adopting official minutes is that sometimes heads of government may be more inclined to make concessions if these are not put on record. As it stands now, heads of government enjoy the freedom of putting their own interpretations on events within the European Council. If necessary, they can minimize concessions they made in the European Council in front of the national press and accentuate their gains. This was the pattern followed by Mrs. Thatcher in the past when British public opinion was not favorably disposed to a powerful EC.[13] Mrs. Thatcher's nationalistic approach appeared outmoded as the 1992 project increased public acceptance of the Community in all member countries. However, sustained support for the EC throughout Europe is not guaranteed. A commentator recently warned of new outbreaks of "Euro-scepticism," ironically explained as a backlash against an EC decisionmaking process in which "government leaders negotiate far-reaching commitments in lofty heights, which can then no longer be controlled or reshaped by national parliaments."[14] Danish leaders had more difficulty than expected convincing their public to accept the Maastricht Treaty on European Union. In addition to more specific objections, discomfort with federalism and "the Community's undemocratic way of taking decisions" were at the root of the opposition.[15] As citizens realize the momentousness of EC decisions, like those taken on EMU at the Maastricht European Council of December 1991, the closed nature of the process becomes more objectionable. On one hand, the secrecy of the European Council facilitates agreements, which might be impossible to conclude in a more transparent setting. On the other, it threatens to raise suspicions, especially now as the EC attracts more serious public attention.

Returning to the reporting system used to inform national delegations, it is not only calculated with an eye to secrecy but is also a remnant of the anti-bureaucratic bias of the heads of government who established the European Council, notably President Giscard d'Estaing and Chancellor Schmidt. The thirty minute time lapse before officials receive the report of the state of progress in the European Council means that they may be too late to affect developments. This does not mean, however, that officials cannot influence European Council developments. To a great extent, the tradition of discouraging bureaucratic participation in a European Council has faded. As observed by Holt and Hoscheit:

It appears that the initial intention of Heads of State and Government to create a debureaucratized environment by excluding experts and civil servants has revealed itself to be somewhat of an illusion.16

On the request of heads of government, officials may enter the European Council. The only restriction is that they are forbidden to linger in the room without purpose. Anticis are linked to prime ministers by a direct telephone line and a paging system. When summoned, Anticis are freely admitted into the European Council. Some Anticis are hardly ever called upon whereas the presence of others is continually requested. A prime minister's purpose may be completely mundane, such as a craving for a cup of coffee, or it may involve a matter of policy. The prime minister might ask the Antici directly for precise information. Via the Antici, he might relay a message to or request advice or facts from a member of the national delegation. Anticis have earned the title *agents de liaisons* because they shuttle communications between prime ministers and national delegations at European Councils. Additional officials are admitted to the room whenever needed by prime ministers.

From the above description, it can be seen that the traditional arrangement of isolating heads of government and their foreign ministers in a room of their own does not constitute a definite barrier to input from officials. The extent of bureaucratic participation in European Council matters will depend on the preferences of individual prime ministers. It appears less desirable to deny heads of government the assistance of their experts now that the European Council focuses on technically sophisticated issues instead of, as originally intended, the general orientations of EC policy and trends in the international economy.

Organization, Quality, and Scope of Discussion

In keeping with its deceptively lax appearance, the European Council does not have a formal agenda.17 In the beginning the motive behind not having an agenda was to maintain flexibility in discussion. Furthermore, if the European Council was to be a talking shop instead of a decisionmaking body, it had no need of an agenda. Traditionally, a letter in the name of the president of the European Council, the prime minister whose country holds the presidency, is sent to other heads of government and the president of the Commission shortly before a European Council. This presidency note, suggesting topics for discussion at the forthcoming European Council, provides the prospective agenda. In responding to this letter, heads of government may put forth additional discussion items and state their reactions to points in the letter.

The agenda continues to take shape in the meetings of COREPER and the General Affairs Council preceding the European Council. As explained in Chapter Two, the negotiations in the final days before a European Council are directed to reducing the number of outstanding issues and the extent of remaining differences on those issues. The presidency circulates a paper through the Antici Group several days before the European Council reflecting the progress made in preceding negotiations and informing participants about how it plans to conduct the European Council.

The London European Council of December 1986, was unusual in that it fell during a relatively idle period for the Community. Heads of government had time to recuperate from the tasking responsibility of negotiating amendments to the Treaty of Rome a year earlier at their meeting in Luxembourg, December 1985. The hard feelings that had developed between the British and French over the British budget dispute had also had time to subside. The Commission had not yet formulated its proposals for restructuring Community financing and rearranging budget priorities, which eventually became known as the Delors Plan. The Commission, therefore, only planned to introduce the subject of financial worries in London. As a result, the London European Council represented a breathing space before the next big negotiation on the Delors Plan was ready to begin at the next European Council in Brussels.

The agenda for London was not predetermined by unresolved issues that were still hanging or by pressing problems that could not be ignored. As for the latter instance, it was not that there were not severe problems but that strategies for addressing them had not fully matured. Consequently, the British had the opportunity rarely open to Presidencies of mostly writing their own agenda. The British were able to use their presidency to stress several themes of particular concern to Mrs. Thatcher, themes which were also not objectionable to other member countries. Mrs. Thatcher sent the customary letter of a page and a half in length to her fellow heads of government indicating that she would like the European Council to address strategies for relieving unemployment, such as creating jobs by measures to stimulate small businesses and by the timely completion of the internal market.[18] She also wanted the European Council to deal with themes related to a frontier free Europe, such as combatting terrorism, controlling drug traffic and supervising immigration. She enclosed two discussion papers totalling four pages in length covering these subjects, these intended to guide discussion at the European Council. Most of the content of this presidency communication eventually found its way into the conclusions agreed in London. The London European Council was exceptional in that it went according to plan with discussions producing the intended results. It resembled earlier gatherings of heads of government by its constructive discussion on commonly perceived problems and as it arrived at general conclusions meant to guide future action.

Unlike the London European Council, most of the European Councils of the 1980s had to bridge wide differences among the participants on precise questions. They had to be difficult negotiating sessions on policy details, instead of sessions devoted to fruitful and informed discussion on broad principles. The presidency, faced with issues that continue to hopelessly divide participants as a European Council approaches, has several strategies it might pursue. The management of a European Council depends on the individual style of the country serving as president as well as on the personality and particular concerns of the president. It is also affected by the intensity of conflict involved in the issues, especially if the presidency is an important party to such conflict. As a management option, the presidency might decide to present a note to the European Council that makes clear recommendations about what conclusions should be decided. The presidency is not expected to remain non-committal and opinionless. It is desirable for the presidency to take a position as long as it is acting without apparent self-interest or without deliberately helping the cause of an ally. A Brussels official expressed his belief that a silent presidency frequently does not accomplish its purposes.[19] Sometimes it is necessary for the presidency to give the lead if progress is to be made.

All Presidencies do not choose to give a specific lead in negotiations, especially if their particular interests are too closely linked to the issues at hand. The presidency may be uncomfortable taking a stance because it fears the appearance of bias. It is also possible that the presidency does not feel the issues are ripe enough for decision. In such cases, it may be preferable for the presidency to present a note to the European Council that outlines the range possible of solutions which have come up in preliminary negotiations without committing itself to any of them.

The presidency note will form the main basis of discussion in the European Council. It is often supplemented by other submissions. Sometimes a previous European Council has requested the Commission to prepare a memorandum on a specific policy question in time for consideration at its next meeting. Less frequently, member governments that have a serious stake in an issue or are keenly interested in promoting a viewpoint will submit a paper to the European Council.[20] Larger countries have the resources to develop initiatives and are more prone to make individual submissions than their smaller counterparts. A regular discussion paper prepared by the Commission is a report on the state of the economy in the Community, which has traditionally been the first item of discussion at European Councils. Differences in economic points-of-view have greatly narrowed in this decade so that heads of government usually agree with the Commission's economic findings as expressed in this report. The Commission chose to dispense with its economic report in Copenhagen, December 1987, in favor of giving fuller concentration to the Delors Plan.

The primary thrust of the first day's discussions is to try to get enough agreement on the main issues to enable the presidency to prepare conclusions with a good chance of being accepted during the next day's session. It is customary that the presidency with the technical assistance of the Council Secretariat prepares draft conclusions following the first day's discussions. These are released to official delegations at a late night or early morning hour. The second day's discussion in the European Council will resume on the basis of these draft conclusions. If the outcome of the European Council is promising, the second day's session will be devoted to small battles over the wording of conclusions. As the second day's session normally lasts half a day, a lot of time does not remain to resolve wide differences.

That the presidency has control over the wording of conclusions explains in part why the conclusions of the London European Council adopted much of the wording in the original Thatcher letter inviting heads of government to London. A member country wanting to challenge the content of conclusions has to make his appeal to the presidency. Sir Michael Butler recounts the time at the Stuttgart European Council of June 1983, when he, as Britain's permanent representative, realized that the word "net" was missing from a text specifying the amount of Britain's budget refund for 1983.[21] Even though Mrs. Thatcher had purposefully gotten the European Council to agree to writing net into the text, it was not in the conclusions being circulated at the end of the European Council. This omission could have made a significant difference in the amount of money returned to Britain. Butler, aware of the potential consequences of this omission, was able to convince the German Presidency to make the insertion, which he considered essential. Even though the conclusions had already been seen by the national delegations, the revision was made just before they were released to the press.

The actual discussion within the European Council has had to become more structured than in the past. Some degree of organization has to be a requisite if the contributions of twelve member governments are to be accommodated. In addition, a more technocratically oriented European Council has to strive for precision, evident in that the public texts of the European Council sometimes employ language suitable for regulations.

A *tour de table* will normally entail each country's spokesperson addressing a point for approximately three to five minutes. Heads of government and foreign ministers usually rely on speaking notes and are not very inclined to elaborate on a subject without the aid of notes. Officials confirmed that direct, personal, and spontaneous exchanges do occur in European Councils. For example, a debate broke out over South African sanctions following remarks made by Greek Prime Minister Papandreou at The Hague, June 1986.[22] This debate lasted for several hours. Even so, unprepared discussion is not the rule in the European Council.

Earlier summits and European Councils were designed with the idea that heads of government should perform the role of probing problems in the international economy and political disputes in the world and considering the broad lines of the future of the EC. Heads of government seemed content with a more distant involvement in the EC, seeing themselves as the theoreticians of Community development, the ones most capable of conducting the intellectual survey of global events, the *tour de grand horizon*. The decade that began with the British budget dispute and ended with the 1992 internal market program changed the role of heads of government in the EC. Specific problems had to be solved, definite and specialized options considered, and concrete decisions made.

Informal Exchanges of View

A variety of informal contacts takes place in the European Council's "margins," the popular term for the periods the European Council is not in formal session. The informal side of a European Council is potentially important for developing relationships of trust among EC politicians and officials and providing alternative negotiating arenas to the more formal sessions. Informal contacts permit the exchange of select information and the deliberate conveying of certain attitudes. An information-provider may choose privacy for delivering a piece of information because, as we have seen, the European Council is not leak-proof. However, a confidence shared with another official or politician might be considered sufficiently safe. In addition, the person who initiates intimate dialogue, especially the exchange of restricted information, confers privilege on the participants. A feeling of alliance, if not actually a proposal of an alliance strategy, may be the result. Intimate exchanges may be used to signal a variety of constructive attitudes, such as goodwill, sincerity, and seriousness of intent, where these have previously been absent. Thus, personal contacts may spur movement in a deadlocked negotiation or contribute to confidence-building for future uses. In general, the opportunities discussed above might not be as great in the pre-cooked negotiations, which tend to predominate, in the European Council's formal sessions.

The London Declaration, issued by heads of government at their meeting in London, June 1977, specified "types of discussion" the European Council could be expected to enter into.[23] Three discussion areas were designated: (1) informal discussions; (2) discussions that involved goal-setting, decisionmaking or that were intended to result in adopted texts; (3) discussions on issues that could not be settled at lower EC levels. "Informal exchanges of view" led the list, an indicator of their importance to heads of governments. They were described as being "of a wide-ranging nature held in the greatest privacy and not designed to lead to formal decisions or public statements." This quasi-formal description is of the fireside chat and dinner, not necessarily held in that order, which occurs the first evening of a European Council. These discussions are restricted to the heads of government and the president of the Commission. Not meant to be converted into public texts, they do not require extensive preparation, if any preparation at all.[24] The letter inviting heads of government to attend the European Council only briefly refers to the subjects which will be covered in informal discussions.

Mrs. Thatcher's invitation to the London European Council of December 1986, mentioned that the dinner conversation would be used in part by Mr. Delors to present his views on the Community's financial situation. As it turned out, this topic was covered during the fireside discussion. Mrs. Thatcher's letter continued that the heads of government would explore events affecting East-West relations at dinner, and, at that time, she would also inform the others about her recent visit with President Reagan. It is not unusual for heads of government to use the occasion of a European Council to report on the important state visits that have occurred in the interim between their EC meetings.[25]

International events were foremost on the minds of leaders at the London European Council, following as it did the Rejkjavík Summit between Gorbachev and Reagan. In Rejkjavik, Reagan had amazed European leaders by discussing deep cuts in European-based weaponry without previously consulting them.[26] To add to European anxieties, Reagan had publicly addressed the Iran-Contra scandal for the first time in the week preceding the European Council. Weakened leadership in the United States was extremely undesirable in the face of Gorbachev's vigorous leadership of the Soviet Union and his overtures to the West.

The heads of government in London could not help but address the rapidly changing international climate. Not surprisingly, the conversation at dinner concerned disarmament issues and the leaders' impressions of Gorbachev, including their assessment of the chances for his proposed reforms in the Soviet Union.[27]

The European Council in The Hague, June 1986, had a significant international dimension that provided the focus for informal discussions. Dinner at The Hague was devoted to attempts to reach a compromise on a sanctions package against South Africa.[28] In his post-European Council statement to the press, Delors commented on the usefulness of the fireside chat on the issues of East-West relations, problems in Latin America and tensions between Greece and Turkey.[29] The reference to Greece and Turkey was surprising in so far as the conclusions agreed at The Hague included no mention of this subject. Obviously, public knowledge about informal discussions is limited to what is deliberately or unconsciously exposed by the participants in press statements and in addresses to parliaments after participants return home.

If the European Council's agenda is overcrowded or sessions have not progressed as planned due to disagreements, unfinished work may spill over into the fireside and dinner contexts. Under such circumstances international issues will go by the wayside. Bulmer and Wessels recognized that the EC's internal focus, which became especially problematic with the British budget dispute, "restricted the value of informal discussions for exchanging views on broader issues."[30] This was true during the 1980s when political cooperation was purposefully neglected in favor of getting the EC back on track and setting the EC's future policy course, this development more fully explained in the next chapter. The internal agenda clearly took precedence in Luxembourg, December 1985, with heads of government so intent on completing the treaty reforms comprising the Single Act, that they extended their meeting by twelve hours.[31] Altogether they devoted thirty scarcely interrupted hours to the task at hand.[32] They became so directly involved that they actually participated in drafting some of the texts of the reforms.[33]

The British budget dispute was another all-consuming subject. In Brussels, March 1984, Mrs. Thatcher evidently carried the Treaty of Rome to dinner to help her argue her case.[34] As it turned out, a bitter argument lasted for several hours. So as not to repeat the experience of this dinner in Brussels, at Fontainebleau, June 1984, the heads of government refused to let their dinner conversation be monopolized by arguments over the British budget dispute. They instead referred the subject to the foreign ministers, who always hold a separate dinner while the prime ministers dine together.[35]

While the European Council is in session, groups of officials may participate in parallel meetings. Political Directors of the twelve member countries meet on the first day while the EC is in session to prepare draft texts of political statements. Their texts are considered for adoption by the European Council on the second day, as will be seen in Chapter Five. If so desired by the presidency, special working groups of officials from the twelve member countries and the Commission may also be set up to prepare specific issues for the European Council. In 1979 the Report of the Three Wise Men on institutional reform referred to the frequency of these parallel meetings at European Councils. It recommended that they be controlled by the presidency to avoid "duplications of effort."[36]

The activities in the margins of narrower groups of officials frequently influence the outcome of policy debates in the European Council. This is especially true if a problem reduces to a conflict between a few member countries or concerns the objections of one member country. Behind-the-scenes meetings between key officials, and sometimes their political masters, working at odd hours to avert failure, appear to be a regular feature of European Councils concerned with large negotiations. Quiet diplomacy involving President Mitterrand, Chancellor Kohl, their agricultural ministers and officials, meeting in various combinations and settings over the course of the Brussels European Council of June 1987, finally produced the long-awaited agreement on phasing out MCAs.[37] Kohl and Mitterrand put the finishing touches on what amounted to a bilateral agreement over breakfast before the second day's session began. This agreement was then ratified by the European Council.

The following year at the Brussels European Council of February 1988, Mrs. Thatcher surprised many observers by making a late hour decision to accept the settlement proposed by the other member countries. Mrs. Thatcher had responded to urging from officials, notably British Permanent Representative Sir David Hannay and the British Secretary-General of the Commission David Williamson, who convinced her that she had secured the best possible offer.[38] The way was cleared for decisions on the Delors Plan the following morning in the European Council. The above examples show the capacity of European Councils for continuous negotiations and the sometimes decisive nature of informal decisionmaking.

Meetings in the margins have developed around special relationships among certain member countries. A customary breakfast meeting between the German chancellor and the French president takes place before the second day's session of the European Council. This meeting can be used to sort out differences or to produce a common strategy to be pursued in the European Council. The disagreement between the French and Germans over MCAs, previously mentioned, was the subject of the breakfast meeting in Brussels, June 1987. Both France and Germany have cooperated in the symbolism of solidarity since the Community's earliest days. This symbolism is so far unaffected by the improved relations between Britain and Germany during the Major premiership and France's hurt pride as Germany begins to wield its influence in the EC and Eastern and Central Europe. In traditional form, France and Germany announced in May 1992 their creation of a Franco-German force. This move seemed designed to preempt attempts by other countries to influence defense plans during this period of adjustment in the NATO role.

Another special relationship exists among the Benelux countries, which hold their own meeting before the second day's session of the European Council. This meeting, also available for alliance-building and strategizing, has symbolic value. In the Europe of the Six, the Benelux countries feared French domination, and as Germany recovered, the prospect of a Franco-German *directoire* commanding the EC's institutions. The threat seemed especially real for institutional arrangements that minimized the role of the Commission, such as the European Council and the institutions of EPC. Benelux unity continues from this traditional fear and the well-developed habit of cooperation in the EC and other contexts.

Countries with troubled relations, such as Ireland and Britain, may find the margins of the European Council convenient for discussing their difficulties. Partially owing to their participation in the European Council, former Irish Taoiseach Garret FitzGerald and Mrs. Thatcher developed a rapport. The margins of the European Council provided the security and privacy for them to proceed with work on the Anglo-Irish Accord. Mrs. Thatcher and former Irish Taoiseach Charles Haughey, at least, continued the tradition of talking, by confronting tense issues in, most likely, tense bilaterals.[39] When Mr. Haughey was head of government previously, relations had become so strained between their countries that Mrs. Thatcher refused to share an interpreter during meals, which would have required their being seated together.[40] With a favorable political climate, European Council and wider EC contacts are used for damage control and even marked improvements in Anglo-Irish relations.

If intimacy is lacking in the more business-like sessions of the European Council, the margins of a European Council have heads of government rubbing shoulders together at mealtimes. Whereas notetakers and interpreters may cramp communications in the formal meetings, the margins provide a safe haven for information exchanges.

Effects of Socialization and Bureaucratization

The interactions that occur at a European Council enhance the already familiar relationships among leaders of EC member countries. A round of bilaterals usually precedes European Councils, in which the head of government, serving as President of the European Council, makes a tour of capitals to inform himself of (and try to influence) the positions of the other heads of government. State visits and other kinds of summitry (such as that of NATO, OECD, the French and German Cooperation Council, and the UN) bring together a portion of the Twelve. Some heads of government maintain friendly telephone contact. For instance, Chancellor Kohl and Prime Minister Major, who reportedly relates to Kohl as he would to a European uncle, have taken to telephoning each other.

EC foreign ministers, mainly because of their EC involvement, are in more frequent contact with each other than cabinet members in the United States. The intergovernmental conferences (IGCs) on EMU and political union throughout 1991 meant that foreign ministers' EC roles were more demanding than ever. Sir Geoffrey Howe describes the knowledge EC foreign ministers have about each others' perceptions as "complete provisional foresight as to the opinions of others."[41] Foreign ministers shoulder much of the burden of participation in regional and international organizations. With the recent changes in Europe, regional organizations, such as the Conference on Security and Cooperation in Europe (CSCE) and the Western European Union (WEU), have new significance and meet more frequently. At present, there is not an official meeting of the WEU at the summit level (unless the European Council is considered the informal equivalent). Therefore, political operations of the WEU are delegated to joint meetings of foreign ministers and defense ministers.

Undoubtedly, the European Council has served very well some relationships among EC politicians. In the past, German Foreign Minister Hans Dietrich Genscher and French Foreign Minister Roland Dumas were "thick as thieves," holding advance consultations and coming to each other's defense in EC meetings.[42] Genscher was not nearly so Anglo-oriented. The unusually strong personal relationship between Prime Minister Major and Chancellor Kohl was in evidence at the Maastricht summit of December 1991. Ignoring Genscher's obvious prodding, the German chancellor refused to criticize his British friend on policy differences, in regard to which their two countries' positions were actually very far apart.[43] By now the friendship of President Giscard d'Estaing and Chancellor Schmidt is legendary; they were used to sitting beside each other in European Councils. No longer, however, are the

French and German seats located next to each other. The seating in the European Council is by alphabetical arrangement of country seats, with the national spelling of country names being used. When Greece joined the Community, Helas fell in between Bundesrepublic and La France and interrupted their cozy seating arrangement.

Participating in the European Council may enhance the good feelings leaders naturally have toward each other just as it may accomplish the opposite. Even though Mrs. Thatcher and Chancellor Kohl served together in the European Council for over half a decade, disappointments with each other tended to recur and prevented a really good relationship from cementing. Nonetheless, Mrs. Thatcher overcame her inherent suspicions and cooperated (albeit reservedly) with German unification. The experience of working with Kohl in the European Council, no doubt, informed her decision and helped develop her ability to trust him.

The minimal function of a European Council is that of a social club. Contacts between heads of government are the tip of the iceberg, as seen by the description in this chapter of the literally hundreds of national representatives who attend European Councils. The result is that a maze of multi-national linkages is forged through work-related and social encounters through the European Council, and as a part of the entire EC process.

The European Council's maximal function is that of decisionmaking, which the large bureaucratic presence signifies. Heads of government need expertise on a wide range of subjects at their fingertips to conclude the large package deals, which they no longer hesitate to negotiate. Leo Tindemans, having repeatedly served as Belgium's prime minister, made the observation that heads of government are "limited in their intellectual capacities" to deal with the technicalities of EC issues.44 Mirroring this concern, the Report of the Three Wise Men, of which Tindemans was the principal author, recommended that technical ministers be asked, whenever needed, to participate directly in European Council discussions.45

With the European Council's present organization, bureaucrats need not hamper discussion in the European Council because they do not hover in the conference room. At the same time, heads of government need not experience trepidation in face of highly complex issues because they are well-served by their national delegations. The technocratic orientation, once seen as being undesirable on the part of the European Council, is perhaps its greatest contribution in recent years, as will be seen in the discussion of the European Council's role in the Delors Plan in the next chapter. Bureaucratization of the European Council enhances political control over an extremely bureaucratic EC decisionmaking process.

The special mix of personnel and the multiple environments assure that subjects of all kinds can and do receive serious, and potentially significant, treatment in the course of a European Council.

Notes

1.   For a brief description of the original conception of the European Council, see Holt and Hoscheit, "The European Council and Domestic Policy-Making," pp. 7-8. On the subject of excluding officials from participation in the European Council, see also Bulmer and Wessels, *The European Council*, p. 49.

2.   Christopher Bo Bramson discusses the objections to excluding foreign ministers from participation in the European Council in, "Le Conseil Européen: Son Fonctionnement Et Ses Resultats De 1975 A 1981," *Revue Du Marcheé Commun*, 25 (1982), p. 627. Leo Tindemans refers to the Netherlands as especially having a problem with excluding foreign ministers from meetings where international affairs would be discussed in, "Le Conseil Européen," *European Yearbook*, 28 (1980), p. 7.

3.   "Seatless Minister," *The Times*, 6 December 1986, p. 5.

4.   Interview by the author at the Commission in Brussels, 16 November 1987.

5.   Information concerning the officials stationed in the European Council is based on various interviews by the author of Community and member country officials in Brussels, 3 November 1987. See also Bulmer and Wessels, who account for seven officials in the conference room in *The European Council*, p. 50. The number reported to the author was ten.

6.   Interview by the author at a Permanent Representation in Brussels, 10 November 1987.

7.   Details of this dispute were reported by Jacques Almaric, "Le Sommet De La Haye; Une seule voix, trois bouches," *Le Monde*, 27 June 1986, p. 3.

8.   Interview by the author at a Permanent Representation in Brussels, 10 November 1987.

9.   The information is first translated into the languages of the notetakers, then into the language of the Antici of the Presidency, and lastly, into the languages of the Antici Group.

10.   Hilary Barnes, "Doubt on Denmark pledge," *Financial Times*, 9 July 1987, p. 3, records an example of confusion in the aftermath of a European Council. Danish Prime Minister Poul Schlüter had signed the communiqué from the Brussels European Council of June 1987, which had expressed support for the Commission plan to link member countries' budget contributions to gross domestic product (GDP). Yet, he represented it to the Market Relations Committee of the Danish Parliament, the Folketing, as only a "symbolic" commitment while the Danish foreign minister had left the public impression that Denmark did not support the Commission plan exactly as it was proposed.

11.   Interview by the author at a Permanent Representation in Brussels, 17 November 1987.

12.   Interview by the author at the Commission in Brussels, 17 November 1987.

13.   "Britain and Europe; Excuse me, is this the right bus?" in *The Economist*, 17 December 1988, p. 52, captures the past flavor of domestic pressures, which supported Mrs. Thatcher's role as the antagonist of the EC, in the following lines: "In Britain fights against Brussels are popular; in most other countries they are not. Those who berate Mrs. Thatcher for her hostility to European integration have missed the point. If Mrs. Thatcher were not there, somebody else would be: less shrill perhaps, but driven by the same homegrown imperatives."

14.   Michael Charlier, "A change of understanding about the state and politics," reprinted in *The German Tribune*, 1 May 1992, pp. 1,3.

15.   "Denmark; Take it or leave it," *The Economist*, 23 May 1992, p. 58.

16.   Holt and Hoscheit, eds., "The European Council and Domestic Policy-Making," p. 8.

17.   On the subject of European Council agenda formation, see Bonvicini and Regelsberger, "The organizational and political implications of the establishment of the European Council," pp. 9-13.

18.   A copy of Mrs. Thatcher's letter inviting the other heads of government to attend the London Summit, December 1986, was made available to the author during the course of interviews in Brussels, November 1987.

19.   Interview by the author with an official from a Permanent Representation in Brussels, 11 November 1987.

20.   For example, Britain submitted a memorandum for discussion at The Hague European Council of June 1986, which laid out measures for stimulating employment, a favorite theme which Mrs. Thatcher's, stressed again at the next European Council in London. See "Le Sommet De La Haye; Vers une aide aux Noirs sud-africains," *Le Monde*, 28 June 1986, p. 1.

21.   Butler, *Europe: More than a Continent*, p. 102.

22.   Interview by the author at the Commission in Brussels, 4 November 1987.

23.   For the London Declaration on the European Council (1977), see Appendix 2, Bulmer and Wessels, *The European Council*, pp. 148-49.

24.   The European Council's informal exchanges of view are described by the "Report on European Institutions," more commonly known as the Report of the Three Wise Men, presented by the Committee of Three to the European Council, October 1979, p. 21.

25.   At the Luxembourg European Council of December 1980, Chancellor Schmidt shared with the other heads of Government his impressions from his recent meeting with newly-elected President Reagan. See Richard Eder, "Common Market Warns Russians Not to Take Action Against Poland," *The New York Times*, 3 December 1980, p. A8.

26.   Chirac mentioned the "disquiet" in Europe caused by Rejkjavik in his statements to the press following the London European Council, December 1986. See Francis X. Clines, "European Leaders Voice Concern That Iran Affair Impairs Alliance," *The New York Times*, 7 December 1986, p. 1; Guy de Jonquieres, "Challenge to the post-war world order," *Financial Times Survey*, 17 November 1988, p. 4.

27.   Interview by the author at a Permanent Representation, 9 November 1987, and at the U.S. Mission to the EC, 4 November 1987, in Brussels. See also Andrew McEwen, "EEC backing for Britain's crusade," *The Times*, 6 December 1986, p. 1.

28.   Richard Owen, "EEC summit deadlock on sanctions," *The Times*, 27 June 1986, p. 1.

29.   *The Bulletin of the EC*, 6 (1986), p. 12.

30.   Bulmer and Wessels, *The European Council*, p. 56.

31.   Richard Owen, "EEC agrees on reform deal after marathon," *The Times*, 4 December 1985, p. 1.

32.   *Bulletin of the EC*, 11 (1985), p. 7.

33.   Interview by the author at the Commission in Brussels, 10 November 1987.

34.   Butler, *Europe: More than a Continent*, p. 106.

35.   Ian Murray, "Mitterrand takes summit guests on tour of his European dream world," *The Times*, 25-26 June 1984, p. 6.

36.   "Report on European Institutions," p. 22.

37.   Monetary Compensatory Accounts (MCAs) refer to an extremely complex system that came into being to offset the effects of exchange rate fluctuations on EC farm prices. Because the system tended to benefit Germany and was costly to France, it was a terribly divisive issue for these two countries.

38.   David Buchan and Tim Dickson, "An end to the nay-saying," *Financial Times*, 15 February 1988, p. 17.

39.   "What's European for Justice?" *The Economist*, 3 December 1988, p. 52.

40.   Tugendhat, *Making Sense of Europe*, pp. 169-70.

41.   "Europe's top club of frequent flyers," *The Economist*, 2 May 1992, p. 64.

42.   *Ibid.*

43.   *Ibid.*

44.   Tindemans writes, "In effect, the heads of government are also limited in their intellectual capacities," in "Le Conseil Européen," p. 9. (Translated from French by the author).

45.   *Ibid.*, p. 11.

4

The Delors Plan and Technical Decisionmaking

The British budget dispute of 1980-84 marked the period in which the European Council became deeply involved in internal Community matters. In undertaking this involvement the European Council opened itself to criticism for taking on a role for which it had no apparent aptitude and certainly lacked a legal basis for what it was doing. There was, however, precedent for the European Council to become involved in community internal decisionmaking, precedent pre-dating the British budget dispute. According to Bulmer and Wessels, from its first meeting in March, 1975 to December, 1984, the European Council was involved in internal issues, and not just in the general way of setting guidelines (the more legitimate function of the European Council).[1] Bulmer and Wessels identify 1980-84, the years spanning the British budget dispute, as a distinct phase in which the European Council's focus on Community affairs departed from previous practice. Prior to this, the European Council was more outward looking; its discussions leaned more to the international economic and political situation.

The British budget dispute of 1980-84 created widespread negative perceptions about the European Council's decisional role in Community matters. The Delors Plan of 1987-88, however, amounted to a renegotiation of several of the issues contained in the British budget dispute. The European Council's handling of the Delors Plan contrasts sharply with how it handled the British budget dispute. The Delors Plan suggests the heightened potential of European Council decisionmaking in Community matters, a potential all the more interesting because the issues dealt with were similar to those in the British budget dispute.

The British Budget Dispute

British dissatisfaction with its EC budgetary situation bedeviled the Community from the moment Britain joined the Community. When Mrs. Thatcher's Conservative government came to power in 1979, that situation became the subject of an especially bitter contest between Britain and her partners. Mrs. Thatcher developed her reputation for being "unEuropean" because of her unrelenting drive to see Britain's budgetary complaints satisfied. The member governments did not share Britain's sense of immediacy and concern. Thus, the dispute embodied Britain's special circumstances. Events would later bear out "that the description 'the British problem' is to some extent a misnomer," as the other EC member countries began to feel discomfort with the shoe that pinched Great Britain.[2]

Britain's budgetary problems were twofold.[3] Britain believed it was at a disadvantage in both contributions to and receipts from the Community budget. Until later amended by the Delors Plan, budget contributions were determined by the system the Council of Ministers established in April 1970. This system designated three kinds of resources as the Community's "own resources": (a) custom duties on imports from non-EC countries on products covered by the Common Customs Tariff; (b) agricultural levies on food imports from non-EC countries administered under the Common Agricultural Policy (CAP); and (c) a percentage of value added tax (VAT) subject to EC call-in but not to exceed a 1% VAT ceiling (later revised upwards at Fontainebleau). By remaining outside of the Community until 1973, the British had a late start in reorienting their trading patterns and, thus, relied heavily on non-EC imports, the effect of which was to increase their budget bill.

A more serious problem arose in the area of budget receipts or "net transfers" from the Community to Britain. To put it quite simply, Britain felt that it was not benefitting as much as it should from Community policies given the high level of its budget contributions. The sticking point for Britain, was that a disproportionate amount of Community expenditure went to the CAP. The European Agriculture Guidance and Guarantee Fund (EAGGF), the Community instrument for farm support, consumed between 65% and 75% of overall Community resources over the decade ending in 1984.[4] With its smaller farming population, Britain did not stand to benefit to the same extent as member countries such as Denmark, France, and the Netherlands. Britain found itself a net contributor to the Community budget because of its import position and its inability to claim a compensatory amount of Community expenditure.

The British budget problem came under consideration in the negotiations for Britain's accession to the Community. During these negotiations the Commission offered the famous assurance that "should unacceptable situations arise within the present Community, or in an enlarged Community, the very survival of the Community would demand that the institutions find equitable solutions." The Labour Government installed in February 1974 rekindled the budget problem renegotiating Britain's accession to the Community. It secured an instrument for reimbursement to Britain in the event of excessive contributions, but the so-called "Financial Mechanism" never returned any funds to Britain. The early efforts to rectify Britain's budgetary situation differed from those that would follow in that the focus was on excessive gross contributions. Once the renegotiation was concluded, Prime Minister Harold Wilson and Foreign Minister James Callaghan announced they were satisfied that all of Britain's problems, even those having to do with the Community budget, had been settled.[5]

When the position of Britain as a net contributor became especially pronounced in 1978, Callaghan as prime minister found himself in the unfortunate position of having to begin the second "renegotiation."[6] Mrs. Thatcher took over in May 1979. By this time the British Government had arrived at its definition of the British budget problem, targeting "the main issue of the short-fall in receipts and the excessive net contribution."[7]

At her first European Council in Dublin, December 1979, Mrs. Thatcher ruffled European feelings by stating the purpose of her mission as getting "my money back."[8] Her position was clear, "We are not asking for a penny piece of the Community's money," and she might have continued, but only what is rightfully ours.[9] The purpose of giving the Community its own resources had been to create a financial base independent of member governments. Community devotees saw Mrs. Thatcher's demand for her money as a claim to something that belonged not to Britain but to the Community. It was, in essence, "an attack on the whole principle on which the Community's 'own resources' system of financing is based."[10]

At Dublin, Mrs. Thatcher introduced the other heads of government to her preference for practicalities over philosophical abstractions, which became the much-criticized Thatcher style in dealing with the EC. She relentlessly stressed that the sanctified principle, the Community's resources belong to no one but the Community, was fine for the member countries materially benefitting from the EC, but Britain would have no part of it.[11] She would have a hard time reconciling herself to the view of the other member countries and the Commission that British contributions had no relation to Britain's entitlement to sums contained in the Community budget. "A longstanding dispute of an almost theological nature" ensued between Mrs. Thatcher and the others over whose resources were whose in the budget, the others repeatedly insisting that they were the property of the Community.[12] Who owned the Community resources derived from agricultural levies and customs duties was a contentious element of informal exchanges among heads of government during dinner at the Brussels European Council of March 1984, indicating that the dispute dragged on for years.[13]

The dispute reached the most serious proportions when it became embroiled with the question of reforming the CAP. Deciding on a mechanism for refunding money to Britain at first offered the most promising solution. Eventually, however, Mrs. Thatcher could not accept a solution which did not curb CAP spending. The CAP's wastefulness was contrary to all Mrs. Thatcher's domestic policies of economic efficiency, and the spending, wasteful or not, did not greatly benefit Britain.

The CAP was not only one of the original cornerstones of the Community, but for integrationists, it represented a policy sector in which a high level of integration had been achieved. CAP expenditure, so objectionable to the British, represented a financial commitment on the part of member governments. The CAP had also been a model of successful integration in the large extent to which decisionmaking was transferred to EC institutions. Mrs. Thatcher and the British disturbed the mystique surrounding the CAP. They questioned whether Community resources could not be better spent and whether EC agricultural decisions had produced the best results.

In criticizing the CAP, the British faced a difficult opponent. The French were not willing to countenance any change. The dispute became hopelessly embedded in the politics of the Community from the Dublin European Council of December 1979, until it was put to rest at Fontainebleau, June 1984. Tugendhat, who was present as Vice-President of the Commission for most of this period likened it to a "ball and chain round the Community's ankle."[14]

The European Council became Mrs. Thatcher's preferred forum for pressing the British cause. European Councils turned into exercises in frustration as the scope of the issue grew along with compounding technical complexities and the impossibility of a quick and easy solution. Aside from the mushrooming of the issue, competing conceptions of the development of the Community were at stake as well as decisions about how benefits would be shared. Tugendhat noted, "The personal prestige of each of the big three was bound up with it."[15] Hijacked by fiercely guarded national interests, lacking the skills to manage technical negotiations, vesting undue influence in a head of government who lacked sympathy for the ways of the Community, the European Council found itself the target of criticism and negative assessments of its decisionmaking capacity.

The Fontainebleau European Council of June 1984, finally broke the impasse as the result of progress made at previous European Councils and impending circumstances. By the time the heads of government met at Fontainebleau, the EC desperately needed new resources. The Community budget was already overspent by the time of Fontainebleau, and the Commission planned budget expenditures for the next year in excess of available resources.[16] The situation had become so dire that President Mitterrand approached Mrs. Thatcher the week before Fontainebleau to ask her to participate in a stop-gap loan to the EC, which she refused to do.[17]

The Community needed a medium-term solution for the budget shortages. The only long-term solution was to raise the percentage of VAT available for Community use. But, raising the VAT ceiling past the 1% level previously agreed required the unanimous agreement of member governments. Mrs. Thatcher's strongest lever in the dispute was her refusal to grant approval for additional EC resources until British demands were satisfied. She held to this strategy late into the night before the second day's session of the Stuttgart European Council of June 1983.[18]

At Fontainebleau, Mrs. Thatcher won redress of the excessive net contribution through a mechanism to reduce British VAT contributions according to a formula taking effect from 1985. The agreement would operate as long as the EC stayed within a new VAT ceiling, raised from 1% to 1.4%. No one knew how long the Community could meet its needs within the new VAT ceiling, but the EC would probably need a new negotiation before 1988.[19] The correction mechanism supplied the automaticity the British desired until the VAT ceiling had to be renegotiated. The press conference following Fontainebleau revealed a gap in the expected duration of the correction mechanism. President Mitterrand stated that he assumed the mechanism was for a "limited period of time." Mrs. Thatcher's goal was permanence.[20] Fontainebleau offered a respite in the dispute but not a final resolution. After Fontainebleau, Commission President Gaston Thorn predicted that the Commission was "going to be up against the wall and facing these budget difficulties," even with the agreed increased resources.[21]

The British had not achieved a long-term solution. They were, however, comforted knowing that the member governments and the Commission recognized and provided redress for a situation in which a member country sustained a "budgetary burden which is excessive in relation to its relative prosperity."[22] Fontainebleau established the principle that a national contribution can be excessive measured in terms of national wealth. This principle provided support for future British arguments to redress its budget problem, as long as Britain could demonstrate that its contribution was too high in light of its national income relative to that of other member governments. Obviously, an improvement in Britain's GDP would undercut this argument as could a revised financing system.

The principle defined an excessive contribution to be one based on the imbalance between gross contribution and national income, and decoupled it from a consideration of net contributions. The Commission could, therefore, maintain several years later in the lead-up to negotiations on the Delors Plan:

> ... that the idea of a budget excess or shortfall [i.e., net gains and losses in the member countries from the Community budget] is inconsistent with that of the own resources of the Community. Nor can the budgetary benefit (or disadvantage) a country may draw (or suffer) from its membership in any circumstances reflect, much less measure, its interest in belonging to the Community.[23]

In summary, if a member country made a claim for a budget correction based on net contributions, it was not sufficient. The EC could thus safeguard the principle of own resources. But, if a member country demonstrated the other conditions relating to gross contribution and national income, it had a sufficient claim.

Even though the problem of net contributions was not specifically involved in the correction mechanism, the reduction in the total contribution removed much of the pressure. Mrs. Thatcher could claim before the House of Commons that budgetary discipline would be respected.[24] To Mrs. Thatcher, "budgetary discipline" meant that increases in agricultural spending would not outstrip the new EC financial base agreed in Fontainebleau. Reform of the CAP was supposed to lead to an eventual curbing of the upwards spiral of agricultural spending. Mrs. Thatcher maintained that budgetary discipline should be "legally binding." As this would encompass amendments to the Treaty of Rome, her proposal ran into staunch resistance. Mrs. Thatcher had to content herself with "guarantees," the word she used in comments to the press after Fontainebleau, that budgetary discipline would be enforced.[25]

Butler, who saw the entire working out of the dispute as Britain's permanent representative in Brussels, summed up the results in this way:

So the final package contained some progress on budget discipline and the beginning of agricultural reform as well as a budget mechanism for the UK in return for allowing other member states to increase their contribution.26

Britain had tried to convince the other member countries and the Commission that it was not only in the interests of Britain but also in the interests of the Community to find solutions to all of the issues in the dispute. Mrs. Thatcher liked to point out that the public deserved to have Community spending brought under control. She argued that if decisive action were not taken, other member countries would also find themselves in an unfavorable net position in relation to the EC budget.27

The art of Community compromise seemed to be alien to Mrs. Thatcher's nature. She wanted the whole package and would not accept a compromise for part of it, even if that part comprised most of it. The other countries were not ready to deal. Mrs. Thatcher got nowhere by simply presenting the merits and justice of her case. Determined to have her way, she resorted to extracting concessions from the others by such means as withholding her approval to agricultural pricing packages. This strategy got Mrs. Thatcher ad hoc rebates, but the permanent settlement remained elusive. The atmosphere soured: Mrs. Thatcher could not get the longer-term solution she wanted, and she became frustrated with her lack of progress. The others resented their being railroaded into making concessions, particularly when the ad hoc rebates returned far greater sums of money to Britain than originally estimated. The other nations prepared to stand more firmly against Mrs. Thatcher during the next round. It was a "no win" situation. What each side sought did not permit a solution all the member governments could live with. Mrs. Thatcher could not have the whole package as long as all the advantage would go to Britain. Denying Mrs. Thatcher what she wanted did not make "winners" out of the others because she would not admit defeat and get on with the work of the Community.

This standoff between Mrs. Thatcher and the others meant non-decision in the European Council, which tended to carry over to the Council of Ministers, lacking the political go-ahead from the powers that be. Non-decision in the European Council did not necessarily have to be an inappropriate means of handling the dispute. If Mrs. Thatcher ever became convinced that she lacked the means to force a settlement, the dispute could quietly fade out of sight without creating the impasse in the European Council and in the Council of Ministers.

The British budget dispute discredited the European Council. The years of "non-negotiability" of the dispute left the impression that the European Council did not have the capacity to make decisions, except for temporary measures. When the crucial medium-term solution came, it was too late to rectify this image of the European Council. That it took five years diminished the feat of reaching a settlement. The European Council's involvement with the British budget dispute suggested that it was ill-prepared to handle negotiations on internal EC affairs for a variety of reasons. It was not a body that adhered to Treaty procedures designed to overcome national obstacles to decision. Heads of government seemed stumped by the technical details they had been asked to deal with during the British budget dispute. The European Council had tried unsuccessfully to usurp the powers of the Council of Ministers, which was far more experienced in these matters and the rightful decisionmaker. The European Council had demonstrated a tendency to take matters into its own hands without accepting direction from and acting on initiatives of the Commission. Considering the uncertainties surrounding the decisional ability and propriety of the European Council, it is surprising that in 1987 the Delors Commission would ask the European Council to involve itself in complex negotiations that recalled the issues of the British budget dispute.

The Delors Plan

At the London European Council of December 1986, Commission President Jacques Delors explained to heads of government the severity of the financial crisis facing the Community. Even though the Fontainebleau European Council of June 1984, had settled the British budget dispute by producing commitments to budgetary discipline and reform of the CAP, the financial requirements of the Community once again exceeded available resources.

In February 1987 the Commission unveiled a document entitled "Making A Success Of The Single Act; A New Frontier For Europe." The document was the Commission's strategy for addressing Community finances. It proposed to reorient budget priorities and increase resources to enlarge the impact of the Community. The Delors Plan, as the Commission proposals came to be called, at base consisted of four major headings (1) CAP reform; (2) structural funds; (3) new financing; and (4) budgetary discipline.

CAP Reform

In terms of CAP reform, the Commission reiterated the position it had maintained since Fontainebleau, that is, an end to agricultural surpluses and the consequent spending increases. The most controversial part of CAP reform was the Commission's intention to introduce more flexibility into the intervention mechanisms to discourage overproduction. The Commission committed itself to controlling surplus production and curbing increases in agricultural spending. The major exception was the Commission's commitment to the preservation of the countryside. To meet this goal, the Commission was prepared to make special arrangements to insure the survival of the small farmer. Nonetheless, the Commission entered a reminder that it could not "solve all the problems arising in this area."[28]

Structural Funds

The second element of the Delors Plan, the Structural Funds, encompassed three specific funds. The European Regional Development Fund (ERDF) was dedicated to assistance for underdeveloped and declining regions. The European Social Fund (ESF), the Social Fund in Community jargon, centered around employment objectives. The third fund, the EAGGF Guidance Section, targetted rural development. Together, these funds operated to assist member countries and regions which were less well-off or experiencing economic troubles.[29]

The ultimate goal of the Commission in its proposals for the Structural Funds was to make them "part of an ambitious macro-economic growth strategy with an eye to 1992."[30] The key to this strategy was the Commission proposal that the resources belonging to the Structural Funds be doubled by 1992, the year in which the EC was supposed to have completed its internal market. Linking the doubling of the Structural Funds to 1992 tacitly admitted that the underdeveloped regions would not be ready to face new competition in 1992 (especially that of the economically powerful EC member countries) without an injection of resources. In preparing less developed countries for 1992, the Commission also proposed to focus the benefits of the Structural Funds on the poorest regions. The Commission named Portugal, Ireland, Greece, southern Italy, areas of Spain, Northern Ireland, and the overseas territories of France as deserving consideration as among the "least-favored regions."[31]

New Financing

Obviously, to double the Structural Funds would mean increasing the existing EC budget. The projected EC budget required new resources not only because the Commission proposed deepening the financial commitment to existing Community policies but because the EC budget had already exhausted its resources by the beginning of 1987. This shortfall occurred even though the Fontainebleau Agreement was supposed to avoid such a financial disaster. Indeed, the Commission maintained that since 1983 the Community had experienced annual shortfalls which accounting tricks had concealed.

The situation was all the more urgent because the Community had set out on a new policy direction as a result of the Single Act, which amended the Treaty of Rome in 1986. The Commission insisted the Community lacked the financial base to fulfill these new commitments in such areas as research and technology, the environment and completing the internal market.

The Commission needed new resources, and it wanted a new way of raising funds, believing that the old financing system had basic weaknesses.[32] The Commission summed up the deficiencies in the old system of financing as providing "neither the volume, nor the stability, nor the flexibility which the Community needs now and in the future."[33] The Commission proposed to create a new resource (called the "fourth resource," as there were already three other resources in place) for acquiring new income for the Community. Under the new system, budget contributions would be linked more closely to national wealth. The new system would respond to the old British complaint that its contributions were excessive in terms of its relative wealth. At the same time, the proposed system was sensitive to underdeveloped member countries. It would also permit the Community budget to grow at a rate closer to that of Community GNP, a linkage not possible under the old system.

The Fontainebleau Agreement had made a special arrangement for Britain, providing it with a rebate on its budget contributions, otherwise known as the "correction mechanism." Under budgetary reform, the Commission recommended that the British rebate be continued for the time being but be reduced. The Commission expected the new financing system, once implemented, to reduce Britain's budget contributions. The Commission did stop short of stating that the British budget rebate should be discontinued after 1992.

Budgetary Discipline

It was inconceivable that the member countries would agree to the new financing system proposed if the Commission could not keep expenditures within budgetary limits. The Commission, therefore, had to deal convincingly with budgetary discipline. A crucial pillar of budgetary discipline would be the enforcement of its own resources ceiling, that of 1.4% of Community GNP.

The Commission had to tie budgetary discipline to CAP reform if discipline were to be effective. To bring greater balance to agricultural spending, the Commission asked for the authority to enact "binding" and "even automatic" stabilization measures when surplus production threatened to cause spending excesses.[34] This echoed the "stabilizer" proposal included in the CAP reform section of the Delors Plan and which became one of the most disputed elements of the package. Furthermore, the plan enunciated the important principle that agricultural spending should not exceed the increase in the Community's resources.

The Commission insisted the entire Delors Plan was indivisible. CAP reforms would require difficult adjustments in the regions most negatively affected and the Structural Funds would ease the adjustments. The increase in the Structural Funds and the accumulation of past deficits in agricultural spending needed financing, and, thus, the proposal for a new financing system. The member countries would not agree to a new financing system unless they were certain that the Commission could enforce budgetary discipline. The negotiability of the Delors Plan, moreover, hinged on its allocation of sacrifices and rewards for the trade-offs necessary to gain the member countries' acceptance.

Brussels European Council of June 1987

Negotiations on the Delors Plan at the European Council level began at the Brussels meeting in June, 1987. The Council's objective was agreement on broad guidelines which would then form the basis of negotiations on the Delors Plan. The Belgians held the EC presidency, and planned their presidency in close consulation with the Commission, respecting the indivisibility of the Delors Plan.

At Brussels the doubling of the Structural Funds proved to be a critically problematic item in the package. There was no progress on this item except that Commission President Delors said that "each country's concerns had been given a sympathetic hearing."[35] Brussels succeeded in delaying hard negotiations on the Structural Funds.

The British had particular problems in these Brussels negotiations. The Belgian Presidency intended that only guidelines would be agreed at Brussels, not final and binding conclusions. Nonetheless, Mrs. Thatcher took this project seriously. She insisted on having satisfactory wording in the conclusions to be made public at the end of the meeting. She hesitated over two parts of the conclusions.[36] She did not want to make a firm commitment to a new financing system linked more closely to relative wealth. As she later explained to the House of Commons, she was not willing to see an increase in British contributions until she was satisfied with measures to achieve budget discipline. She would be satisfied only with seeing draft regulations designed explicitly for budget discipline, which she expected the Commission to have ready for the next European Council in Copenhagen.[37] Her other hesitation concerned the base year for calculating the rate of growth of farm spending. Mrs. Thatcher did not want the base year to be redefined to take into account the increased costs of agricultural spending owing in part to the falling dollar.[38] Mrs. Thatcher explained to the House of Commons that it was unacceptable for future agricultural spending to rest on an inflated basis.[39]

The British reservations did not represent insuperable barriers. Regulations for budget discipline were on the agenda as part of the process of concluding the Delors Plan. Member countries also had become more amenable to CAP reform since the British budget dispute (with the serious exception of West Germany), and the Commission had replaced Britain as the leader in this cause. Britain might well be satisfied with the general orientations of the Brussels conclusions, especially the commitment to stabilizers. Described by one observer as "pure Thatcherism," the stabilizers the Commission requested would give it the authority to intervene immediately and decisively to cut prices once production began to overrun previously agreed ceilings.[40]

To explain Mrs. Thatcher's refusal to sign parts of the conclusions, one must note she had pushed for negotiations to continue in Brussels until the few British objections were satisfied. Several minutes could have produced the minor changes of wording the British insisted on. At the urging of Spanish Prime Minister Gonzalez, the Belgian President made a "take it or leave it" offer to Mrs. Thatcher. At this point she refused to be party to certain commitments, eventually included in the first annex of the text published after Brussels. By refusing to continue negotiations until there was unanimous agreement, the others signalled Mrs. Thatcher that they were not inclined to tolerate further obstructionist tactics.

In the follow-up negotiations at the level of the Council of Ministers, the British took the position that commitments made by the other member countries at Brussels should hold, even though Britain had opted out of these commitments. British Foreign Minister Sir Geoffrey Howe reminded the others that they had committed to negotiating stabilizers on a product by product basis in Brussels, demonstrating that the Brussels conclusions had well served British interests.[41]

On the whole, Brussels accomplished what the Commission had wanted. It gave European Council endorsement, Britain excepted, to the broad objectives of the Delors Plan, the softest commitment being the doubling of the Structural Funds. The European Council agreed on a set of general instructions for the Council of Ministers. These instructions indicated the decisions the Council of Ministers needed to take in relation to the Delors Plan on the basis of Commission proposals. Some confusion about how to reform the CAP remained, although there was agreement that some variety of CAP reform clearly had to be on the agenda. The Brussels conclusions put noticeable emphasis on a prices policy, the Commission's preferred means of CAP reform. The conclusions also mentioned the possibility of implementing a set-aside program as an additional means of coping with agricultural problems. It would entail adopting a scheme that had been tried in the United States with farmers being paid to take land out of production. Because of the proliferation of half-solutions and because of the complete lack of fully satisfactory solutions, CAP reform would remain one of the most problematic parts of the Delors Plan.

Copenhagen European Council of December 1987

The national effects of the Delors Plan became more evident during the negotiations leading to Copenhagen. In instituting a new financing system linked to GNP, the budget contributions of Germany, the Netherlands, Denmark and Italy would increase.[42] Italy would feel the effects as it had lately published new GNP figures, inflated by including the activities of Italy's large black market. Potentially, Britain could lose with the new financing system requiring a renegotiation of the terms of its correction mechanism. If not the correction mechanism, Britain would gain from a system that relied on national income as a measure for contributions.

Britain, France, the Netherlands, and Germany resisted the doubling of the Structural Funds. They received slight benefits from this source of EC outlays.

Germany took an extremely cautious approach to agricultural savings. Politically important to the governing coalition, cereals farmers in the south of Germany viewed the proposals as threats.[43] It was, of course, in the often stated British interest to insist on very strict controls of agricultural spending. France's interests were cross-cutting. Like Germany, France faced a strong farmers' lobby and tried to side with Germany where possible. On the other hand, once she became a net contributor France committed to CAP reform. Therefore, France experienced ambivalence toward CAP reform, wanting to bring agriculture more in line with market forces but not willing to accept some of the stricter Commission proposals designed to cut farm costs. Large net contributors — Britain, France, and Germany included — were naturally interested in budgetary discipline, even if it conflicted with their positions on other parts of the package as in Germany.

At Copenhagen the bargaining became more intricate and refined. As with the Belgian Presidency, the Danish Presidency stayed close to Commission proposals. The Danes also maintained the indivisibility of the Delors Plan. A high level of coordination between the Commission and the Danes took place, surprising in that the Danes were, with Britain, among the least integrationist member countries, as the Danes were to show in their 1992 vote against the integrationist Maastricht Treaty. The Danish Presidency proved its objectivity by offering proposals counter to Denmark's interests. Reviewing his country's term as president, Denmark's Prime Minister Poul Schlüter noted "it was therefore not easy for us to put forward proposals which will undoubtedly be painful for the agricultural sector and in our country as well."[44] A Eurobarometer poll in early 1988 showed the CAP to be most popular among the EC publics of Denmark and the Netherlands.[45] The poll demonstrated the extent to which the Danes subordinated national interests to their presidency responsibilities in throwing their weight behind CAP reform.

Member governments busily postured in the week preceding Copenhagen. The British let it be known that they would not tolerate any rise in their EC budget costs.[46] Delors maintained that Britain had to contribute, along with the others, to the increased costs of enlargement. He asserted that Britain was better able to afford increased contributions than in 1984.[47] British officials defended their position by stating that Fontainebleau had allowed for the costs of enlargement in its financial settlement and that Britain's contributions had already gone up.

Germany also sent strong signals on CAP reform. On 26 November 1987, Farm Ministers had finally abandoned their task of coming to terms on CAP reform after six meetings, some of them all night sessions, over a ten-day period. Germany opposed stabilizers with the same intensity that Britain insisted on them. Germany objected to the form of stabilizers the Commission and Britain envisioned.[48] The Farm Council referred CAP reform to the Foreign Ministers who also failed to find the essential compromise. By the time of Copenhagen, the German position was well established. They had a special preference for including a set-aside program in CAP reform. For Britain, stabilizers continued to be an essential part of any package of measures to control agricultural spending. Otherwise, budgetary discipline could not occur. Mrs. Thatcher mistakenly had believed that she had reached an understanding on CAP reform with French Premier Jacques Chirac in a meeting before Copenhagen, which would have been surprising considering their normally fractious relationship.[49] As it turned out, the French would be of no help to the British on farm questions and would, instead, support the Germans.

In its position on stabilizers and budgetary discipline, Britain had the support of the Netherlands and the Commission. Mrs. Thatcher and Dutch Prime Minister Ruud Lubbers enjoyed a good working relationship and held an informal meeting after they arrived in Copenhagen.[50] Britain's allies on CAP reform and budgetary discipline were, conversely, opposed to the British position of refusing adjustments to the correction mechanism. Despite the friendliness between Mr. Lubbers and Mrs. Thatcher, he along with Chancellor Kohl, would have liked to see the British correction mechanism eventually discontinued.

Previous to the summit, French President Mitterrand had little sympathy for British and Italian financial worries over the new financing system. In a meeting with the Italian Prime Minister Giovanni Goria before Copenhagen, President Mitterrand had even suggested that the time had come for Italy to give up some of the developmental aid it received from the EC.[51]

Such extensive differences among member countries did not bode well for the Copenhagen European Council. Indeed, Copenhagen failed to achieve the breakthrough on the agricultural issues, necessary for the rest of the package to achieve final form.

The first day's negotiations were unsuccessful in finding a solution to the problem of surpluses in the cereals sector. Mrs. Thatcher wanted a more restrictive ceiling in this sector, which once exceeded would bring about price penalties. She reportedly would not yield on the figure of 155 million tons for the cereals ceiling because this figure already permitted a greater level of production than the level of EC consumption of cereals.[52]

Throughout the night the presidency worked with the Commission to develop a compromise. When the presidency presented the compromise to the European Council on the second day, the Germans immediately rejected it because of the slight attention it gave to a set-aside program. Reportedly, the reference to the set-aside alternative was so deemphasized in the presidency's compromise proposal that it appeared only in a footnote referring to an annex.[53] With support from the French, Kohl also still objected to the central role stabilizers had come to play in surplus management and the severity of the stabilizers the Commission proposed. In light of this impasse, Kohl was able to secure the agreement of the others for an extraordinary European Council to be held during the German Presidency.

At Copenhagen a consensus finally emerged for increasing the Structural Funds, but member governments had different margins of increase in mind. The British seemed prepared to see a 35% increase in the Structural Funds, while Germany was willing to go up to 50%, with the Netherlands and France closer to the British figure.[54]

Differences among the member countries had not narrowed enough to make it possible for a decision to emerge at Copenhagen. Neither Germany nor Britain were solely responsible for the failure at Copenhagen. Each country had an ally, the French staying with the Germans and the Dutch with the British. The elements needed for a final compromise were not yet in place.

Progress had been made at Copenhagen, however. Clearly, both British and German concerns required a mixed strategy for CAP reform. In reporting on the outcome of Copenhagen to the Bundestag, Kohl indicated that the other member countries had come around to the view that leaving farmland idle (the set-aside alternative) was one viable solution for coping with the financial pressures of agriculture.[55] Although the presidency issued no conclusions at the end of Copenhagen, informal decisions on agricultural stabilizers, with the exception of those sectors such as cereals where views most diverged, were prepared for eventual inclusion in the final agreement. The presidency's refusing to publish conclusions was not merely out of respect for the Commission's desire to keep the Delors Plan whole. It was also politically wise, at least for Germany, to avoid attracting too much attention to the stabilizers agreed at Copenhagen. Immediately following Copenhagen, the President of the West German Farmers' Association, Mr. Constantin Heeremann, expressed the hope that "the introduction of automatic price cuts was no longer under discussion" by the time of the extraordinary European Council.[56]

Copenhagen clarified the outlines of possible solutions and showed that all of the participants accepted the Delors Plan's general orientations. Still, decisions on the major elements of the Delors Plan remained in the air.

Brussels European Council of February 1988

During the preparations for the extraordinary European Council in Brussels, neither the Germans nor the British, at least publicly, strayed very far from previous positions. The postponement of the finalization of the Delors Plan to February moved the French closer to presidential elections scheduled in the spring where Mitterrand and Chirac would be competing candidates. Chirac, especially, had become increasingly conscious of the farm vote pushing the French even closer to the Germans on farm issues.

In January the Commission showed itself willing to respond to German preferences concerning agricultural reform. During a meeting between Kohl and Delors on January 7, 1988, the centerpiece of discussion was the Commission's authorization for Agricultural Commissioner Andriessen to prepare proposals outlining a set-aside plan.[57] Part of the Commission's strategy behind introducing proposals for set-asides was to make stabilizers more tolerable for the member countries that opposed them.[58] The Commission was also anxious to begin fence-mending with Germany, which now held the EC presidency. The Commission realized that it would have to depend on the German Presidency to conclude the Delors Plan. The new Commission proposals were the focus of the first meeting of Farm Ministers after Copenhagen on January 18, 1988. A brief discussion indicated that the Farm Ministers agreed that a set-aside scheme was an indispensable element of CAP reform. Various details still remained to be worked out, but the set-aside plan received the wide acceptance it needed.

There was much less progress on stabilizers. At the next Farm Ministers' meeting, January 24, 1988, the Germans tabled a compromise proposal on agriculture.[59] The compromise would have, among other things, fixed the ceiling for cereals production at 160 million tons. The British, however, were still firm on the lower ceiling of 155 million tons. Commissioner for Agriculture Andriessen announced himself ready to accept a ceiling of 158 million tons. In an important turn of events at this meeting, the Commission became amenable to German proposals. The new Commission flexibility on CAP reform signified that Britain was losing its most formidable ally. Following on the heels of the Farm Council meeting was a Foreign Minister's meeting on January 25, 1988. The tide seemed to be turning against the British. Britain was losing supporters, as the Dutch were more sympathetic to German compromise proposals than the British. The Germans showed few signs of accommodating British demands on CAP reform. The French position hardened in light of the upcoming national elections. Therefore, Germany could more confidently rely on France to lead the resistance against British agricultural demands. To raise the pressure on the British, German Foreign Minister Genscher made noises about the difficulties which lay ahead in negotiating the British budget correction mechanism. It was a bargaining maneuver that the French Agricultural Minister Françoise Guillaume also used. Referring to Britain's being practically isolated in the Farm Council meeting of January 24, 1988, Guillaume said it was time to begin discussing the correction mechanism.[60] In the preparations for Brussels, the German Presidency also pressured Britain to concede a more generous increase in the Structural Funds, while Spain remained entirely serious about receiving no less than a doubling of the funds.[61] Undoubtedly, the presidency was preparing for Britain to be the obstacle to agreement at Brussels.

All of the main issues of the Delors Plan were still outstanding. With the exception of finding a consensus on a set-aside plan in CAP reform, the small progress made in the interim since Copenhagen did not lend itself to high expectations for Brussels.

With so complicated a negotiation and with so many unresolved issues before it, the European Council went into a marathon meeting. It took twenty-six hours for the Twelve to come to terms, the European Council finally ending at midnight on the second day. Mrs. Thatcher was extremely reluctant to give her consent to the final agreement. Late into the night of the second day's session Kohl, as Chairman, was ready to abandon negotiations and call an end to the meeting. Had it not been for the persistence of Spanish Prime Minister Felipe Gonzalez, the meeting could have ended with Britain in solitary opposition as happened at Brussels the year before. Gonzalez was not willing to risk the concessions he had won on the Structural Funds, which generously exceeded most expectations. He asked for additional time for all of the member governments to reflect. At this point Mrs. Thatcher consulted with her advisors outside the conference room. When she returned, she was ready to accept the package.

Britain lost on the threshold for cereals which was finally decided at the level of 160 million tons (155 million tons being the British negotiating figure). Britain could be satisfied, however, with a package of stabilizers.[62] These stabilizers covered seven farm sectors including milk, sheepmeat, wine, sugar, tobacco, cotton, fruit and vegetables. The stabilizers represented the maximum concessions the British won on CAP reform and budgetary discipline.

Britain was partially satisfied on the Structural Funds. The compromise here was that the doubling of the entire budget of the Structural Funds would be delayed to 1993, but the amount committed under the Commission's first objective, the advancement of underdeveloped regions, would be doubled by 1992. In other words, Spain, Portugal, Ireland, Southern Italy, the French overseas departments could anticipate a doubling of EC regional assistance by 1992.

The measures agreed in Brussels for budgetary discipline were also off the mark from the British negotiating position. The guideline for agricultural spending for 1988 was fixed at 27.5 billion Ecu compared to the figure of 27 billion which the British had advocated.

The arrangements for new financing provided the EC with additional resources of between 1.2% and 1.3% of Community GNP, well over the increase Britain had wanted.[63] The Brussels agreement on giving new finances to the EC did not disappoint the Commission.[64] Undoubtedly, the Commission had come very close to acquiring the sums it wanted, over the more restrained financial attitudes of the British.

Why did Mrs. Thatcher consent to an agreement which obviously fell short of many of her objectives? She had few hopes of repeating the previous success in the British budget dispute by prevailing over the other member countries and the Commission. Among member countries, the feeling had persisted that Mrs. Thatcher got a better deal than the British deserved in the settlement of the British budget dispute at Fontainebleau. The rhetoric of the French and Germans about phasing out the British budget rebate during negotiations of the Delors Plan clearly showed their feelings. If the British had prolonged the negotiations on the Delors Plan, it is likely that they would have encountered less favorable German and French positions, and perhaps even more arguments over stabilizers. Further, Britain would likely have been unable to count on the support of the other member governments that had helped secure the Copenhagen stabilizers. A particularly unattractive prospect for the British was losing the Dutch as allies. After all, the Dutch had been ready to concede to the final agreement before the British. The Commission would also be unavailable as an ally for the British since it had cooperated closely with the German Presidency in presenting options to the Brussels European Council and was ready for a conclusion to the package. Although Britain did not accomplish many of its objectives in the final settlement, it won important victories. The shape of the Delors Plan was a credit to the British, emphasizing as it did budgetary discipline and CAP reform, subjects the British introduced to the Community through their budget dispute. Germany gave little ground on CAP reform in Brussels but the concessions it made carried political costs. The results of Brussels were unpopular with the German farmer because they included stabilizers based on price reductions, the most bitter of the medicines prescribed for overproduction.[65]

The greatest consolation Britain was granted at Brussels was that its budget correction mechanism reemerged barely altered. Known to have a good understanding of finances, Mrs. Thatcher was not willing to see the budget rebate get lost or significantly diminished. Whereas the savings Mrs. Thatcher pressed for in agriculture would not accrue directly to Britain, the savings resulting from the budget correction mechanism were Britain's alone.

In Brussels, other countries won concessions. Potentially facing the most disadvantages in the new financing system, Italy saw her interests specially addressed. Luxembourg and Ireland got answers for their particular budget concerns. Portugal received a special bonus in the decisions on the Structural Funds, amounting to receipts of 500 million Ecu over five years.[66]

The Commission was satisfied with the similarity of the Brussels conclusions to the Delors Plan. Unquestionably, the heads of government were faithful to the grand design as well as to many of the details of the Delors Plan. The eventual deviations from the original Commission proposals were dwarfed by the heads of government's acceptance of the large majority of the package. As one Commission official put it, the Brussels Agreement was equivalent to "Com 99.5," indicating its close similarity to the original Commission document, numbered "Com 101."[67] While making concessions, in the end the Commission managed to overcome significant political pressures. The Commission unquestionably achieved success in holding the member governments to its agenda throughout the negotiations.

The European Council, an intergovernmental body, had produced decisions which must be described as integrative. These decisions also strengthened the authority of the Commission. Swinbank observes that stabilizers agreed by the Brussels European Council of February 1988, "enhance the powers of the Commission, and diminish those of the Council."[68] The irony was inescapable that the European Council, long suspected of being anti-integrationist, would benefit the major integrative institution of the Community.

The European Council's decisions on the Delors Plan were not easy to arrive at. The Delors Plan was extremely ambitious in the subjects it covered and in the potential for conflict involved in the allocative decisions it asked the member governments to make. The Plan in essence asked member governments to set the future course of the EC for at least the next half-decade. Before European Council meetings, efforts to sort out the technical details were far from successful. The Brussels conclusions, parts of which included the language of near-regulations, demonstrated that this negotiation was as permeated with technicalities as any negotiation which preceded it. Thus, it was not avoiding technical details which facilitated agreement. Nor did the Commission significantly lower its expectations to meet those of the member governments to reach agreement. On the contrary, member countries made large sacrifices to achieve the success of the Delors Plan. Why did the European Council succeed here when it had stumbled so miserably on the British budget dispute?

Formula for Success

The Delors Plan was not the seemingly impassable obstruction at the European Council level that the British budget dispute was. From the beginning, all the participants negotiated the Delors Plan in good faith. A certain number of staged national battles for domestic audiences seemed always to accompany European Councils, but even this posturing was minimal. Improved relations among EC political leaders and working habits learned from previous serious and difficult negotiations favorably influenced the negotiations of the Delors Plan.

One of the most important elements of the Delors Plan's success was the Commission's role. As the Commission conceived the Delors Plan, from the outset it provided a legitimate agenda for the European Council. This was not the case during the British budget dispute which had the immediate appearance of being Mrs. Thatcher's agenda, and seemed to be pure national interests. As for the Delors Plan, its automatic legitimacy was enhanced because it was the program of a Commission with growing influence. The same Commission had recently shown great skill in managing the negotiation of the Treaty amendments in the Single Act at the Luxembourg European Council of December 1985. The recent policy successes of the Community increased the reliance of the member countries on the Commission. That the Community had more well defined policy goals of considerable importance to the member countries meant that member countries had to look to the Commission to see these policies carried out.

The Commission accommodated national interests at the point they served Community interests and used a variety of tactics to make the required sacrifices acceptable to member governments. The Commission attempted to minimize sacrifices, tried to force sacrifices with the threat that even greater sacrifices would be imposed if the lesser sacrifice was rejected, and offered compensation for sacrifices in a trade-off arrangement. Widely distributing rewards was also part of the strategy that led to the success of the Delors Plan, not only to cushion sacrifices but to multiply the stakes the member countries had in it. The Delors Plan had a high degree of calculated relevance to the member countries which contributed to its negotiability. The Commission's success centered on presenting a package that drew some member countries in as enthusiastic advocates while other member countries, which faced potential losses from the Delors Plan, found themselves able to tolerate it.

Enlargement increased the Commission's ability to play the political role it assumed in European Council negotiations. This became particularly true with the accession of Spain and Portugal to the Community in 1986, bringing the number of member countries to twelve. Numerically, enlargement meant greater opportunities for coalition-building. In a Community of Twelve, it is rare for the Commission to be without allies. In a package as extensive as the Delors

Plan, the Commission was able to alter its group of supporters according to each issue so that it had an interest or interests in common with most of the membership. The Commission was not alone in realizing the importance of allies, as we have seen how essential Dutch support was for the British and French support was for the Germans throughout the Delors Plan negotiations. Part of the political success centers on Delors, himself. A high-ranking politician in France before he came to the Commission, Delors personally possessed the political sophistication for which the Commission got credit throughout the negotiations. Delors confidently used the European Council to advance Commission goals. In comments to the press, Delors even made the analogy of the European Council to the "political engine" of the Community, suggesting that he recognized its constructive potential, particularly if its political prestige graced Commission proposals.

That member governments made important concessions during negotiations on the Delors Plan was also critical. The revitalization of economies prone to recession in the previous decade partly explained a willingness to compromise. The Delors Plan asked member governments to make financial decisions which they now could afford during a period of healthy economic growth.

The cooperation between the Commission and each of the three Presidencies undoubtedly contributed to the success of the Delors Plan. The Delors Plan was well launched in February 1987 because the Belgian Presidency treated the package as a whole and stayed close to Commission proposals throughout negotiations. The Danish Presidency cooperated in the same way. It was likewise advantageous that concluding the Delors Plan fell under the German Presidency. The Germans were essential to the settlement of any large negotiation. The desire to conduct an objective and successful presidency allowed the Germans to make compromises they could then justify to their domestic population. Entering into Mrs. Thatcher's calculations in accepting the Brussels agreement could have been a desire to avoid being the spoiler of the German Presidency. Quite possibly Mrs. Thatcher wanted good relations between Germany and Britain to deal with upcoming defense issues in NATO.

Even though successive Presidencies played parts in the success of the Delors Plan, the Commission deserves the most credit. It conceived a highly negotiable package and applied a workable political strategy to get it through negotiations. Furthermore, the Commission maximized its increasing influence by building on the momentum and content of recent policy developments, including the member countries' higher valuation of the Community and its revitalized policy potential. Most of these elements were missing during the British budget dispute, a phase marked, instead, by perceptions of a declining Commission and a stagnating Community.

Once ill at ease with the European Council, a more influential Commission came to encourage its participation. Greater cooperation and interaction between the European Council and the Commission became a feature of Community successes of recent years.

Notes

1.   Bulmer and Wessels, *The European Council*, Chapter 4, pp. 59-73.

2.   Geoffrey Denton, "Re-Structuring the EC Budget: Implications of the Fontainebleau Agreement," *Journal of Common Market Studies*, 23 (December 1984), p. 117.

3.   *Ibid.*, pp. 117-22. I rely chiefly here on Geoffrey Denton's excellent explanation of Britain's disadvantages in relation to the Community's previous financing system.

4.   *Ibid.*, p. 120.

5.   Tugendhat, *Making Sense of Europe*, p. 119.

6.   Denton, "Re-Structuring the EC Budget," p. 121.

7.   *Ibid.*

8.   Tugendhat, *Making Sense of Europe*, p. 121.

9.   Michael Hornsby, "Mrs. Thatcher ready for crisis action after rebuff by EEC," *The Times*, 1 December 1979, p. 1.

10.   *Ibid.*

11.   *Ibid.*

12.   Denton, "Re-Structuring the EC Budget," p. 123.

13.   "A Drama, but not a crisis," *The Times*, 22 March 1984, p. 13.

14.   Tugendhat, *Making Sense of Europe*, p. 122.

15.   *Ibid.*, p. 123.

16.   Ian Murray, "Summit deal has bought time but Thorn sees tough bargaining ahead," *The Times*, 28 June 1984, p. 5.

17.   Julian Haviland and Ian Murray, "Europe's leaders gather in new mood of hope," *The Times*, 25 June 1984, p. 1.

18.   Butler, *Europe: More than a Continent*, p. 101. See also Ian Murray, "Thatcher determined not to give way at summit; 24 hours that can settle EEC future," *The Times*, 19 March 1984, p. 6.

19.   Murray, "Thatcher claims good EEC deal for Britain," *The Times*, 27 June 1984, p. 1. See also Denton, "Re-structuring the EC Budget," p. 125.

20.   *Ibid.*

21.   Murray, "Summit deal has bought time," p. 5.

22.   "The Single Act: A new frontier for Europe," *Bulletin of the EC*, Supplement 1, 1987, p. 19.

23.   *Ibid.*

24.   "Parliament June 27, 1984; Kinnock invites Tories to join fight against deal," *The Times*, 28 June 1984, p. 4.

25.   Murray, "Summit deal has bought time," p. 5.

26.　Butler, *Europe: More than a Continent*, p. 110.

27.　Julian Haviland, "A Summit perspective from London, Paris, Rome and Bonn; British war on waste," *The Times*, 17 March 1984, p. 6.

28.　*Bulletin of the EC*, Supplement 1, 1987, p. 12.

29.　The developmental dimension of the Community, represented by the three funds, is commonly referred to as "cohesion."

30.　*Bulletin of the EC*, Supplement 1, 1987, p. 14.

31.　*Ibid.*

32.　The old system of financing was made up of three resources which included custom duties, agricultural levies and Value Added Tax (VAT) call-ins. For various reasons, both custom duties and agricultural levies became shrinking parts of the total sum. That left only VAT to make-up the difference. The European Council, however, imposed a ceiling on the percentage of VAT subject to Commission call-ins, a ceiling that could only be lifted by national parliaments. Therefore, the Commission proposed a "fourth resource" that would automatically make additional income available to the Community as member countries experienced economic growth.

33.　*Bulletin of the EC*, Supplement 1, 1987, p. 18.

34.　*Ibid.*, p. 21.

35.　*Bulletin of the EC*, 6 (1987), p. 13.

36.　Quentin Peel, "Surprising degree of accord at the EC Summit," *Financial Times*, 2 July 1987, p. 3.

37.　"Thatcher stands by position on budget controls," *Financial Times*, 2 July 1987, p. 1.

38.　Peel, "Surprising degree of accord," p. 3.

39.　"Thatcher stands by position," *Financial Times*, p. 1.

40.　Peel, "Surprising degree of accord," p. 3.

41.　Peel, "Bonn hardens position on farm demands," 30 November 1987, p. 24.

42.　Peel, "An explosive cocktail of national interests," 2 December 1987, p. 26.

43.　For Germany's political concerns over farmers, see Tim Dickson, "High expectations recede as ministers bow out of talks," *Financial Times*, 27 November 1987, p. 2; *The Economist*, 12 December 1987, p. 56; James M. Markham, "For Europe, Talks Fizzle: Community's Summit Seen as Disappointing," *The New York Times*, 7 December 1987, p. 5.

44.　*Bulletin of the EC*, 12 (1987), p. 87.

45.　Dickson, "European poll finds backing for CAP," *Financial Times*, 3 February 1988, p. 2.

46.　Peel, "Thatcher rejects deal on EC rebate," *Financial Times*, 3 December 1987, p. 1.

47.　Richard Owen, "EEC farm crisis: Thatcher showdown is looming," *Financial Times*, 25 November 1987, p. 9.

48.　Dickson, "High expectations recede," p. 2.

49. Owen, "Britain offers 'clean slate' scheme to end EEC food surpluses," *Financial Times*, 24 November 1987, p. 10; "Praying for a European farm reform miracle," *Financial Times*, 30 November 1987, p. 7.

50. Peel, "Plea for summit flexibility," *Financial Times*, 4 December 1987, p. 28.

51. John Wyles, "France and Italy divided over budget," *Financial Times*, 28 November 1987, p. 2.

52. Dickson and Peel, "Hopes of EC summit deal rise," *Financial Times*, 5-6 December 1987, p. 1.

53. Peel, "Kohl's explosion dooms passionless summit," *Financial Times*, 7 December 1987, p. 2.

54. *Ibid.*

55. *The Week in Germany*, 11 December 1987, pp. 1-2.

56. Peel, "Bonn plans compromise on EC finance," *Financial Times*, 8 December 1987, p. 2.

57. Wilhelm Hadler, "Gesture value in farmland reduction plan," reprinted in *The German Tribune*, 17 January 1988, p. 3.

58. Dickson, "Accord on EC set-aside plan likely today," *Financial Times*, 18 January 1988, p. 4.

59. Dickson and William Dawkins, "EC welcomes German farm compromise," *Financial Times*, 25 January 1988, p. 1.

60. Owen, "Howe sticks to his guns on farm plan," 26 January 1988, p. 6.

61. An interview by the author at a Permanent Representation, 6 November 1987, revealed that the increase in the Structural Funds was of such importance to Spain that the Delors Plan had been discussed in Cabinet many times. Spain was more attached to the Commission proposal for a doubling of the Structural Funds than the Commission itself. See David Buchan, "UK and Bonn edge towards EC budget deal," *Financial Times*, 3 February 1988, p. 2.

62. Andrew McEwen and Nicholas Wood, "Divisions remain on EEC crisis," *The Times*, 30 January 1988, p. 24.

63. Expressed in VAT, the Brussels agreement meant an increase from the Fontainebleau ceiling of 1.4% of VAT to a level between 1.9% and 2.0% of VAT. Britain had been extremely difficult about the relatively narrower rise in the VAT ceiling from 1.0% to 1.4% at Fontainebleau.

64. Buchan, "EC bureaucracy claims summit deal as its own," *Financial Times*, 16 February 1988, p. 2.

65. A declaration by the German Farmers' Association, 7 July 1989, opposed future reforms to bring the EC farm market in line with the world market. See *German Information Center*, 14 July 1989, p. 6.

66. Diana Smith, "Cavaco Silva expects an Es500bn bonanza," *Financial Times*, 16 February 1988, p. 2.

67. Buchan, "EC bureaucracy claims summit deal," p. 2.

68. A, Swinbank, "The Common Agricultural Policy and the Politics of European Decision-Making," *Journal of Common Market Studies*, 27 (June 1989), p. 315.

5

The Train of History

The original charge of the EEC did not include cooperation in foreign policy or in military policymaking. Only gradually did the Community undertake European Political Cooperation (EPC).[1] Until the end of the 1960s, divisions over what role, if any, the Community and its institutions should play prevented any basic policy or procedure from emerging. Finally, a heavily compromised arrangement permitted the structures and procedures of EPC to begin developing in the Community background throughout the 1970s and 1980s. Even though the past two decades have seen progress in conceptualizing and reaching agreement on ultimate goals, foreign and security policies remained in an immature state. Delors' assessment of EPC in a 1988 book he co-authored was the following:

> Although this movement towards a "homogeneous foreign policy" has continued, however, it has only intermittently shown the strength needed if Europe is to speak with one voice. Too often, Europe has hung about arguing on the station platform while history's trains have departed.[2]

The train of history, which European elites seem determined to drive, is the decommunization of Eastern and Central Europe in 1989. Inspired by the momentum of history, European decisionmakers began building on two decades of serious efforts and giving even more consideration to the EC's international role. The EC has the opportunity to be a major actor, if not the major actor, in Eastern and Central Europe. EC member countries are keenly interested in reforming traditional security arrangements and having a greater impact on global affairs. Difficult questions now pose themselves.

- How much political influence should the EC aim to exert in the former Communist bloc?
- How much military power is required to support that level of political influence?
- Relatedly, what are the political and logistical considerations involved in establishing a European army, especially in its relationship to NATO and, also important, the recently upgraded (at least in terms of security) UN and Conference on Security and Confidence-building in Europe (CSCE)?
- In addition, what EC institutional adjustments are needed to support an enhanced EC security role (a reopening of the decades-old debate about whether decisionmaking in EPC should be supranational or intergovernmental)?
- Finally, how can EC decisionmakers reconcile their plans to the idiosyncratic requirements of member governments, such as those that are sovereignty-conscious, are ready to forego military preparedness in the post-cold war era, are neutral, or have different geo-political commitments?

For de Gaulle, only a country's highest political executives could decide questions like these because they alone have the primary interest in maintaining the state. In this respect, the Gaullist perspective had a special bias against other national and supranational institutions. Faith above all is in the President, "the guarantor of national independence, of the integrity of the territory...," according to Article 5 of the French constitution. Even Delors showed this bias. Mapping out a plan for his Commission presidency in January 1985, he considered whether the EC should expand into defense. He decided, "Not only were minds not ready for this, but the subject was *ultra vires* for the European executive."[3] In other EC countries, the highest executive is not elevated to the same extent the French head is by presidentialism. National security matters are also an executive affair, but with varying dependence on the skills of the foreign minister and parliaments' reaction.

European federalists disagree with the concept of conducting international relations by subjecting the most important decisions to intergovernmentalism or, rather, the diplomatic efforts of politicians and their officials. For the Community to acquire a foreign policy capability and responsibilities for security, federalists had to compromise their ideals. The crux of the compromise is that the European Council is the highest organ of political cooperation. It decides questions that, in Gaullist fashion, heads of government feel they must take.[4] Even though the Commission and the European Parliament are now associated with

EPC, their influence is not decisive. The frequency of contacts among EC member countries, their many points of connection on a vast network, are novel elements in their intergovernmental relations. However, dominance of the EC's foreign policy and security apparatus by a restricted elite follows most closely national traditions.

An official interviewed in 1987 about the role of the European Council in political cooperation put it quite simply that the European Council wore two hats, one for political cooperation and the other for internal EC matters; however, it wore the latter hat most of the time.[5] A new departure was begun at Rhodes, December 1988, where heads of government expressed their determination "to strengthen and expand the role of the European Community and its Member States on the international political and economic stage...." Since then, European Council participation in world affairs has been characterized by extraordinarily high visibility. To have reached this point, however, a number of significant events took place. To understand the current role of the EC, we must review these events.

EPC Evolves Its Distinct Identity

Prior to the founding of the EEC, in 1954 the French parliament defeated the plan for a European Defense Community.[6] This blow stopped even the most minimal developments in political cooperation for over a decade and a half, while the prevailing Gaullist view stressed the inappropriateness of supranational institutions being involved in issues of national security. With the launch of the EEC, 1 January 1958, integrationists had to accept that only economic matters, assumed to be more "technical" than "political" in nature, were available for common policy-making.[7] The establishment of an economic organization did not extinguish the hopes of federalists, who faithfully adhered to the view that the Community, teleologically, was a "political union." Ultimately, with a chipping away of sovereignty, they believed member countries would extend the Community's authority into more politically significant areas. Resistance to the federalist view persisted.[8]

In the early 1960s, "institutionalized summitry was regarded as an integral part of political co-operation."[9] For de Gaulle, the connection between summitry and political cooperation was essential. Aiming to insure national control, he proposed implementing political cooperation outside of the Community structure. The vehicle for this was the Fouchet Plan, including the blueprint for a European Political Union. To plan for political cooperation was the reason for the original summits (Paris, February 1961; Bonn, May 1961). As heads of government accepted the responsibility to decide how political cooperation should be organized, a council of heads of government would have assumed the leading role in decisionmaking in the new organization. As it turned out, the smaller member countries blocked the Plan. Sentimental attachments and the influence small countries enjoyed under supranational arrangements would not let them abandon the Community.[10] Member countries' competing conceptions of European integration prevented any progress on political cooperation until the end of the 1960s.

At The Hague Summit of December 1969, the heads of government instructed the foreign ministers "to study the best way of achieving progress in the matter of political unification, within the context of enlargement" of the Community.[11] On 27 October 1970, the foreign ministers presented the organizational scheme for EPC in "The Luxembourg Report."[12] Henceforth, foreign ministers would meet at least every six months to consult on foreign policy issues. The report allowed for heads of government to substitute for foreign ministers if a foreign policy situation deserved higher level attention. A committee of directors of political affairs (presently known as the Political Committee or "PoCo" in Community jargon) would routinely meet, at least quarterly, and prepare for ministerial meetings. The report planned for political directors to constitute specialized working groups, as the need arose. This basic structure has survived intact, albeit in a more complex form, to process EPC issues.

The establishment of EPC did not resolve ideological differences among EC member countries. During the 1970s the French were on guard that the normal EC institutions did not become intentionally or accidentally associated with EPC. Since it was the foreign ministers who would consider EPC issues, following the Luxembourg Report, the French did not want it to appear the Community institution, the Council of Ministers, was in charge of EPC. Therefore, the practice developed in which foreign ministers, meeting in an EC capacity, could not discuss EPC issues in the same sitting. Furthermore, foreign ministers' EPC meetings had to be held in the capital of the presidency, out of range of the influence of Brussels, which the French so mistrusted. On an occasion in November 1973, most memorable to the travel-weary ministers involved, the French insisted that the foreign ministers change their venue from Copenhagen to Brussels on the same day so as to make a shift from the EPC agenda to the EC agenda.[13] The French insistence on maintaining the distinction between EC and EPC issues and procedures finally relaxed with the presidency of Giscard d'Estaing.[14]

EPC has experienced an impressive institutional development. The agenda of EC foreign ministers may now simultaneously include both EC and EPC issues. The Single Act even went so far as to mention political cooperation and the Community institutions in the same breath: "The Commission shall be fully associated with the proceedings of Political Cooperation." (Article 30.3b) The next paragraph guarantees "the European Parliament is closely associated with European Political Cooperation." (Article 30.4) Even though the linkage between Community institutions and those of EPC existed in practice, the Single Act's formalization of this linkage shows the growing acceptance of EPC as a legitimate Community activity. That acceptance is further reflected in inclusion of the EPC text in the body of the Treaty.[15] An official German statement neatly pinpoints the compromise contained in the Single Act's manipulation of the EPC text: "Enshrining EPC in a single treaty brings it nearer the Community institutions without depriving it of its independent character."[16] Albeit lessened, however, the distinctness of EPC survives in its unique structures and procedures.

Normally, preliminary discussions prepare political issues almost to the point of agreement before they come to the European Council. The process begins in the Political Committee (PoCo) composed of a political director from each country's foreign ministry and a Commission representative. In advance of a European Council, the Political Committee prepares preliminary texts that cover the gamut of major tension areas in international relations. The presidency may take a special interest in a foreign policy issue and encourage work on it before a European Council. For instance, during the Dutch Presidency the first-half of 1986, Foreign Minister Hans van den Broek, drew attention to the situation in South Africa.[17]

More often than not, the texts the Political Committee prepares tend to be "pretty anodyne," in the words of an official close to political cooperation.[18] The undramatic nature of the great majority of these texts follows from the circumstances of the EC. European Councils do not often coincide with major international events. In addition, the requirement of unanimity means that even if an event is so important that it deserves comment, the European Council may be unable to respond.

As noted in Chapter Three, when the European Council meets, the Political Committee holds a parallel meeting. The Political Committee reviews the draft texts or, if necessary, creates new texts. In the evening, these texts resurface at the foreign ministers' dinner, held separately from that of the heads of government. Foreign ministers might make minor changes in the wording of a text, but it is rare that prolonged discussion takes place or that texts undergo significant alteration. The same is usually true for heads of government. When the texts come before the European Council during the following day's session, heads of government are prone to give a nod to the final text.

The pattern of European Council involvement in EPC just described is not unlike that of the Cabinets of member states in policy decisions. Given the time constraints on cabinets and the abundance of issues that require their attention, it is all the better if differences of opinion are sorted out at lower levels and issues prepared to the point where only the formal agreement of Cabinet members is needed. As a rule, national cabinets devote time to only the most controversial and important issues, which we will see is the case with the European Council's processing of EPC issues.

Political Cooperation at the Venice and The Hague European Councils

The European Council did not play a visible role in EPC throughout most of the 1980s. There were, however, two notable exceptions. At Venice, June 1980, and at The Hague, June 1986, the European Council devoted significant attention to EPC. Both European Councils sought to deal with highly controversial political issues: tensions in the Middle East (Venice) and apartheid in South Africa (The Hague). Decisions on these issues were likely to lead to an EC position different than that of the United States. Because of international pressures and internal differences, no pre-cooked agreement was at hand at either European Council. Enough agreement existed, however, that these were issue areas in which the EC could contribute distinct perspectives and, ultimately, establish and develop distinct policies. Therefore, there were extra efforts to try to reach a compromise at both European Councils.

The Middle East, especially, had been a testing ground for EPC. Not only were Europe's vital interests at stake in this region, but an independent European perspective from that of the United States began to emerge. Only three years old when the first oil crisis occurred in 1973, EPC was still defining its focus. At that time, the United States was not at all prepared to share influence with the EC. When U.S. and EC interests nearly collided over the oil crisis, EC foreign ministers worked out an informal agreement to avoid future controversies and enable the U.S. to live more comfortably with EPC. Named from "Gymnich" in Germany, in June 1974 the agreement provided for consultations to link the various official and political levels of EPC with their equivalent offices in Washington.[19]

The European Council of June 1980, provided the setting for the Venice Declaration on the Middle East. Significantly, the Declaration charted a course in the region separate from U.S. policy. Undisguisedly pro-Palestinian, it proposed that the PLO "be associated with negotiations" for peace in the region.[20] Also significant was that the Venice Declaration would be followed up with diplomatic activity. Lord

Carrington, the British foreign minister at the time, was especially concerned about the faltering Camp David process and had urged EC involvement to spur dialogue in the region.[21] It is suggested that, ultimately, Carrington "was so beguiled by trying to 'sort out the Israelis' that he lost sight of how urgent it was to keep a close focus on the Argentine threat to the Falklands in the last fateful days of March 1982."[22] This oversight precipitated his resignation.

The idea of an active EC role in Middle Eastern affairs set well with neither Israel nor the United States. Israel, especially, mistrusted the motives involved in the EC statement. Former Israeli Foreign Minister Abba Eban responded to the Venice Declaration in *The Times*.[23] He linked the EC member countries' position on the Palestinian question to their interest in securing access to Arab oil. The U.S. administration had tried in vain to dissuade the EC member countries from making the Venice Declaration. Both President Carter and Vice-President Mondale extensively pressured the EC not to stir up the already troubled waters around the Camp David process.[24] Arab counter-pressures added to the delicacy of the situation. Arab states worked against the EC's caving in to U.S. and Israeli pressures. Additional complications resulted because the EC member countries differed about the extent to which they should support the Palestinians. The British pushed for a limited statement, not wanting to part ways too obviously with the United States In contrast, the press described the French as preferring no statement at all to one that was watered-down.[25] The Germans were in the position they most dislike, their loyalties stretched between France and the United States. EC member countries' different sensitivities to the United States pushed the Venice Declaration to the forefront of the European Council agenda. In their conclusions at Venice, the heads of government noted their "comprehensive" discussion on the Middle East, indicating that EPC had been the main item of business at the Venice European Council.[26]

As in Venice, heads of government at The Hague European Council could not easily determine a common policy in regard to South Africa. Reflecting the U.S. position, Britain and Germany were reluctant to go along with any form of sanctions. France, Italy, and Spain staked out the middle ground. The Netherlands led a group which was in favor of sanctions, including Denmark, Greece, and Ireland.[27] By the close of the European Council, the Twelve had apparently reached a fragile behind-the-scenes agreement, which certain heads of government preferred to keep secret. Prime Minister Ruud Lubbers of the Netherlands, acting president of the European Council, drew strong protests from Mrs. Thatcher and Chancellor Kohl when he alluded to this informal understanding in his closing remarks. He revealed that sanctions would be applied after three months if diplomatic overtures had failed to convince the South African regime to moderate. This compromise strategy could be directly traced to Mrs. Thatcher. She had taken the position that positive measures be tried first before resorting to punitive ones. Having promised in advance of The Hague to stand firm on her no sanctions position, Mrs. Thatcher faced protests from Parliament on her return to Britain. The British government wasted political credit in the Council of Ministers tiresomely resisting sanctions while support grew for the policy. The EC eventually imposed limited sanctions. These were later relaxed after the South African regime took steps to conform to international demands for reform.

Aside from these two examples, European Councils, for most of the 1980s, did not make political cooperation a high priority. Issuing political declarations was no longer the automatic process it had been in the past. Occasionally there were no preparations made for the European Council's political statement, especially if the presidency did not want to pursue a political theme. Even when the European Council issued a political statement, usually the ministers had spent only a few minutes discussing the subject. Heads of government also left the impression that they scarcely concerned themselves with political cooperation during the private moments of their meetings.28

The European Council's Evolving External Emphasis

At the Athens European Council of December 1983, the Council did not include a political cooperation text in its final conclusions — a departure from usual practice. Despite officials' and ministers' laborious extra-preparations in advance of this summit, heads of government failed miserably to agree on issues related to the reform of the CAP. Former Greek Prime Minister Papandreou said that to have made political proclamations, given such blatant failure in other areas, "would have simply betrayed [the member countries'] nakedness."29 At this time, there was a wide agreement that the EC needed to get its own house in order, or else expect a cynical response when it told outside countries how to manage their affairs. Following Athens, the European Council began to act on a long list of housekeeping chores, the major tasks including the resolution of the British budget dispute, addressing institutional reform (which had been an irritant to EC inter-institutional relations since the 1970s), making adjustments in the CAP and rearranging Community spending priorities, participating in planning and completing the Single Market, and working toward monetary union. While activating, negotiating, and supervising the internal agenda, the European Council chose not to devote valuable time to political cooperation. Whenever the European Council could not get through the entire agenda, they dropped the political statement. Furthermore, as the emphasis was on the optimal use of the European Council, heads of government felt most needed to make decisions and spur action in other EC institutions to deal with pressing Community problems. If the European Council could not get to political cooperation, that did not mean its abandonment but its delegation to foreign ministers.

The European Council also wanted its words to carry more weight. Thus, once having defined its position on a crisis, it aimed to avoid repetitious and seemingly perfunctory statements, if the crisis situation persisted. Thus, the European Council stopped making its often repeated objection to Soviet intervention in Afghanistan. It saved comment for the London European Council of December 1986, which coincided with the seventh anniversary of the Soviet occupation of Afghanistan.[30]

Not only practical reasons for the European Council's seeming inattention to political cooperation were at work. Political reasons were as important. In the past, EC internal politics and international politics, both separately and in their various combinations, affected the scope of Community action in international relations. Certainly, Mrs. Thatcher's formidable presence in the European Council limited independent (in relation to the United States) EC postures in international relations. Were EC influence to be identified as such in world politics, it would require independence from the United States at least from time to time. Indeed, policy emphases and strategies alternative to those of the United States frequently reinforced the distinctness of the European character of EPC. As noted by Jean De Ruyt, practitioner and major author in the EC field, "when EPC manages to produce a specific and definite policy of its own, the policy often contrasts with the U.S. position." Furthermore, he describes the insufficiency of communications links that have developed between EPC and U.S. officials and politicians:

> These U.S.-EPC meetings are very casually prepared and usually are little more than a superficial diplomatic chat about current issues. There is no working group in EPC discussing relations with the U.S., and there is no appropriate structure in the State Department to consider EPC issues as such. Moreover, the EPC dialogue remains totally separated from the close and permanent relations which have developed between the U.S. and the EEC on commercial policy issues.

This, he explains, is not the result of "a procedural problem" but owing to "the well known ambiguity in the U.S.-European relationship."[31] Recognizing the insufficiency of links between EPC and the U.S. foreign policy process, former President Bush and Secretary of State James Baker called for an improvement in communications.[32]

The "ambiguity" in U.S.-EC relations manifests itself in a large variety of ways. There may be the most intimate cooperation, including exchange of intelligence, between the United States and Europe when it serves both sides' interests, as in the Gulf War and the crisis of Yugoslavia. Otherwise, the GATT negotiations have shown that Europeans persistently reject U.S. demands when they appear too excessive and out of tune with EC concerns and interests. France, in particular, reacts to any minimization of its power by the United States and can influence Germany to react with a show of strength, such as the Franco-Germany army corps of recent invention.

West-West relations is a topic at every European Council, even though not always reflected in the published texts of the meetings. Most recent public acknowledgement of the European Council's concern with West-West issues is its frequent statements on the GATT negotiations. These statements avoid expressing the tension that exists in economic relations with the U.S. and which is certainly discussed among the participants in European Councils. Public texts restrict comment to mutually shared values, such as the Community's aim for the GATT negotiations "to strengthen the multilateral trading system".[33] As one of the few highly influential multilateral institutions that excludes the United States, the European Council has a special vantage point on West-West relations. Either in the margins or during its organized sessions, disturbing events in U.S.-European relations come under discussion along with the impact on Europe of policy and political changes in the United States.

Whereas other leaders sought "separateness" in European positions, Mrs. Thatcher was comfortable espousing European views but preferred them to be complementary to those of the United States. Undoubtedly, Mrs. Thatcher aimed for an important international role for Britain. She supported Britain's realizing this goal through more foreign policy activism on the part of the EC. Nonetheless, from her point of view, everyone was better off if U.S. and EC foreign policy goals were mutually supportive.

Mrs. Thatcher neither had the complications in her relations with the United States of other of her European partners nor did she share their convictions that integration in all its possible forms was desirable. She valued conducting foreign policy through bilateral relations with the, then, Soviets and, especially, the United States. Her view of the structures of power in the international system translated into loyalty to NATO and tolerance of the unequal relations between the United States and other members of the Alliance, especially as Britain had been "less unequal" than others. As for the EC, she had a utilitarian view of it as the sum of its market potential and not much more. Her experience with the EC was personally bitter. Mrs. Thatcher's devoted press secretary, Bernard Ingham, must have come close to expressing her sentiments in describing how "she suffered the abuse of small men" in the context of the EC.[34] Cutting a swathe in global affairs was for her and men of the stature of Reagan and Gorbachev. In comparison, the efforts of the EC must have seemed feeble.

Nonetheless, at Fontainebleau, June 1984, the British government presented a paper suggesting practical improvements in the Community's foreign policy machinery.[35] Britain needed to make a peace offer at the close of the British budget dispute and procedural improvements appealed to the instincts of "Maggie the Manager."[36] Equally important, British Foreign Secretary Sir Geoffrey Howe's enthusiasm for EPC dampened the prime minister's skepticism in this instance.

Ironically, Mrs. Thatcher several times was more in agreement with the EC on security issues than with U.S. President Reagan and tried to convince him of the European perspective. During her first Camp David meeting with him, December 1984, she sought and received specific guarantees on key points of concern to her and other European leaders about the Strategic Defense Initiative (SDI). Primarily, Europeans wanted to preserve the nuclear security doctrine of deterrence. Ultimately, SDI would void deterrence if it provided to one side the credible nuclear defense it promised. President Reagan gave assurances, but Europeans continued to be wary of SDI. SDI represented to Europeans enormous subsidies to U.S. high technology industries already leading the international competition. Europeans were so concerned that this, and other controversies with the United States, spurred the rebirth of the exclusively European security organization, the Western European Union (WEU). The WEU eventually set up an expert working group to monitor the effects on Europe of developments in SDI.[37]

Mrs. Thatcher represented renewed European concerns during her second visit to Camp David, 15 November 1986. The previous month, 12 October, President Reagan had almost negotiated his vision of a nuclear-free world with Soviet leader Gorbachev at Rejkjavík, with U.S. allies completely uninformed of his intentions. Rejecting this as a dangerous lack of realism, Europeans insisted on disarmament (as opposed to total denuclearization) and grew more determined to influence issues of East-West relations affecting European concerns. At Camp David, Mrs. Thatcher actually based her discussions with the U.S. president on common positions of Britain and its WEU partners, these made public at a WEU ministerial meeting, 13-14 November 1986.[38] As mentioned in the previous chapter, Mrs. Thatcher wrote heads of government that Rejkjavík and Soviet reforms would be on the agenda for informal conversations at the London European Council of December 1986. Undoubtedly, this European Council was an ideal opportunity for a purposeful exchange of information on subjects vital to security. An official referred to the role of the European Council at that time as the Community's "senior voice" on East-West relations.[39]

However much Mrs. Thatcher shared certain positions of her European partners, she did not have great expectations for the EC's lofty ambitions. Out of office, she remained particularly skeptical about Europe's being able to manage its own military security, which is significant for the "unEuropean" way in which she shaped her argument. Mrs. Thatcher insisted on Europe's continuing to rely on U.S. forces, originally stationed against the Soviet threat, because they "provide similar comfort against the rise of Germany today."[40] Her tolerance for developing the EC's international role stopped at defense cooperation. It is not surprising, then, that the post-Thatcher European Council showed new activism on global political and security issues. Furthermore, Prime Minister Major, her successor, was faithful to and made personal contributions to thinking about European international positions.

One must also consider the predominance of nuclear issues in the hierarchy of international issues in the past. Nuclear politics encouraged more agreement-building on secondary issues between the United States and the EC than would have otherwise existed, and dampened disagreements. In addition, the regions the EC might have hoped to influence were either within the sphere of one or the other of the superpowers or off-limits as a dangerous breeding ground of superpower conflict, which if unleashed could always turn nuclear. In its assessment of the G-7 summit, July 1992, an article in the German press implied greater world influence for Germany by proclaiming a new currency in foreign relations:

> The summit underscored that foreign policy is no longer made with missiles and nuclear weapons. In these times, after the end of the great ideological confrontation, the old adage is more valid than ever: money rules the world.[41]

A wider interpretation of the changing requirements of a post-Cold War world is that political influence has displaced military influence in importance. Changed circumstances seem designed for the preferences and talents of the Europeans. EC member countries are neither confident nor comfortable exercising military power. Wielding political influence is something they feel they can do at least as well as the United States. Generally, they see themselves as having abundant experience in nurturing political links with other countries through multilateral organizations, the EC having served as a training ground and now supplying a model for the development of future relations with Eastern and Central European countries. Germany is already applying the lessons of its EC interactions, as told by one observer:

"Germany has consciously based its policy toward Poland on a process of reconciliation like that achieved with France."[42] Secretary General of EPC Giovanni Jannuzzi described the first effects of changes in Eastern and Central Europe as having "spurred hopes that the strictly military aspects of defence might gradually give way to political security, bringing essentially politically oriented structures like the Community to the forefront."[43]

In more hopeful times, the EC sensed the opening of a new era in European politics. At the Rhodes European Council of December 1988, hosted by the Greek Presidency, heads of government agreed to intensify, expand, and redirect the Community's external emphasis. The text that supplied this agreement bore the title, "International role of the European Community." This text was significant in several respects. First, it clearly signalled the beginning of a new stage of political and economic global activism on the part of the Community and heads of governments' willingness to encourage this tendency."[44] Second, it predicted a climate of international relations more favorable to the EC's assuming new regional responsibilities. Anticipating the destruction of the Berlin Wall, it recommended a four point course of action that should be taken in the "renewed hope to overcome the division of our continent."[45] Third, the European Council recognized the increasing relevance of the processes of international organizations, especially the UN contributions to human rights and peacekeeping. The EC could assume new international responsiblities by participating in a revitalized UN.

The Spanish Presidency, the first-half of 1989, saw itself as assuring the implementation of Rhodes. In presenting the program of the presidency to the European Parliament, January 1989, Spanish Foreign Minister Francisco Fernández Ordóñez devoted the biggest part of his speech to external matters. This emphasis certainly had the encouragement of Spanish Prime Minister Felipe Gonzalez. As early as October 1987, Mr. Gonzalez had advocated more defense cooperation among EC member countries in a much publicized lecture he delivered at the European University Institute.[46]

The Madrid European Council hosted by the Spanish Presidency, June 1989, delivered on its promise to emphasize the external dimension. The political texts from Madrid read like a menu of EC involvement in international issues. A declaration on East-West relations highlighted the importance of the CSCE process to healing the European rift. Taking note of their increased efforts to cooperate on security matters, EC member states stressed the value they attached to the arms reduction negotiations and other security-related discussions in process. The European Council surveyed issues in a number of regions, including the Middle East, Latin America, Asia, Southern Africa, and the Maghreb. Where peace efforts were underway, the European Council offered support for the process. This was the case in relation to Lebanon, Angola, Cambodia, and the Israeli-Palestinian conflict. Where the peace process was in trouble, the European Council expressed concern, for instance, over the failure of ethnic groups in Cyprus to reach a UN-mediated solution and Afghanistan's difficulties in forming a legitimate and stable government. Confronted with violations of human rights, such as China's continued persecution of student activists and other countries' hostage holding, EC heads of government issued condemnations. The European Council repeated established policies, as in its anti-apartheid stance in relation to South Africa. In addition, it applauded the regional integration efforts of other groups, such as the Maghreb Union.

Member countries' historical and cultural linkages to countries and regions also served to focus the European Council. Conflict among subnational groups in Cyprus was a matter of concern because of affected ethnic Greeks. The Spanish Presidency made it a priority to include a political cooperation text sympathetic to the interests of Latin America. Among other items, it emphasized the economically depressive effects of the debt crisis, a speedy solution to which heads of government pledged their support.

The most developed foreign policy statements of this European Council were in relation to Lebanon, the Israeli-Palestinian question, and China. Precise objectives were outlined in all three cases, with detailed texts on the Israeli-Palestinian situation and China elaborated in two annexes to the "Conclusions of the Presidency."

Almost a decade had passed since the European Council's Venice Declaration, June 1980. Foreign Ministers continued to develop the policy toward the Middle East but left it unamended at the highest level until Madrid. By then the EC had established itself as an important actor in the peace process in the Middle East. It had gained access to both sides of the dispute, no longer completely ignored by Israel and, for other interested actors, providing a link to Palestinian representatives.

Indicating the active role of the EC in Middle Eastern diplomacy, the European Council referred to the contacts the presidency had made under the "troika" arrangement.[47] Whereas EC Middle Eastern policy had been consistent since the Venice Declaration, there had been a change in the U.S. policy position. Moving closer to the European view, the United States became more willing to talk to the PLO. In contrast to the traditional diplomacy of a decade ago, one that was mainly restricted to major powers and their clients, the actors and possibilities had changed. Especially interesting was that the UN, with active EC participation, had passed resolutions that could form the basis of negotiated solutions. The EC strategy was one of coordinated action with the UN and through international treaties. Therefore, the European Council expressed approval for the actions of the Arab League and the Palestinian National Council in conformity with various UN prescriptions. At the same time, it sought to put pressure on Israel to submit to specific UN resolutions, as well as being governed in its actions in the Occupied Territories by the Geneva Convention. In this, the European Council showed its desire to establish an international legal regime for conflict resolution and create precedents for its use.

The European Council directed its China policy against the Communist authorities' continued persecution of regime opponents. The policy combined punitive measures against the regime with positive measures for students. The sanctions against China consisted of temporarily cutting off political and high official contacts, an embargo on EC arms sales to China, discontinuing military and other kinds of cooperation (with a view to not harming students' interests in the process), and a campaign against China's human rights abuses in international organizations. Chinese students studying in EC member countries could extend their visas. For the victims of persecution, the EC would make efforts to get neutral observers into prisons and students' trials in China.

The French Presidency, the second-half of 1989, continued to take advantage of the momentum on EC international involvement. The coincidence of the traditionally outward-looking French Presidency with changes in Eastern and Central Europe assured the external thrust of EC policy. The French Presidency had ample opportunities to try to influence international events, chairing the G-7 Economic Summit in Paris in July, followed by the extraordinary European Council in Paris in November and the regular meeting in Strasbourg in December. At the economic summit, U.S. support was crucial to make the Commission the coordinator of aid to Eastern and Central Europe for the Group of 24. U.S. support for the Commission signalled the important role the EC would be permitted to play in the region. An organization to promote economic reforms in the emerging democracies, the Group of 24, with the Commission as its agent, initially sought to influence events in Poland and Hungary. Almost immediately, the Commission's mandate broadened to include other countries as they chose the path of reform.

Similar to the previous European Council in Madrid, the foreign policy agenda in Strasbourg, December 1989, was full. It included monitoring developments in areas of established foreign policy (*i.e.*, Lebanon, the Occupied Territories, Cyprus, Southern Africa). Events dominating newspaper headlines also elicited responses. With Chilean general elections planned within days of the EC meeting, heads of government tried to nurture this democratic development with promises of future economic assistance.

The European Council made two major contributions to the evolving EC international identity: the "Declaration on Central and Eastern Europe" and "Press statement on the activity of the Twelve in the field of human rights."

The immediate political significance of the Declaration on Central and Eastern Europe was to express support for Gorbachev. As important were the messages for the people taking to the streets to demonstrate against Communist authorities: to convince them that economic assistance was forthcoming and to show moral solidarity with them. This was done as well to encourage continued popular backlashes against remaining Communist regimes. For Germany, the European Council accepted in a public text of the highest order that unification would take place: "We seek the strengthening of the state of peace in Europe in which the German people will regain its unity through free self-determination."[48]

Aside from tactical political maneuvers, the Declaration on Central and Eastern Europe, formally, anchored an aspiring dimension of the EC international role: "It [the Community] remains the cornerstone of a new European architecture and, in its will to openness, a mooring for a future European equilibrium."[49]

The European Council's statement on human rights promised an increased commitment in this area. While the subject of planning by bureaucrats and pro-European politicians for two decades, human rights had not been a major priority of the European Council until recently. The European Council's emphasizing the human dimension was equally appropriate for the development of the Community's international personality as for internal political reasons. Externally, this emphasis reflected priorities agreed on in the past between the "two Europes" in the Helsinki Final Act. Begun in the early 1970s as a part of the CSCE process, a pan-European dialogue on human rights led to the conclusion of the Final Act, laying one of the first bridges between the divided

Continent. This bridge, perhaps, did the most to reveal the moral bankruptcy of Communist rule. It led dissenters to appeal to the Helsinki Final Act for international law protection against the authoritarian actions of their regimes. Eventually, the liberation of Eastern and Central Europe convinced the European Council to make human rights an even more prominent foreign policy consideration. It now stands as "one of the cornerstones of European cooperation as well as of relations between the Community and its Member States and other countries."[50]

To give greater effect to human rights policies, European leaders have strived for a more contemporary expression of the international law principle of "non-interference in the internal affairs of a state." The Luxembourg European Council of June 1991, maintained that actions taken in pursuit of human rights" cannot be considered as interference in the internal affairs of a State, and constitute an important and legitimate part of their dialogue with third countries."[51] This was a conscious effort to promote the revised conception of "non-interference" and influence its legal standing. Renewing the commitment taken at Strasbourg a year and a half earlier, the Luxembourg European Council issued the "Declaration on human rights."

As the European Parliament had consistently put human rights at the front of its concerns, the European Council followed the Parliament's lead. This provided the European Parliament with the rare opportunity to influence political cooperation, once jealously guarded by the Council institutions. Not only could the internal politics of the EC benefit from this sharing of responsibilities, but domestic publics concerned with human rights could see evidence of the EC carrying out their interests. The German public recently demonstrated the seriousness of its expectations on humanitarian issues. March 1992, it was revealed that, in violation of a parliamentary ban, Germany supplied Turkey with a shipment of tanks. Reacting to public pressures, German Defense Minister Gerhard Stoltenberg had to resign even though he did not accept direct personal responsibility. Because of Turkey's flawed human rights record, in particular the mistreatment of its Kurdish minority, Parliament had passed the ban.[52]

The European Council's contributions to promoting the positions and raising the global influence of the EC also carried over in the individual actions of its members. In a visit to the United States, June 1992, British Prime Minister John Major represented British and French points of view. Major received assurances from President Bush that, in the event Russian President Yeltsin suggested to the U.S. president that British and French nuclear forces be counted with U.S. forces in arms reduction negotiations, the leaders would leave the subject for the responsible governments. Indeed, France and Britain made it clear in "The WEU Platform on European Security Interests," that they do not want their nuclear forces negotiated away, especially by others. This seminal document agreed, 27 October 1987, during the post-Rejkjavík rethinking states, "The independent [nuclear] forces of France and the United Kingdom contribute to overall deterrence and security."[53]

Major also brought up with the U.S. president an issue of critical importance to the Germans, that of the G-7 summit's making a financial commitment to bringing Soviet-made nuclear facilities up to the safety standards of the West.[54] Evidently, EC countries were not entirely successful in persuading former President Bush of this necessity at the following month's G-7 summit in Munich, 5-8 July, 1992. The final summit communiqué underlined the danger but did not allocate specific monies to reactor safety.

In addition to advancing European views in quiet diplomacy, Prime Minister Major also engaged in public diplomacy. He prepared an initiative to rescue the Kurds from Saddam Hussein's persecution after the ceasefire in the UN-sponsored war against Iraq. Major formulated his plan en route to the Luxembourg European Council of April 1991. European Council approval of the proposal was immediate, according to a perceptive observer, "partly because it appeared to be upstaging the Americans."[55] Because of time constraints the British prime minister had not sought the pre-approval of the U.S. president. Therefore, Major secured the objective of making his a European proposal, even if unintentionally. The defense of human rights became even more a European monopoly as events surrounding the EC's initiative for a Kurdish enclave unfolded. The EC's use of the term "enclave" was a difficult point for the United States reminiscent of the Gaza Strip.[56] Palestinians had languished there since 1949 even though it was supposed to be a temporary home, their despair continuing to fuel tensions in the Middle East. The United States saw its main objective of a smooth and swift withdrawal from Iraq being undone by the Kurdish rebellion and Iraq's reprisals, not to mention, oddly enough, the EC initiative. The caution of the U.S. administration was probably legitimate, and the United States eventually participated in relief efforts and protective measures for Iraq's religious minorities. Initially, however, the U.S. appeared singularly unsympathetic to the Kurdish plight and had been outdone politically.

Maastricht: Strengthening Foreign Policy and Security Capabilities

At Maastricht, December 1991, the European Council tried to match its new assertiveness in international relations with organizational and procedural reforms to strengthen the EC machinery in common security and foreign policies. Constitutionally, the European Council's defining the role of EPC was not unprecedented. Prior to Maastricht, European Councils provided the legal underpinnings for EPC in the Solemn Declaration at Stuttgart, June 1983, and the Single Act at Luxembourg, December 1985. In addition, Maastricht committed the European Council to review the state of an EC common defense policy by 1998 (on the basis of a paper submitted by the Council of Ministers by 1996), at the time the WEU conducted its own parallel review.

Most striking was the constitutional development of EPC in security. Throughout the 1970s member governments denied the EC's propriety in the security field. At the time, however, it was impossible to isolate security issues from the economic and political ties developing with Eastern and Central Europe, especially considering the coordinated EC strategy pursued in the CSCE Measures and Conference on Disarmament in Europe. Certain member countries had problems with encouraging the security dimension. Neutral Ireland and anti-federalist Denmark feared the disapproval of their publics when the Greek foreign minister revealed, in September 1983, that the Council of Ministers discussed "the deployment of American missiles in Germany."[57] Together the Solemn Declaration and the Single Act expanded the EC's competence to the "economic" and "political" aspects of security, omitting the "military" aspect. This formality kept the most important NATO subjects off the EC agenda, or at least the formal agenda, and soothed U.S. apprehensions about EC interference in and rivalry with NATO. Initially, the WEU provided an alternative forum for defense issues that could not be comfortably raised in the EC context. Ireland's neutrality, Denmark's suspicion of militarism in a post-Cold War world, and Greece's reputation for going against the consensus in EPC created special problems for these countries, the only EC member countries who remained, for the time being, outside of the WEU. The British were leery of French plans that would have the WEU duplicate the functions of NATO. Britain, however, did not prevent the steady revitalization and refinement of the role and the structures of the WEU during the second half of the 1980s. Spain, Portugal, and Greece have now joined the organization, presaging even closer links between the WEU and EC and, perhaps, their eventual merger.

A partial merger resulted from the intergovernmental conference (IGC) on Political Union held throughout 1991, culminating in the Maastricht Treaty on European Union. The European Union, the renamed and refederalized EC, received full jurisdiction in security discussions and looked forward to the "eventual framing of a common defense policy."[Article D(1)][58] In addition, Maastricht agreed that the

European Council could specify certain subjects of foreign and security policy for "joint action." Thus, a process came into being for transferring sovereignty on these subjects to the European Union. At the same time as enlarging the Community's security dimension, Maastricht kept the WEU organizationally separate from the EC but described it as "an integral part of the development of the European Union." [Article D(2)] Two concepts of security, which might be thought of as "soft" and "hard" security, influenced the division of responsibilities between the EC and the WEU. In an annex to Maastricht, the European Council listed the subjects to be considered immediately for "joint action": CSCE matters, European regional arms and security negotiations, nuclear non-proliferation policies, and the international trade in arms and military technology. In contrast to these peace-building responsibilities, Annex V on the WEU prepared for its militarization, for the eventual assignment of forces and making provisions for strategic planning and decisionmaking. WEU foreign ministers and defense ministers met in Bonn, 19 June 1992, to issue the Petersburg Declaration. The Declaration implemented the Maastricht defense plans in the non-binding annex or, according to one minister, the agreement in the "margins" of Maastricht. A text separated from the body of the Treaty, the agreement would proceed even if all of the member countries failed to ratify the Maastricht Treaty. In response to a journalist's question, the British foreign secretary indicated that further upgrading the WEU did not depend on the success of Maastricht.[59]

Even so insulated from direct public pressures, European politicians have always faced difficulties agreeing on the texts with which to build the European foreign policy and security dimensions. The proposals that did not find their way into Maastricht were revealing. Whereas the French and Germans aimed to bring the EC dialogue with North America under joint action, it did not make the list.[60]

Maastricht gave the European Council another chance to put EPC under the normal decisionmaking process. One could have anticipated that the European Council was intent on keeping EPC under the Council system, even though the Commission did not walk away empty-handed. The Commission's new right to share in making proposals in EPC did not compare with its exclusive right of initiative in EC affairs. However, after many years of not having an established means of input in EPC, the Commission definitely benefitted. The Treaty provided for the Council to use majority voting on select issues of "joint action," if it opted to do so. It was highly unlikely that the European Council would agree to cede decisionmaking authority in EPC to the Commission and the European Parliament or see majority voting adopted across the board in EPC matters. Very simply, if the European Council were to "normalize"

EPC, the argument could be made that the European Council should also submit to Treaty rules and procedures. As a result of the Dane's initial rejection of Maastricht (now overturned by the 1993 Danish referendum), federalizing according to the old formula of giving more sovereignty to the most integrative institutions experienced a set-back. Community and national elites had already become more amenable to pragmatic arrangements, especially if they were integrative in the sense of enhancing and allowing for more common policies.

The refusal, so far, of the European Council to see the EC mode of decisionmaking applied to EPC should not be confused with whether it is willing to support the development of EPC. The mechanisms of EPC have so gradually fallen into place and become compatible with other supporting mechanisms (for instance, in NATO, the WEU and the CSCE) that the deliberateness of this progression may have gone unnoticed. EPC is still growing. Community insiders are convinced of its value and aware of the deficiencies. Overall, EPC has been less confrontational than some policy areas that might qualify as "low politics," notably reforming the CAP. Community insiders feel that EC member countries are converging in their foreign policy and security outlooks, and politicians agree on the necessity of this convergence. Strictly from a constitutional standpoint, the outlook for EPC is positive.

Testing Procedures in the Gulf War and Yugoslavia

Speaking of the Yugoslav crisis, British Foreign Secretary Douglas Hurd told parliament, 8 May 1992, "We also have testing new work in hand on the security of Europe."[61] This was in reference to the variety of informal activities, new measures painstakingly negotiated, and the meticulous coordination of roles of all of the security-related organizations: the EC, WEU, NATO, CSCE, and the UN Security Council. The original stimulus for the new procedures was the East-West conflict. The expanded regional possibilities of EPC after the embrace of Western influence by Central and Eastern Europe only reinforced this tendency. The renewed regional focus of EPC was a natural extension of its efforts throughout the 1970s in the mainly peace-building CSCE process. The evolution developed so favorably in Eastern and Central Europe that it seemed only to require coaching and coaxing. Thus, EPC was not prepared for a Third World dictator to threaten blackmail with vital oil supplies and for Yugoslavia to revert to age-old nationalities crises.

The Gulf War exposed the immature state of the military capability, insofar as Europeans were weak in arrangements for defense cooperation. For the United States it revealed the decline of the effectiveness of U.S. unilateralism, but certainly did not celebrate what might be called "equal multilateralism." The WEU played an important role in political symbolism; as reported by one observer,

> Paris took delight in organizing back-to-back WEU and EC meetings during both the Persian Gulf and Yugoslav crises, not only because it made substantive sense but also to rub Anglo-Saxon noses in the fact that the two organizations already are part of the same entity.[62]

Despite the WEU's visibility at the time, the U.S. strategic lead was not negotiable and not as much influenced by European participation as might be the case in the future.

Evidently, cooperation on political matters eventually worked well during the Gulf War, although it failed in the beginning stages. The disarray of the Community at the outset was apparent in Belgium's flatly turning away the British who tried to purchase ammunition for their Gulf involvement.[63] Britain did not delay joining the U.S. effort until the EC adopted its position.[64] During later political consultations there was more agreement and common policy-making. We have already seen that the European Council pressured the U.S. administration on the issue of humanitarian assistance to Iraq's Kurdish minority. All indications suggest the British and French seats on the UN Security Council have been "Europeanized," an arrangement that Germany has insisted on in lieu of a seat of its own at this time. German Foreign Minister Kinkel alluded to this arrangement, in relation to UN sanctions against Serbia, when he said that EC interests could be "represented" by the Community members participating in the Security Council.[65] Therefore, the active role of Britain and France in UN resolutions against Iraq was closely linked to EC political cooperation.

Because it occurred in the European house, the crisis of Yugoslavia emerged as an even greater test of the new security architecture than the Gulf War. The United States decided to take seriously EC ambitions to be the regional power. In unprecedented fashion, the United States faded into the background, while offering support for European efforts in the crisis, including sharing intelligence. According to a U.S. official for Balkan relations, such detachment on the part of the United States from a European conflict had not been seen since the 1930s, and, therefore served to signal a new policy direction and new global interests introduced by the Bush administration.[66] The United States was prepared to see whether Europe could manage the new regional security challenges and, at the same time, relieved itself of responsibility for a "tar baby."[67]

Consensus-building was a slow process in the EC. Member governments disagreed over initial objectives. Germany felt the dismembering of Yugoslavia was inevitable and that the new states should be recognized as they emerged. Britain and France favored trying to save as much of former Yugoslavia as possible so as not to set the precedent that borders in the region were transmutable. Maintaining this position was difficult as Serbia became more rapacious. Germany, finally, succeeded in persuading the EC to give official recognition to the first of the breakaway states, Croatia and Slovenia. Unwilling to wait on the EC timetable with internal political pressures building, Germany "broke ranks" by recognizing the new states before the EC. Even though informed of Germany's intentions, the Community objected to Germany's unilateralism, and France, in particular, resented the pressure tactics. As none of the remaining regions of the rump state were powerful enough to counter Serbian influence, other secessions were made inevitable. The independence vote of Bosnia and Herzegovina created fears for the Serbian minorities in this region. Internal ethnic conflict erupted and was followed by territorial aggression by Serbia. In the EC uncertainty remained about whether the policy of recognition aggravated the situation.

There seems to have been a consensus, in the U.S. administration as well, that a large scale military intervention was not practicable for a variety of reasons, including the sheer difficulty of the task given geophysical conditions and the deep national antipathies that fuelled the morale of the combatants. Therefore, political solutions took top priority. An EC-sponsored mediation process lurched from ceasefire to ceasefire. UN mediators were also closely involved. As peacemakers offered constitutional remedies, the violence increased.

The U.S. administration decided to seek a solution more actively in May 1992. Facing a presidential election, then-President Bush could not afford the appearance of inaction. U.S. officials recognized EC weakness in the midst of the worsening situation. Throughout the summer of 1992 Serb regulars and irregulars assaulted Bosnia and Herzegovina. Civilians suffered not only war-related injuries but ethnically motivated attacks, deprivations, and expulsions. The U.S. public and members of Congress began to grasp the extent of the tragedy. In August 1992 Bush found himself having to explain to Congress and the U.S. public his opposition to U.S. forces entering the conflict. The recent demonstration of U.S. military power in Iraq made the president's task all the more difficult.

U.S. observers have often disparaged the EPC process as a limited capability, at best. History seems to support this evaluation. EPC does not have a stunning victory to parade, as the U.S. administration has had in the Gulf War. Against the example of the Gulf War, the EC's lack of decisive action during the first year of the Yugoslav crisis is hard for Americans to understand. A syndicated U.S. journalist has concluded, "Politically a united Europe is one more fictional creature that walks without clothes.... The European concept of unity will never be an equal or a substitute for the strength and flexibility of the American constitutional system."[68]

The EC's problems with military issues are due not only to procedural deficiencies and confusing overlap with U.S. structures and responsibilities. Also significant are the limits European public opinion places on military action, especially if such action is unilaterally initiated by the United States. The military language in Europe has to be one of "peace-keeping" and "peace-building" and is different from that of the United States. European politicians are very familiar with the constraints and licenses of the security framework they have constructed, as Sir Geoffrey Howe so unambiguously noted:

> The point of using WEU is that the conclusions will have been arrived at by Europeans themselves and on the basis of their own analysis of Europe's best interests. The effect will be to demonstrate more clearly, for our own publics as well, that the Atlantic arch truly does have two pillars and that one of these is truly European.[69]

Instead of proving the utility of national military force, both crises have shown its shortcomings. The United States alone possessed the force, but wanted to have international legitimation for its actions. While not guaranteeing the United States will seek cooperation from the international community in every military action, it does establish the ideal if force is to be used effectively. In the case of Europe, individual countries lack sufficient force, and they lack sufficient legitimation as well.

Notes

1.   Sources on European Political Cooperation (EPC) include David Allen, Reinhardt Rummel and Wolfgang Wessels, eds., *European Political Cooperation: Towards a Foreign Policy for Western Europe* (London: Butterworths, 1982); Philippe de Schoutheete, *La Cooperation Politique Européenne* (Brussels: Labor, 1980); William Wallace, "Political Cooperation: Integration Through Intergovernmentalism," in H. Wallace, W. Wallace and C. Webb, eds., *Policy-Making in the European Community*, pp. 373-402; Françoise de la Serre, "Foreign Policy of the European Community" in Roy C. Macridis, ed., *Foreign Policy in World Politics: States and Regions*, 7th ed. (Englewood Cliffs, N.J.: Prentice Hall, 1989), pp. 345-73.

2.   Jacques Delors, *Our Europe: The Community and National Development*, trans. by Brian Pearce (London: Verso, 1992), p. 23.

3.   *Ibid.*, p. 26.

4.   See this plan of the organization of EPC which puts the European Council at the pinnacle of the process, de la Serre, "Foreign Policy of the European Community," p. 357.

5.   Interview by the author at a Permanent Representation in Brussels, November 1987.

6.   For the aborted attempt to establish a European Defense Community, see Richard Mayne, *The Community of Europe Past, Present And Future* (New York: W.W. Norton and Company, Inc., 1962), pp. 85-106.

7.   At the time it seemed possible to make a distinction between technical and political matters, most simply, a distinction between economic issues, on the one hand, and foreign policy and security issues, on the other. Governments generally regarded economic issues as secondary in importance (especially in comparison to Cold War nuclearization) and not especially problemmatic during the post-WWII economic expansion in Europe and the United States. Hence, economic issues were non-threatening enough to put under Community authority. In June 1993, Russian President Boris Yeltsin's visit to the United States demonstrated a reversal of priorities. Most prominent were economic themes, such as Yeltsin's trying to convince Congress to speed up passage of the Russian aid package. During one event, Yeltsin had the chance to lobby hundreds of prospective U.S. investors. All of this took place as the Russian and U.S. leaders agreed the deepest cuts, yet, in their nuclear arsenals. John Dickie provides evidence of a similar trend in Britain. He finds the allocation of resources in Britain's Diplomatic Service gives the main priority to "commercial work," which includes efforts to advance the country's economic interests. It takes up the largest part of resources, some twenty-nine per cent, twice as much as that given to "political work." See *Inside the Foreign Office* (London: Chapmans Publishers Ltd., 1992), p. 45.

8.   Throughout much of the 1980s the British press revealed its anti-federalist bias as it continued to refer to the organization as the EEC and the Common Market, even though EC had entered common usage.

9.   Bulmer and Wessels, *The European Council: Decision-Making in European Politics*, p. 122.

10.   The smaller EC member countries are often suspicious when the larger countries advance schemes outside of the EC framework, as was the Fouchet Plan. Holt and Hoscheit mention the smaller countries' fears of having imposed on them a *"directoire*-type of decision-making," "The European Council and Domestic Policy-Making," p. 5. The old suspicions were aroused again with the announcement in 1988 of the development of a Franco-German Defense Council. A German official felt it necessary to give assurances that the Defense Council represented "neither an axis nor a *directorate.*" See David Marsh, "Bonn soothes fears on French defence link," *Financial Times*, 22 January 1988, p. 2.

11.   See the "Luxembourg Report" on EPC in *European Political Cooperation (EPC)*, 5th ed., Translation published by the Press and Information Office of the Federal Government, Bonn, 1988, pp. 24-31.

12.   *Ibid.*

13.   Wallace, "Political Cooperation: Integration Through Intergovernmentalism," in H. Wallace, W. Wallace, and C. Webb, eds., *Policy-Making in the European Community*, p. 381.

14.   Bulmer and Wessels, *The European Council*, p. 42. See also Morgan, *From Summit to Council*, p. 6.

15.   Head of intergovernmental cooperation between member states in the Secretariat-General of the Commission, Simon Nuttall revealed that "voices had been raised for the negotiation of the EPC Treaty as a separate exercise ... with no link to the Community. See "European Political Co-operation and the Single European Act," *Yearbook of European Law*, no. 5, 1985, p. 206.

16.   "Memorandum of the Federal Government on the Single European Act of 28 February 1986," excerpts in *European Political Cooperation (EPC)*, p. 355. The European Parliament did not agree with the assessment that, included in the Single Act, EPC had become a more normal aspect of Community life. In a resolution, Parliament noted the "very slight" impact the Community institutions had on political cooperation and expressed "serious doubts" over the continuing distinction between the Community sphere and EPC. See "Resolution adopted by the European Parliament on the Single European Act," 11 December 1986, also in *European Political Cooperation*, 395-97.

17.   Former foreign minister Hans van den Broek is now commissioner in charge of the newly created Directorate-General of Political Affairs, formed in anticipation of Maastricht's ratification. Maastricht gave the Commission the right to share the initiative in EPC. The crisis of Yugoslavia certainly had a bearing on the Commission's new role as well.

18.   Interview by the author of an official responsible for political cooperation in Brussels, November 1987.

19.   For a description of the variety of U.S.-EC consultations on political cooperation provided for by the Gymnich Agreement, see Jean De Ruyt, "European Political Cooperation: Toward a Unified Foreign Policy," *Occasional Paper of The Atlantic Council of the United States*, October 1989, p. 34.

20.   "Declaration by the 17th European Council on the Euro-Arab Dialogue, Lebanon, Afghanistan and the situation in the Middle East, Venice 12-13 June 1980," in *European Political Cooperation (EPC)*, p. 130.

21.   Roger Tomkys, "European Political Cooperation and the Middle East: a personal perspective," *International Affairs*, 63 (Summer 1987), p. 432.

22.   Dickie, *Inside the Foreign Office*, p. 112.

23.   For an example of the Israeli reaction to the Venice Declaration, see the article by Israel's foreign minister from 1966 to 1974, Abba Eban, "The West Bank: why have Europe's diplomats played such an unimpressive role?" *The Times*, 13 June 1980, p. 14. The official reaction of Israel was sent to the permanent representatives of the EC member countries. In a clear attempt to affect the

German position, it stated that the Venice Declaration had asked Israel "to involve in the peace process the Arab SS called the Palestine Liberation Organization," reported in "Israel bitter over EEC Middle East peace plan," *The Times*, 15 June 1980, p. 1.

24.   Carter had publicly asked the EC to refrain from any move to involve the PLO in negotiations for peace in the region, as reported by Michael Hornsby, "Europe says PLO must have voice in peace quest," *The Times*, 14 June 1980, p. 1.

25.   R.W. Apple, Jr., "Western Europeans Urge Role For PLO in Mideast Parley," *The New York Times*, 13 June 1980, p. 1.

26.   "Declaration by the 17th European Council on the Euro-Arab Dialogue," p. 129.

27.   For EC member countries' positions on the sanctions discussed at The Hague, June 1986, see the following: Richard Owen, "South African Crisis: Caution in Europe despite growing clamor for action; EEC shies away from complete embargo," *The Times*, 16 June 1986, p. 7; Owen, "Howe plans EEC Pretoria *troika*," *The Times*, 25 June 1986, p. 1; Owen, "EEC summit deadlock on sanctions," p. 1; Owen, "Thatcher averts immediate EEC sanctions at summit; Howe in solo mission to Pretoria," *The Times*, 28 June 1986, p. 1.

28.   Interview by the author with a Commission official responsible for political cooperation in Brussels, November 1987.

29.   *Bulletin of the European Communities*, 12 (1983), p. 7.

30.   "London European Council," *Bulletin of the European Communities*, 12 (1986), pp. 11-12.

31.   Jean De Ruyt, "European Political Cooperation," p. 34.

32.   The Trans-Atlantic Declaration now provides for EC-U.S. contacts on the official, ministerial, and highest political levels; the first bi-annual EC-U.S. summit between President Bush, President of the Council, Prime Minister Major, and Commission President Delors was held in December 1992.

33.   "Rhodes European Council," *Bulletin of the EC*, 12 (1988), p. 11.

34.   Bernard Ingham, *Kill The Messenger* (London: Harper Collins Publishers, 1991), p. 265.

35.   "Europe — the Future," paper presented by the British prime minister to the Fontainebleau European Council of June 1984, reprinted in *Journal of Common Market Studies*, 23 (1 September 1984), pp. 73-81.

36.   This title is borrowed from Frank P. Sherwood, "Maggie the Manager: Administrative Reform in Britain," *The Bureaucrat*, 20 (Summer 1991), pp. 39-44.

37.   WEU working groups include one for Mediterranean security issues and another for collective defense resources. See Alfred Cahen, "The Western European Union (WEU) and NATO: Strengthening the Second Pillar of the Alliance," *Occasional Paper of The Atlantic Council of the United States*, 1990, p. 14.

38.   *Ibid.*, p. 28.

39.   Interview by the author of an official at a Permanent Representation in Brussels, 9 November 1987. Consistent with this official's view, the German foreign minister cited the "need to clarify the new prospects for East-West issues," at the upcoming Hanover European Council, June 1988. See "Report on

the German Presidency of the European Community by Foreign Minister Hans-Dietrich Genscher to the European Parliament," *Statements and Speeches,* no. 11, 17 June 1988, p. 6.

40.   Quoted by Robin Oakley and George Brock, "Thatcher warns of growing German power," *The Times,* 16 May 1992, p. 1.

41.   *The Week in Germany,* 10 July 1992, German Information Center, p. 3. The group of seven industrialized nations (G-7) are Britain, France, Germany, and Italy of the EC countries, and United States, Canada, and Japan.

42.   Edwina S. Campbell and Jack M. Seymour, Jr., "Franco-German Relations in Post-Cold War Europe," *Bulletin of the Atlantic Council of the United States,* 10 July 1992, p. 4.

43.   Giovanni Jannuzzi, "Europe and a security dimension," *NATO review,* no. 2, April 1991, p. 3.

44.   "Rhodes European Council," *Bulletin of the EC,* 12 (1988), pp. 10-11.

45.   *Ibid.* The four points included (i) further utilizing the CSCE process; (ii) continuing the negotiations aimed at increasing security on the Continent; (iii) concentrating on the human dimension of East-West relations, including encouraging more contacts between citizens of both regions; (iv) pursuing a "political dialogue" with the East.

46.   "Gonzalez backs closer EC ties on defence," *Financial Times,* 20 October 1987, p. 2.

47.   To insure continuity in the foreign policies of successive EC presidencies, collaboration takes place among representatives of past, present and future presidencies. This "troika" arrangement is utilized at various political and official levels. For instance, foreign ministers participate in diplomatic representations as members of the "troika" just as embassy and mission heads do. The Strasbourg European Council, December 1989, referred to the many intercessions with foreign governments to bring up human rights offenses carried out "most often through the Ambassador of the presidency or heads of mission forming the Troika." See *Bulletin of the EC,* 12 (1989), p. 18.

48.   *Ibid.,* p. 14.

49.   *Ibid.,* p. 15.

50.   *Bulletin of the EC,* 6 (1991), p. 17.

51.   *Ibid.,* p. 17.

52.   See "Stoltenberg Resigns, Ruhe Is New Defense Minister," *The Week In Germany,* 3 April 1992, p. 1.

53.   See the text of The WEU Platform on European Security Interests in the appendix, Cahen, "The Western European Union (WEU) and NATO," p. 36-44.

54.   "Major discovers that everybody loves a winner," *The Times,* 10 June 1992, p. 8.

55.   The details of the so-called "Major Plan" could only be elucidated by a studied insider in Britain's foreign policy world such as Dickie, *Inside the Foreign Office,* p. 226-27.

56.   *Ibid.,* p. 227.

57.   Tugendhat, *Making Sense of Europe*, p. 67. During the referendum campaign on the Single Act, the Irish Government stressed the minimalist nature of the Act's commitment to EPC. A government booklet prepared specifically for the campaign stated, "It is quite clear [from Article 30.6 (a)] that cooperation on military aspects of security is not appropriate to European Political Cooperation." See *The Single European Act; A Government Information Booklet*, published by The Stationery Office, Dublin, May 1987, p. 29. The Irish referendum on Maastricht succeeded without much difficulty despite the Treaty's commitment, ultimately, to a common defense policy.

58.   "Provisions on a Common Foreign and Security Policy" of the "Maastricht Treaty," *Europe Documents* 1750/1751. Subsequent references to Maastricht are based on the same documents.

59.   Policy Statement, British Information Services, 23 June 1992, p. 6.

60.   "Return fire," *The Economist*, 19 October 1991, p. 54.

61.   See the speech of British Foreign Secretary Douglas Hurd in the debate on the Queen's speech in the House of Commons, 8 May 1992, British Information Services, Policy statement 18, 1992.

62.   Jenonne Walker, "Fact and Fiction about a European Security Identity and American Interests," *Occasional Paper of The Atlantic Council of the United States*, April 1992, p. 13.

63.   Howard LaFranchi, "The World From Brussels," *The Christian Science Monitor*, 2 April 1991, p. 4.

64.   Hypothetically, under the Maastricht regime, the European Council could label Middle Eastern security matters a subject of "common policy," and, thus, legally bind the EC member countries to coordinate their related actions. Under such circumstances, Britain would have been prevented from immediately declaring its loyalty to the United States during the Gulf crisis.

65.   "Kinkel Appeals to Serbian Leadership to 'Stop Murder and Destruction'," *The Week in Germany*, 12 June 1992, p. 1.

66.   David Binder, "The Yugoslav Crisis: Why U.S. Is Bearing Down on Belgrade," *The New York Times*, 27 May 1992, p. A4.

67.   Walker, "Fact and Fiction About a European Security Identity," p. 16.

68.   A. M. Rosenthal, "The Grim Lesson of Yugoslavia," *The Miami Herald*, 26 May 1992, p. 11A.

69.   Sir Geoffrey Howe, "The European Pillar," *Foreign Affairs*, 63 (Winter 1984-85), p. 341.

6

When Politicians Become Eurocrats and Eurocrats Become Politicians

Two perspectives have dominated most discussions of the European Community. One of these, the "European Federalists," mainly focused upon a particular type of constitution-building. Throughout the history of the Community, federalists pushed for institutional changes to increase the decisionmaking capacity and powers of EC institutions out of the conviction that Europe could only be built in great leaps. From this point of view, giving the EC a strong constitutional basis provided the most protection against national backlashes. In addition to aspiring for the federation they call "European Union," federalists have also been concerned about how to further democratize the process of integration, a concern closely related to their desire to turn the European Parliament into an authoritative decisionmaker. In the final analysis, federalists aimed to politically empower the Community.

As many of its adherents are active in the European Parliament, European federalism has been a political movement as well as a theoretical perspective on integration. Passionately committed to this cause since his days as a WWII partisan, Altiero Spinelli led federalists in the European Parliament to renew their momentum. They set forth their brainchild, the Draft Treaty of European Union, adopted by the European Parliament in February 1984, with 237 supporting votes, thirty-one negative votes, and forty-three abstentions. Bieber described the extent to which the draft Treaty emphasized institutional rigging:

> The institutions and the decisionmaking process occupy a central position in the approach chosen by the European Parliament toward European Union. Their key role is apparent for the fact that the relevant articles (19) cover more than one-third of the entire Draft Treaty.[1]

The European Council did not accept the Draft Treaty's proposals for institutional change. Nonetheless, persuaded by the effort, the European Council accepted the more modest reforms in the Single Act, the 1987 amendments to the Treaty of Rome. The Maastricht Treaty, informally agreed by the Twelve, in December 1991, marked another attempt at a great leap showing the persistent influence of federalism in the Community's development.

The second perspective has been that of the "neo-functionalists." The quantity, variety and originality of scholarship related to this school of thought complicates the presentation of a unified perspective. Neo-functionalism is, perhaps, best understood in comparison and contrast to federalism. Whereas the specific institutional goals of federalism required a strict constitutional arrangement of powers, neo-functionalism analyzed existing EC institutions and decisionmaking approaches which would promote integration. More widely focused, neo-functionalists considered every aspect of the Community from legitimacy-building in terms of satisfying the needs of mass consumption to the vital role of the European technocrat and the technocratic orientation in integration. Like the federalists, neo-functionalists measured advances in integration in terms of increases in the supranational institutions' authority. Additionally, they judged progress by "scope enlargement," that is, as the Community took over more and more of the tasks traditionally performed by the nation-state. Scope enlargement did not depend entirely on the favorable political conditions federalists were so interested in but could also be attributed to the more abstract condition of "spillover," a novel concept contributed by neo-functionalists. Spillover posited that "... economic integration per se has a certain internal dynamic whereby areas and tasks are inextricably linked to each other."[2] As a result of issue density, the performance of one task tended to create opportunities and needs for additional tasks. Integration was, to a certain extent, self-perpetuating and therefore semi-autonomous.

Even though each paradigm contributed different insights and priorities in terms of understanding the Community, they tended to share a common view of the institutional dynamics of the Community as national-minded institutions vying against community-minded institutions, anti-integrationists versus integrationists. Each paradigm was also attached to the founders' model of Community decisionmaking: the Commission proposes and the Council decides. Integrationists favored a Commission-driven model of integration. The Council could only be transformed into a partner in integration if it submitted to supranational procedures, such as majority voting. Charged with upholding national interests, the Council had a conflict of interest with the Commission, the translator of the Community view. According to Sbragia,

> Both pro- and anti-integrationists have identified the representation of the Community interest with the Commission and, more recently, with the European Parliament, not with those institutions representing national interests such as the Council of Ministers and the European Council. The Community is thought to be strong to the extent that its policies transcend the collectivity of national interests, and the strength of the Commission has been seen as a rough approximation of such transcendance occurring.3

As early as the 1970s, Helen Wallace observed the narrowing of the distinction between the roles of the Commission and the Council of Ministers:

> The necessity for drawing hard and fast lines of demarcation between the Commission and the Council has become less stringent, given that both are integral parts of a single process.4

Wallace was alluding to the interaction between the Council and the Commission which was far more complex and interwoven than the original model suggested.

As Chapter Two showed, no longer is the Commission the exclusive initiator of policy at the European Council level or, for that matter, any other decisional level. The Commission now shares this role with the presidency and individual member governments. Even though the press is fond of depicting the Commission as regulation-crazed, Commissioners claim that responsibility belongs to national governments, the real source of the majority of Brussels regulations. According to EC Commissioner Karel van Miet,

> At least 85 percent of the initiatives we take up come from demands and instructions from EC summit conferences or the EC Council of Ministers, that means from demands made by the 12 Community governments. Often we reject a request for an EC regulation.5

In the past, critics attacked the Commission for compromising the Community interest when it let consultations with representatives of national governments influence its proposals. The Committee of Permanent Representatives (COREPER) enabled the Commission to take a preliminary stock of national responses to its proposals, a practice which the critics considered detrimental to integration.6 Consultations have become a routine matter between representatives of the

Commission and member governments. Technocracy flourishes in the more than a hundred specialist working groups that support COREPER and the Council of Ministers. The Commission would be hard-pressed and politically naive to do without data and advice from the most advanced civil services in the world. The Commission, moreover, nurtures links with member governments not only from below, but also from above. The Commission president, occasionally, makes a tour of capitals to meet with heads of government before a European Council. These pulse-taking tours monitor the strength of opposition to and support for specific proposals.

The Commission's accomodation of national interests is routine, but not for the mere sake of giving satisfaction to member governments. The Delors Plan demonstrated how the Commission strategically accomodated national interests to win acceptance for the overall integrative package. During the Delors Plan negotiations, we noted how the Commission in the latter stages made specific proposals to accomodate German interests. A meeting between Delors and Kohl opened the way for the Commission to propose the set-aside scheme and thereby meet the German preference for controlling agricultural production.

The Delors Plan showcased the Commission's strength as a policy proposer. By giving it input in foreign and security policies, Maastricht promised to enlarge the Commission's scope in policy initiation. The Commission's increased responsiveness to national interests enabled it to reach compromises and to clear the backlog of proposals from the 1970s. Delors not only facilitated cooperation between France and the Commission; he also provided an essential contact for Franco-German cooperation, a dynamic which the Commission could use for its own purposes. After the 1986 enlargement to include Spain and Portugal, championing the interests of particular member countries gave the Commission another tactical advantage. In coalition with less developed member countries, during the 1980s, the Commission skillfully navigated regional redistributive policies past Mrs. Thatcher. The strategy was so successful that, in the early 1990s, Britain sought a counterweight in opening the Community to the wealthy members of the European Free Trade Association (EFTA).

In its dealings with the European Council, the Commission exploited its expertise in initiation and mediation, making the most of its constitutional role. The unprecedented quality of the Delors Commissions was their political weight: their ability to influence not only the Community agenda but the outcomes of bargaining, largely owing to successful networking with national politicians. Delors was already an intimate of national decisionmakers during his first year at the Commission in 1984. During the first half of that year the French had the presidency of the Community and had to deal with elections to the European Parliament and the conclusion of the British budget dispute. Major decisions of the French Presidency "were made in meetings *à quatre* with Mitterrand, Dumas, Delors, and the French Minister of European Affairs."[7] Known to be sensitive to power and, perhaps hoping to gain influence with him, Mrs. Thatcher supported Delors' reappointment to a second term, 1988-92, to coincide with the completion of the Single Market. She gave this support even though other influential member governments were willing to consider Delors' replacement. Shortly afterward their relationship deteriorated. As a former prime minister Lady Thatcher made known her opinion that the Commission should be stripped of any but clearly administrative functions, no doubt in reaction to Delors' successful wheeling and dealing.

While the Commission became more politically competent, the European Council became more technocratically competent. In the past, a task-oriented European Council had surfaced from time to time. In 1978 technocrats in the European Council, former finance ministers German Chancellor Helmut Schmidt and French President Giscard d'Estaing, responded to a political impulse by then Commission President Roy Jenkins. On the basis of Jenkins' suggestions, the European Council launched the European Monetary System (EMS) in 1978. At the outset of the 1980s, critics of the European Council claimed it was ill-prepared to negotiate technical issues and insisted that the British budget dispute proved such incompetence. By 1988, the Delors Plan taught the opposite lesson. The European Council skillfully negotiated a maze of inter-linkages, resolving numerous difficult distributional issues from grain production thresholds to a revised system of funding the Community.

The ability to negotiate complex details was in part owing to the presence of national delegations of key experts. It was also owing to politicians seasoned in Community bargaining. By the time of the Delors Plan, the three major heads of government, Thatcher, Kohl, and Mitterrand, had been through two previous multiple issue negotiations, the British budget dispute and the Single European Act. Kohl and Mitterrand took the additional experience of the Delors Plan negotiations into Maastricht. After thirty-three European Councils, Mrs. Thatcher did not politically survive to participate in Maastricht,[8] largely out of Conservative party leaders' fears that she would use her formidable negotiating powers to block EC progress. Her replacement, John Major, learned the ropes of EC negotiations as a foreign minister. Indeed, the depth of experience at the foreign ministers' level matched that of heads of government. A near-permanent fixture on the Community stage was

Germany's Hans Dietrich Genscher, foreign minister for eighteen years until 1992. Other foreign ministers also had staying power. Hans van den Broek was Dutch Foreign Minister from 1982 until he moved to the Commission in 1993 to head up the new directorate-general for political affairs. The present Danish Foreign Minister, Uffe Ellemann-Jensen, also rose to his post in 1982. The image of Eurocrats stealing the EC show does not hold up in the light of national politicians' expertise in EC affairs.

The dense technical-political overlap of the issues the European Council faced in the second-half of the 1980s and early 1990s necessitated a technocratic orientation. The initiative to create the Single Market in the Commission White Paper in 1985 oiled the Community machinery and led to a massive policy expansion. The Community's reach expanded to touch on the defining issues of national sovereignty: tax, monetary, and national boundary issues. Although material for number crunchers and economic analysts, these were also intensely ideological issues, as Mrs. Thatcher's resistance to ceding sovereignty and the silent resisters who took cover behind Britain clearly showed.

The European Council's technical problem-solving not only included bold sovereignty-cutting issues; it also included issues which could not be solved at lower levels for political and other reasons. CAP reform regularly found its way to the European Council not only because it raised political concerns, but because it also threatened the traditional landscape of countries trying to preserve their family farms. Britain's attachment to zero value added tax (VAT) on baby items was, partly, a sentimental issue that fortified sovereignty-based objections to harmonizing VAT. After the British budget dispute, the Commission discouraged using the European Council as a "court of appeal" for decisionmaking problems below. Even so, the Maastricht backlash against integration and the politicians who staked their reputations on Europe immediately led to hitches in Community decisionmaking. The European Council faced new pressures trying to balance the EC machinery with decisions palatable to domestic publics.

Even though the European Council has not always been known for decisional efficiency, the Council became integrated with the "normal" Treaty institutions and developed a decisionmaking stride. As the Community gears up for a European Council, seemingly chaotic preliminary preparations follow an often repeated pattern. The object is to be able to present the heads of government with the right conditions for decisionmaking. The "lower" Council is all abuzz; working groups, COREPER, and various Councils of Ministers meet in marathon sessions, if necessary. National administrations coordinate their positions, hushing-up the occasional inter-ministerial dispute, and signal the negotiators. The other executive, the Commission, goes through similar motions. The European Parliament debates in the background, the noise of member governments' posturing sometimes drowning its efforts. Parliament's best hope for influence lies with getting the Commission to sponsor its views in the Council. Expectations of decisional efficiency modelled on the experience of national governments could not possibly take into account the institutional diffusion of power in the EC. The closest approximations would be federal systems, but their political centers are more authoritative than that of the EC. Of course, the participation of national governments, each an authoritative political center in its own right, is the complicating factor.[9] Any complex organization tends toward inertia, but the EC's tendency is amplified owing to the additional complexity of its structure of authority. The leadership of the European Council was important to overcoming the inertia of the 1970s and the early 1980s. A meeting of the European Council stimulates movement in the entire organization. The European Council has succeeded in motorizing the EC, not by replacing the Commission motor, but by systematically bringing political force to bear on a necessarily tedious decisionmaking process. And, as we saw in Chapter Five, the European Council can be a competent decisionmaker when issues cannot be resolved at lower levels.[10]

Ironically, greater cooperation and interaction between the European Council and the Commission spearheaded the revival of integration. Both institutions seemed to revel in the political and technocratic challenges of European construction. Even Mrs. Thatcher was more a part of the enterprise than she generally got credit for. Her behavior in the European Council, before she dug in her heels with European and Monetary Union, was described in the following terms:

> ... she has repeatedly accepted compromises on detail and commitments in principle to the radical development of European integration and cooperation, which contradict her public assertions outside.[11]

The interesting contrast to previous theoretical expectations is that in recent years the Commission and the Council worked closely together and both institutions simultaneously expanded their policy influence. Our focus has been the legislative productivity of the relationship between the European Council and the Commission. An increasingly interventionist European Council supported the work of the Commission, indeed created work for it, and responded to its lead. For its part, the Commission steered the European Council in a more integrative direction, as the Delors Plan demonstrated. Delors regarded the European Council as the "political engine" of the Community and trusted it with the Community's most important decisions. Far from being at cross purposes and detracting from each institution's importance, the European Council and the Commission participated in joint endeavors which were jointly beneficial. The presumed gap in perceptions between the two institutions narrowed to the point that their responsibility in Maastricht was indistinguishable. The public opposed to Maastricht did not know whether to lay blame at the feet of the Commission or national politicians.

This study bears out strongly what other scholars admit: that integration proceeds with intergovernmentalism. Keohane and Hoffmann, for example, concluded,

> There is little doubt that European decisionmaking has since 1985 been more expeditious and effective; we attribute a decisive role in that change not only to incentives for the world political economy and spillover but also to intergovernmental bargains made possible by convergence of preferences of major European states.12

Trends and Prospects

Negotiating the Maastricht Treaty throughout 1991 over the course of two intergovernmental conferences, national officials and politicians once again demonstrated their commitment to the EC. Maastricht's potential impact on EC legislative and regulatory powers was certain. International lawyers observed,

> Although the treaty is more often discussed in terms of its symbolic importance than its substantive provisions, it is an unprecedented agreement substantively. An understanding of the centralization of power called for in the treaty makes clear why the outcome of the ratification process will mark a turning point for Europe.13

Culminating in the European Council's decisions at Maastricht, the EC's revitalization coincided with a period of cabinet stability in the major European governments and a consensus among them to pursue economic growth through the EC. Ideological battles over fundamental economic policy faded. Only skirmishes remained to be settled, whether social policy would be made at the EC or national levels. Attachments to ideologies loosened under the influence of Thatcherism and a new technocratic consensus on economic objectives. Countering the failed economics of the 1970s was the mission of the 1980s. National and EC elites mobilized around a strategy for the twenty-first century designed to put Europe in the lead of the international competition in high-tech and service industries while cooperating in painful economic restructuring.[14] Maastricht marked the height of the elite consensus on what steps needed to be taken to insure economic growth. It included a fitness test for European Monetary Union requiring member countries to satisfy precise conditions in order to qualify for participation.

The new Europe rejected the economic nationalism of the 1970s. EC politicians reacted to the first oil shock in 1973 by trying to rely on their individual contacts with Arab oil suppliers. Iraqi President Saddam Hussein's threat to oil supplies in 1990 not only led to the formation of an international coalition and subsequent military intervention, but to the European Council's laying the foundation for a Community energy policy relying more on Russian resources.

As unprecedented confidence in regional economic strategies crosscut the discord of competing internal strategies, developing Europe became a major component of ideologies of the Left and Right. Socialist parties saw in Europe the possibility of economic growth, on which publics perceived the Left to be weakest, combined with progressive themes. A European Community with social democratic policies was perhaps their only hope for reinventing the Socialist International. Mitterrand made his choice when he permitted his finance minster, Jacques Delors, to de-radicalize economic policy in 1983, even though it meant the Communists leaving the government. Progressively, the French socialists increased their economic stakes in Europe. It was said of Mitterrand, "He arrived in power under the banner of socialism; he'll leave under the banner of Europe."[15] To an equal degree, the allure of pragmatic socialism attracted Spanish Prime Minister Felipe Gonzalez.

Mrs. Thatcher's satisfaction with her own ideology let her resist Europe's appeal. Nonetheless, enough members of her party and government warmed to the EC to make her obstinance over Europe a factor in her replacement. Despite Mrs. Thatcher's problems with Europe the market emphasis of the 1992 agenda was undiluted Thatcherism. Major responded to Europe as a way of cooperating with a natural adjustment in Britain's position in the global political economy, as the different call of his generation. For Germany, Europe neatly accomodated its political spectrum as a consensus between Left and Right. More important, partnership in the Community provided Germany with the legitimation it needed to exercise full sovereignty, as opposed to remaining in the condition of semisovereignty imposed on the country after WWII and not ended until unification.[16] In the final analysis, few political objections could be raised to pursuing economic growth through a non-partisan, future-oriented, mildly social democratic and peace-building Europe.

Absent the paralyzing disagreements over economics of the past and new European issues to inflame party sensitivities, EC decisionmaking revived. The consensus-style decisionmaking of the European Council was vigorous from 1985 through 1991. Heads of government even consented to more majority voting in the Council of Ministers on issues pertaining to the Single Market. Oddly enough, Mrs. Thatcher acceded to majority voting, putting concerns about decisional efficiency on issues that were important to her ahead of objections to more supranationalism. United in their aims, European politicians and Eurocrats enabled the close working relationship between the Council and Commission to flourish. European elites made decisions about Europe with confidence. They believed they knew what was best for European citizens and that they were representing citizens' interests, perhaps in that order.

Relatively unencumbered, national governments supported problem-solving on the regional level. External constraints did not manifest themselves and cause national decisionmakers to question their plans. Whereas determined U.S. opposition to a "fortress Europe" could have threatened to undercut Europe's dynamism, the Bush administration embraced the Community from the outset, even criticizing Mrs. Thatcher for holding up progress. The boldness of the EC agenda made it seem that an autonomous, even powerful, Europe had finally broken out of its nation-state confines. As long as member governments were willing to go along with the EC, this was true; however, the Danish and French referenda in 1992 revealed a strong public desire for their leaders to put checks on the Community.

Throughout a large part of the previous decade until the Danish referendum, the main constituency of the EC had been cooperative national governments. The Maastricht referenda extended the constituency to directly involve public opinion. At the time a mobilized public was anxious to make itself heard for a variety of reasons, not all of them completely related to the EC. For instance, the unpopularity of Maastricht in France was partly the result of President Mitterrand's personal unpopularity, a situation not much improved by other mainstream politicians rallying around the Treaty.

Elites might have been able to avoid the public backlash if they had been able to call upon party loyalties, but as pointed out earlier, elites did not frame recent EC issues in partisan terms. Unbound by traditional party positions and thus able to pursue what they considered to be technocratically feasible national politicians gained freedom of maneuver during the EC revitalization. When public opposition surfaced, politicians found it hard to restore the elite-public link on EC issues. The task was made more difficult given technocracy's association with the failed economic policies and bureaucratic-authoritarianism of Communist regimes.

Denmark realized the significance of the democratic appeal of its Maastricht rejection. At the extraordinary Birmingham European Council of October 1992, under the British Presidency, Danish Foreign Minister Uffe Ellemann-Jensen played to popular democratic feelings. To expose bureaucratic meddling, he carted a box of home-grown Ingrid Marie apples to the summit, forbidden for sale in the Community because their diameter did not satisfy EC requirements.[17] Evidently, the apples passed the summit inspection and, henceforth, would be allowed for sale.

What the early 1990s showed was that the EC remains an "extension" of the concept of the nation-state, not only in the necessity to fulfill public demands but in that the EC experiences the same vulnerabilities as the nation-state.[18] If international events are unfavorable to the nation-states of Europe, they tend to be unfavorable to the EC at least at this stage in its development. The EC barely survived the "international turbulence" of the 1970s, which also rocked the foundations of the European nation-states.[19] The worldwide economic recession of the 1990s equally shook nation-states and the EC.

Certainly EC member governments aim ultimately to increase their capacities to cope with shocks from the international economy, capacities which European elites increasingly believe their small nation-states do not possess on their own. Indeed, the legitimacy of transferring sovereignty to the Community is phrased in terms of "pooling sovereignty," a gain over the shrinking sovereignty of nation-state pygmies in the global political economy. We saw how strongly de Gaulle desired international activism on the part of EC heads of government, mostly to influence U.S. economic policies with repercussions for Europe. Community assertiveness in international trade negotiations and plans for monetary union follow in this tradition. Still, an uncertain U.S. economy, the growing needs of the Third World, and the freedom of Eastern and Central Europe to compete in world trade and appeal for economic assistance (not to mention Community membership) threatens to "overload" the EC, just as "unification" overloaded Germany.

As economies falter, member countries will judge more harshly the costs and benefits of policy positions in the EC. Community politicians and officials tended to regard the British budget dispute as an aberration, mostly the result of Mrs. Thatcher's penchant for being "difficult." It was, however, a truer reflection of the pull of domestic publics than realized at the time. At the end of 1992, Community negotiators reached a compromise with the United States to cut agricultural subsidies and opened the way for the conclusion of the long overdue Uruguay Round of GATT negotiations. As a result of French farmers' opposition to the agreement and pending legislative elections in France, President Mitterrand found himself strangely isolated in the EC (and in the world) in defending national agricultural interests.

In the same year, stung by public suspicions and pessimistic economic forecasts, the Commission had to temper its ambitions. So much success accompanied the negotiations of the Single Act in 1986 and the related budget expansion, Delors I in 1988, the Commission had decided to put this strategy to work again. The Commission planned back-to-back negotiations on Treaty amendments and budget reform. Proposing increased resources to fund the new commitments undertaken at Maastricht, the Commission prepared its Delors II package for the Luxembourg European Council of June 1992. Given the EC's increased commitment to common security and foreign policies and the Commission's extra responsibilities in this area, specifically administering the international aid program to Eastern and Central Europe, Delors II sought a doubling of resources for the Community's external relations. In addition, it contained a proposal for a redoubling of the Community's structural funds, modeled on that of Delors I. To finance these objectives Delors II proposed lifting the ceiling on EC expenditure from 1.2% to 1.37% of Community GDP by 1997.[20] Whereas the negotiation of Delors I benefited from member governments' optimistic assessments regarding EC competition in the international economy and the performance of domestic economies, a recession in Britain and budget deficit in Germany clouded the negotiation of Delors II. In changed economic circumstances and with the difficulties of the ratification of Maastricht focusing an unusual amount of public attention on the Community, heads of government at the Luxembourg Summit objected to so large an increase. Eventually, the Edinburgh European Council of December 1992 agreed to allow EC spending to rise to 1.27% of Community GDP by 1999. The increase was enough to appease Spain's concerns over regional spending. Including reallocations from research, the environment, and transport, funds for the Community's poorest members would almost double. However, the European Council sent a clear message that it recognized a new financial reality.

German unification was unsettling for the Community, as much as European integration had relied in the past on the more equal relations between France and Germany. Undoubtedly, German leaders will emphasize the European dimension of their work and perhaps even magnify it. Even though it would be more difficult to be more pro-European than former German Foreign Minister Hans Dietrich Genscher,

Klaus Kinkel may have more opportunities to realize the ambitions of his predecessor. Expectations in Germany and the world are now adjusting to the necessary acceptance of an expanded international role for Germany. Foreign Minister Kinkel will have to negotiate the particulars with his own domestic public and international leaders, but Germany's new influence will be concretized in a variety of new forms and existing institutions. In combination with its EC commitments, Germany's heightened international role could greatly benefit the Community's foreign policy and global economic strategies.

Even though a unified Germany is prepared to exercise strong leadership in the Community, a dominating member country is contrary to the practices and processes of EC decisionmaking up to now. Equally important, it is contrary to the Franco-German cooperation that supplied the main context of German behavior in European politics. Urwin describes how the partnership of German Chancellor Schmidt and French President Giscard d'Estaing between 1974 and 1982 "dominated" the European Council.[21] The balance of power in the Community changed as Mrs. Thatcher vowed to break the combined control of France and Germany, the Community enlarged, and the Commission ascended in the ranks. Nonetheless, President Mitterrand and Chancellor Kohl made sure that Franco-German relations remained the driving force of integration from the mid-1980s.

Germany did not deny its own policy preferences even though closely identified with the Community, in general, and France, in particular. Through the strong personality of Schmidt, Germany drew limits on its participation in Community spending, an approach that Kohl continued. At present, the specter of Weimar increases German anxieties about its internal situation and will not permit loose spending by the Community or uncomfortable German sacrifices to bolster other economies. In the early 1990s, the German central bank, the Bundesbank, maintained high interest rates to counter the otherwise inflationary effects of government borrowing to finance unification. This action imposed high interest rates not only on the member countries of the European Monetary System (EMS) but on would-be member countries. Countries claimed their economies were flagging from having to pay for German unification while Germany attributed the weakness of other economies to their internal policies. The currency crisis of 1992 caused Britain to temporarily suspend its membership in the Exchange Rate Mechanism (ERM) of the EMS. As a result, public recriminations between British and German politicians starkly contrasted with the exceedingly good relations Major and Kohl enjoyed in the past.

In the final analysis, Germany's EC role is already well-defined and includes necessary compromises. Thus, the Bundesbank inched down interest rates. Furthermore, at the Edinburgh European Council of December 1992, Chancellor Kohl went over the heads of his financially conscious officials and agreed to more Community spending on infrastructure. Ironically, Germany recovered full sovereignty at a time it no longer existed. This country, too, must cope with interdependence.

Unification itself attests to the enduring influence of nationalism. Even more important, the violent internal reactions to the strains of unification show that the process of channeling contending nationalisms through nation-building and, ultimately, supranationalism, is far from complete. Thus, supranationalism is dependent not only on nation-states but stable nation-states.

Events such as the failure of the Community to come to the aid of the breakaway states of former Yugoslavia or the difficulties experienced in ratifying Maastricht recall the dependent condition in which the EC remains. In response to such failures, U.S. observers tend to overlook what the Community has already accomplished, speak of the hopelessness of future plans, and call for renewed U.S. leadership in the world. When mature federalism is the only frame of reference, European integration falls short of expectations. The problem in terms of thinking about the EC from the U.S. perspective is that the only proper and real division of power is through federalism. The Community is admittedly in a pre-federal state, but that is not to say that it cannot exercise the powers of a more federalized entity.

Aside from federalism, a division of power can be effected in any or a combination of the following ways: a transfer of functions, a transfer of decisionmaking authority, and new constituency-based authority.[22] The EC is most advanced in its functional independence whereas, as this study bears out, it depends largely on national governments in terms of decisionmaking and constituency. Therefore, the EC does not exercise the "general power" expected of federations, but the powers it exercises need not be minimal and are as potentially great as those of a federation. The emphasis of this study has been on the more permissive attitudes of national governments in granting the EC functionally specific powers. Significantly, the preceding chapter showed that function has been extended to the security realm, albeit with notable imperfections. Certainly, a litmus test of federations is their competence in security matters.

From currency crises to unsafe nuclear reactors, a plethora of issues are begging for regional solutions. In some cases, such as immigration policy, particular member countries (*i.e.*, Germany) are the ones begging for a Community policy. The revised security concerns of the United States forced the issue of European regional security. By the admission of former President Bush's then deputy secretary of state, "[the U.S.]

economic and political position in the world, still eminent but not dominant, does not so easily permit the luxury of unilateralism."[23] The conviction among Europeans that U.S. hegemony is over led to speculation about how Europe will fill the gap. As the United States refuses leadership in Eastern and Central Europe, the Community faces no other choice but to plan and implement the new European architecture.

So open is the scope for EC policy expansion that it threatens to confound European leaders and fuel public fears of change. Responding to popular pressures, during the second-half of 1992, the European Council turned its attention to curbing the powers of the Commission, making the work of the Council of Ministers more transparent, and defining "subsidiarity" to make it a more discriminating and binding principle for deciding which powers should be performed by the Community. Although it still remains to be seen how EC competences will be affected, subsidiarity suggests that any level of government should perform only those tasks for which it is uniquely suited. Anti-integrationists hope that subsidiarity will be implemented as a de-centralizing principle, but, of course, the opposite effect is possible. Owing to heightened public concerns, the main challenge of the post-Maastricht European Council is legitimation.

Given heightened sensitivities in Europe about human rights, to which the EC has made its own contribution in terms of socialization, it seems the Community can improve its legitimacy with activism in this field. Coupled with the cooperation of the European Parliament, which federalists view as the most democratic of all EC institutions, the human rights emphasis seems a political winner. Successive presidencies and European Councils indicate that they have been convinced of the merits of human rights activism. More pessimism is justified as to whether contemporary circumstances will permit foreign policy to be based on human rights. The economic and security goals of foreign policy loom especially large. It is unlikely that for the sake of human rights European decisionmakers will turn their backs on the opportunities presented by China's expanding internal market or risk becoming involved in a sustained war in the Balkans. However difficult these choices, the cause of human rights will suffer damage as well as elite-public relations, recently sensitized to hypocrisy by the collapse of Communist regimes.

On a closely related matter, the European Council can insist that the EC accept leadership in assisting the transition in Eastern and Central Europe. On the one hand, the Community's expanded regional focus is potentially self-serving. It represents an attempt to take advantage of circumstances extraordinarily favorable to the EC's assuming more power, both regionally, and as a consequence, internationally. In this light, the human rights emphasis and generous tone adopted in relation to the new democracies could cynically be considered as the sanctimonious gloss of power politics. On the other hand, the European Council has to respond to real challenges and problems thrown up by history, many of which it would prefer not to deal with, *i.e.*, the crisis of Yugoslavia and extending more of the profits of the EC trading regime (and eventually membership) to the new democracies. Coping requires new strategies and the development of new capabilities. These are seriously limited by what has already been accomplished in the EC framework, accomplishments too dear to be thrown away and start anew.

The Community has established the process of nurturing political links among its member countries, transforming the techniques of diplomacy, cooperation and policy-making among the Twelve. Europe exists on the level of European politicians and civil servants. It exists not so much as an "idea" but in the complex process of managing all kinds of relations among the member countries and the willingness of decisionmakers to devote themselves to this task. The process itself tends to be legalistic and bureaucratic, which partially explains its recent lackluster appeal to the European public. Subject to pluralism and heightened political sensitivities during an economic downturn, Community decisionmaking breaks down from time to time and only stressfully accomodates new members. Other imperfections include the excessive travel and time demands on government personnel, especially foreign ministers, as a result of their EC and EC-related responsibilities. National politicians' abilities are overstretched with the changing international relations of Eastern and Central Europe, the expanded roles of regional and international organizations, and recent security and economic problems. Yet, one must ask how these changes could be managed at all if not for the EC framework. There, of course, have been failures. Nurturing political links has so far failed to work in the Yugoslav crisis. However, if it should work in terms of EC relations with Russia, in terms of Germany's relations with Poland, and continue to form the basis of Franco-German relations, the EC experience will have been a rewarding one, even if measured only by the success of its diplomacy.

The post-Maastricht reaction has clearly demonstrated that Europe is still a continent of nation-states. Each of those nation-states has a history, a language, a culture, social and political institutions that are not only specific to that nation but often centuries old. Thus, those who look to the federalism of the United States, or Canada, or Switzerland as models must keep in mind the very different historical legacies involved. Regional cooperation, functional cooperation, even shared political institutions do not mean political integration. As this study has shown, one leader has often played a critical role in deciding whether the EC functions well or badly. Thatcher was able to tie the system into knots during the British budget crisis; Delors later was able to bring about extraordinary efficiency of operation. That leaders matter is no revelation to political observers, but the dominating importance of individual leaders in an arena like that of the EC means that the institutions still are only partly formed,[24] still have not fully found their role and their power base.

At the most specific level, it seems certainly true that the Community is evolving, and the evolution is both reflected in and a product of changes in the role of the Commission and the Council. It is possible that as evolution continues, the European Parliament may come to play a more significant role; it may even develop its own independent decisionmaking apparatus, and with its greater links to democratic processes come to be the legitimating and integrating institution in the Community. All that would appear, however, to lie far in the future. In the meantime, the decisionmaking mechanisms we have examined here will continue to wield the real power of the EC, and central to those mechanisms is the European Council. At least in the near term, how well or how badly the European Community deals with the remarkable changes occurring in Europe and the world is going to depend on how well or how badly the European Council performs its role as engine of the Community.

Notes

1.   Bieber, "The Institutions and the Decision-Making Process in the Draft Treaty Establishing the European Union," European University Institute Working Paper no. 164, 1985, p. 12.

2.   Lindberg and Scheingold, *Europe's Would-Be Polity*, p. 118.

3.   Alberta M. Sbragia, "Thinking about the European Future: The Uses of Comparison," in Sbragia, ed. *Euro-Politics: Institutions and Policymaking in the 'New' European Community* (Washington, D.C.: The Brookings Institute, 1992), pp. 269-70.

4.   Wallace, "National Bulls in the Community China Shop," in Wallace, Wallace, and Webb, eds. *Policy Making in the European Community*, 2d ed. (London: Wiley, 1983), p. 52.

5.   Thomas Gack, "Bent gherkin and other tales of the red tape," reprinted in *The German Tribune*, 23 October 1992, p. 6.

6.   See Bieber's and Palmer's analysis of the effects on the Commission's role of the creation of a lower Council, the term they coined for COREPER, in "Power at the top," pp. 310-18.

7.   Andrew Moravcsik, "Negotiating the Single European Act," in Keohane and Hoffmann, eds. *The New European Community* (Boulder, Co.: Westview Press, 1991), p. 69.

8.   Dickie, *Inside the Foreign Office*, p. 275.

9.   "Without the broad access and strong influence of national decisionmakers no decision on the Community level would be taken at all; that is, the effectiveness would be zero." See Wolfgang Wessels, "The EC Council: The Community's Decisionmaking Center," *The New European Community*, p. 150. Wessels developed his considerable expertise in EC decisionmaking as the co-author of the first major work on the European Council.

10.   See the first major legal analysis of the European Council, Jan Werts, *The European Council* (North-Holland: Elsevier Science Publishers B.V., 1992). Werts considers the status of decisions of the European Council, pp. 123-34. The most relevant European Council decisionmaking he characterizes as "the adoption of politically and morally binding (but not enforceable nor sanctionable) decisions later to be brought into force by the institutions within the meaning of the Treaties." (p. 124) Werts finds no instance in which a decision solely emanating from the European Council has been published as "a Regulation, a Directive or a Decision within the meaning of Article 189 EEC." According to Werts, "The European Council nevertheless has at times approached the essential boundary between decision-making in a political sense and *de jure*." On two occasions cited by Werts a text of the European Council was adopted at the next Council of Ministers meeting "without inserting a comma, let alone changing a letter." He finds this to be true of the Brussels Agreement, 1988 (*i.e.*, the agreement on the Delors Plan) and the establishment of the European Monetary System (EMS) at the European Council of December 1978.

11.   Peter Ludlow, *Beyond 1992 Europe and Its Western Partners*, Center for European Policy Studies Paper, no. 38, 1989, p. 18.

12.   Keohane and Hoffmann, "Institutional Change in Europe in the 1980s," *The New European Community*, p. 25.

13.   William Krisel and Christopher Wolf, "Unity in doubt: Maastricht Vote Jolts E.C. Bar," *International Law*, 19 October 1992, p. 31.

14.   British Prime Minister Major's seeming willigness, during a time of personal political weakness in 1992, to see through a fifty percent reduction in coal mining jobs, is incomprehensible unless seen in connection with Europe's future-oriented growth strategy.

15.   Attributed to the Head of the French Institute of International Relations, Dominique Moisi. See Russell Watson with Ruth Marshall, et. al., "In Europe, Three's a Crowd," *Newsweek*, 5 October 1992, p. 54.

16.   For an excellent treatment of Germany's semisovereignty, see Peter J. Katzenstein, *Policy and Politics in West Germany*; The Growth of a Semisovereign State (Philadelphia: Temple University Press, 1987).

17.   William E. Schmidt, "Conference in England Weighs European Unity Plan," *The New York Times*, 16 October 1992, p. A3.

18.   See Stanley Hoffmann, "Obstinate or Obsolete? The fate of the nation state and the case of Western Europe," *Daedalus* 95 (1966), pp. 862-915.

19.   See Ernst Haas, *The Obsolescence of Regional Integration Theory* (Berkeley, Ca.: Institute of International Studies, 1976).

20.   *Europa Yearbook 1993*, v. 2, p. 147.

21.   Derek W. Urwin, *The Community of Europe: A History of European Integration Since 1945* (New York: Longman, 1991). "In many ways the success of the European Council has depended upon the degree of compatibility between French and German interests." p. 176.

22.   Arthur Maass, "Division of Powers," in Maass, ed., *Area and Power; A Theory of Local Government* (Glencoe, Ill: The Free Press, 1959), pp. 10-12.

23.   "Whos's afraid of Europe, now?", *The Economist*, 16 September 1989, p. 22.

24.   This follows Helen Wallace's observation that the Community is "a part-formed political system" quoted in Alberta M. Sbragia, "Thinking about the European Future," in Sbragia, ed. , *Euro-Politics*.

Appendix
European Council Meetings
1975-1993

Dublin	March 1975
Brussels	July 1975
Rome	December 1975
Luxembourg	April 1976
Brussels	July 1976
The Hague	November 1976
Rome	March 1977
London	June 1977
Brussels	December 1977
Copenhagen	April 1978
Bremen	July 1978
Brussels	December 1978
Paris	March 1979
Strasbourg	June 1979
Dublin	December 1979
Luxembourg	April 1980
Venice	June 1980
Luxembourg	December 1980

Maastricht	March 1981
Luxembourg	June 1981
London	November 1981
Brussels	March 1982
Brussels	June 1982
Copenhagen	December 1982
Brussels	March 1983
Stuttgart	June 1983
Athens	December 1983
Brussels	March 1984
Fontainebleau	June 1984
Dublin	December 1984
Brussels	March 1985
Milan	June 1985
Luxembourg	December 1985
The Hague	June 1986
London	December 1986
Brussels	June 1987
Copenhagen	December 1987
Brussels	February 1988
Hanover	June 1988
Madrid	December 1988
Madrid	June 1989
Strasbourg	December 1989
Dublin	April 1990
Dublin	June 1990
Rome	October 1990
Rome	December 1990
Luxembourg	June 1991
Maastricht	December 1991

Lisbon	June 1992
Birmingham	October 1992
Edinburgh	December 1992
Copenhagen	June 1993

Bibliography

Books and Monographs

Allen, D., R. Rummel, W. Wessels, eds. European Political Cooperation: towards a foreign policy for Western Europe. London: Butterworths, 1982.

Bassompierre, Guy de. Changing the Guard in Brussels: An Insider's View of the EC Presidency. New York: Praeger, 1988.

Bulmer, Simon and William Paterson. The Federal Republic of Germany and the European Community. London: Allen and Unwin, 1987.

Bulmer, Simon and Wolfgang Wessels. The European Council: Decision-Making in European Politics. London: The Macmillan Press Limited, 1987.

Butler, Sir Michael. Europe: More than a Continent. London: William Heinemann Limited, 1986.

Campbell, Colin. Governments under stress: Political executives and key bureaucrats in Washington, London and Ottawa. Toronto: University of Toronto Press, 1983.

Carr, Jonathan. Helmut Schmidt: Helmsman of Germany. New York: St. Martin's Press, 1985.

Coombes, David L. Politics and Bureaucracy in the European Community: A Portrait of the Commission of the E.E.C. Beverly Hills, Ca.: Sage Publications, 1970.

De la Serre, Françoise, Jacques Leruez, and Helen Wallace, eds. French and British Foreign Policies in Transition: The Challenge of Adjustment. New York: Berg Publishers, 1990.

Delors, Jacques. Our Europe: The Community and National Development. Trans. by Brian Pearce. London: Verso, 1992.

Dickie, John. *Inside the Foreign Office.* London: Chapmans Publishers Ltd., 1992.

_____. *European Political Cooperation (EPC).* 5th ed. Trans. Bonn: Press and Information Office of the Federal Government of the FRG, 1988.

Fitzmaurice, John. *The European Parliament.* Aldershot, Hampshire, England: Gower, 1985.

George, Stephen. *An Awkward Partner: Britain in the European Community.* New York: Oxford University Press, 1990.

Goehlert, Robert. *The European Parliament: A Bibliography.* Monticello, Il.: Vance Bibliographies, 1982.

Hallstein, Walter. *United Europe: Challenge and Opportunity.* Cambridge, Ma.: Harvard University Press, 1962.

Haas, Ernst. *The uniting of Europe: political, social, and economic forces, 1950-1957.* Stanford, Ca.: Stanford University Press, 1958.

Haas, Ernst. *Beyond the Nation State.* Stanford, Ca.: Stanford University Press, 1964.

Haas, Ernst. The Obsolescence of Regional Integration Theory. Berkeley, Ca.: Institute of International Studies, 1976.

Hennessy, Peter. *Cabinet.* New York: Basil Blackwell, 1986.

Hoscheit, Jean-Marc and Wolfgang Wessels, eds. *The European Council 1974-1986: Evaluation and Prospects.* Maastricht, EIPA, 1988.

Ingham, Bernard. *Kill The Messenger.* London: Harper Collins Publishers, 1991.

_____. *International Political Communities: An Anthology.* Garden City, N.Y.: Anchor Books Doubleday & Company, Inc., 1966.

Jouve, Edmond. *Le Général de Gaulle et la construction de l'Europe (1940-1966).* Paris: Librairie De Droit Et De Jurisprudence: R. Pichon Et R. Durand-Auzias, 1967.

Katzenstein, Peter J. *Policy and Politics in West Germany: The Growth of a Semisovereign State.* Philadelphia: Temple University Press, 1987.

Keohane, Robert O. and Stanley Hoffmann. *Then New European Community.* Boulder, Co.: Westview Press, 1991.

Keohane, Robert O. *International Institutions and State Power.* Boulder, Co.: Westview Press, 1989.

Kirchner, Emil Joseph. *Decision-making in the European Community: The Council Presidency and European Integration.* Manchester, UK: Manchester University Press, 1992.

Kirchner, Emil Joseph. *The European Parliament: Performance and Prospects.* Aldershot, Hampshire, England: Gower, 1984.

Kitzinger, U.W. *The Politics and Economics of European Integration: Britain, Europe and the United States.* New York: Frederick A. Praeger, 1963.

Lindberg, Leon. *The Political Dynamics of European Economic Integration.* Stanford, Ca.: Stanford University Press, 1963.

Lindberg, Leon and Stuart Scheingold. *Europe's Would-Be Polity*. Englewood Cliffs, N.J.: Prentice-Hall, 1970.

Lindberg, Leon and Stuart Scheingold, eds. *Regional Integration*. Cambridge, Ma.: Harvard University Press, 1971.

Lodge, Juliet, ed. *The European Community: Bibliographical Excursions*. Phoenix, Ar.: The Oryx Press, 1983.

Ludlow, Peter. *Beyond 1992 Europe and Its Western Partners*, Brussels: Center for European Policy Studies, no. 38, 1989.

Maass, Arthur, ed. *Area and Power: A Theory of Local Government*. Glencoe, Il.: The Free Press, 1959.

Macridis, Roy C. *Foreign Policy in World Politics: States and Regions*. 7th ed. Englewood Cliffs, N.J.: Prentice Hall, 1989.

Mason, Henry L. *The European Coal and Steel Community: Experiment in Supranationalism*. The Hague: Martinus Nijhoff, 1955.

Mayne, Richard. *The Community of Europe Past, Present And Future*. New York: W.W. Norton and Company, Inc., 1962.

Miller, Charles. *Lobbying Government: Understanding and Influencing the Corridors of Power*. New York: Basil Blackwell, 1987.

Monnet, Jean. *Memoirs*. London: Collins, 1978.

Morgan, Annette. *From Summit to Council: Evolution in the EEC*. London: Chatham House, PEP, 1976.

Norton, Philip. *The British Polity*. New York: Longman, 1984.

Nye, Joseph S. *International Regionalism: Readings*. Boston: Little, Brown and Company, 1968.

O'Nuallain, Colm in collaboration with Jean-Marc Hoscheit, eds. *The Presidency of the European Council of Ministers: Impacts and Implications for National Government*. London: Croom Helm, 1985.

Pentland, Charles. *International Theory and European Integration*. London: Faber & Faber, 1973.

Rose, Richard and Ezra N. Suleiman, eds. *Presidents and Prime Ministers*. Washington, D.C.: American Enterprise Institute for Public Policy Research, 1980.

Sasse, Christoph, et al. *Decision-Making in the European Community*. New York: Praeger, 1977.

Sbragia, Alberta M., ed. *Euro-Politics: Institutions and Policymaking in the 'New' European Community*. Washington, D.C.: The Brookings Institution, 1992.

Schoutheete, Philippe. La Coopération Politique Européenne. Brussels: Labor, 1986.

Shell, Donald. *The House of Lords*. Totowa, N.J.: Barnes and Noble Books, 1988.

Spero, Joan. *The Politics of International Economic Relations*. 3rd ed. New York: St. Martin's Press, Inc., 1985.

154

Spotts, Frederick. *Italy, a difficult democracy: a survey of Italian politics.* New York: Cambridge University Press, 1986.
Tugendhat, Christopher. *Making Sense of Europe.* Harmondsworth, Middlesex, England: Penguin Books Limited, 1986.
Urwin, Derek W. *The Community of Europe: A History of European Integration Since 1945.* London: Longman, 1991.
Wallace, H., W. Wallace, and C. Webb, eds. *Policy Making in the European Community.* 2d ed. London: Wiley, 1983.
Werts, Jan. *The European Council.* Amsterdam: North-Holland, 1992.
Willis, Virginia. *Britons in Brussels: Officials in the European Commission and Council Secretariat.* London: Policy Studies Institute, 1982.
Wilson, Harold. *The Governance of Britain.* London: Weidenfeld and Nicolson and Michael Joseph, 1976.
Young, Hugo. *One of Us: A biography of Margaret Thatcher.* London: Macmillan, 1989.

Scholarly Journals and Other Periodicals

_____. "A Drama, but not a crisis." *The Times* 22 March 1984: 13.
Almaric, Jacques. "Le Sommet De La Haye: Une seule voix, trois bouches." *Le Monde* 27 June 1986: 3.
Apple, R. W., Jr. "Western Europeans Urge Role for PLO in Mideast Parley." *New York Times* 13 June 1980: 1.
Barnes, Hilary. "Doubt on Denmark pledge." *Financial Times* 9 July 1987: 3.
Bebr, Gerhard. "The Balance of Power in the European Communities." *Annuaire Européenne* 5 (1959): 53-79.
Berthoud, Roger. "After EEC's disappearance as a domestic political issue influence of civil servants is likely to increase." *The Times* 21 July 1975: 3.
Bieber, Roland. "The Institutions and the Decision-Making Process in the Draft Treaty Establishing the European Union." European University Institute Working Paper no. 164, 1985.
Bieber, Roland and Michael Palmer. "Power at the top — the EC Council in theory and practice." *World Today* August 1975 310-18.
Binder, David. "The Yugoslav Crisis: Why U.S. Is Bearing Down on Belgrade." *The New York Times* 27 May 1992: A4.
Bohnhof, Klaus. "Europeans fail to agree on farms and money." Reprinted in *The German Tribune* 13 December 1987: 1.
Bramson, Bo. "Le Conseil Européen: Son Fonctionnement Et Ses Resultats De 1975 A 1981." *Revue Du Marché Commun* 25 (1982): 624-42.

Bulletin of the EC. Published by the Commission of the European Communities.

_____. "Britain and Europe: Excuse me, is this the right bus?" *Economist* 17 December 1988: 52.

Buchan, David and Tim Dickson. "An end to the nay-saying." *Financial Times* 15 February 1988: 17.

Buchan, David. "EC bureaucracy claims summit deal as its own." *Financial Times* 16 February 1988: 2.

Buchan, David. "UK and Bonn edge towards EC budget deal." *Financial Times* 3 February 1988: 2.

Bulmer, Simon. "The European Council's First Decade: Between Interdependence and Domestic Politics." *Journal of Common Market Studies* 24 (December 1985): 89-104.

Burch, Martin. "The British Cabinet: A Residual Executive." *Parliamentary Affairs* 41 (January 1988): 34-48.

Cahen, Alfred. "The Western European Union (WEU) and NATO: Strengthening the Second Pillar of the Alliance." *Occasional Paper of The Atlantic Council of the United States* 1990.

Campbell, Edwina S. and Jack M. Seymour, Jr. "Franco-German Relations in Post-Cold War Europe." *Bulletin of the Atlantic Council of the United States* 10 July 1992: 4.

Charlier, Michael. "A change of understanding about the state and politics." Reprinted in *The German Tribune* 1 May 1992: 1,3.

Clines, Francis X. "European Leaders Voice Concern That Iran Affair Impairs Alliance." *New York Times* 7 December 1986: 1.

_____. "Danes' suspicion of Brussels underlined." *Financial Times* 20 June 1989: 6.

_____. "Denmark: Take it or leave it." *The Economist* 23 May 1992: 58.

Denton, Geoffrey. "Re-Structuring the EC Budget: Implications of the Fontainebleau Agreement." *Journal of Common Market Studies* 23 (December 1984): 117-40.

De Ruyt, Jean. "European Political Cooperation: Toward a Unified Foreign Policy." *Occasional Paper of The Atlantic Council of the United States* October 1989.

Dickson, Tim. "Accord on EC set-aside plan likely today." *Financial Times* 18 January 1988: 4.

Dickson, Tim and David Buchan. "The Community tries again." *Financial Times* 11 February 1988: 2.

Dickson, Tim and Quentin Peel. "European Community farm talks collapse in disarray." *Financial Times* 27 November 1987: 26.

Dickson, Tim and Quentin Peel. "Hopes of EC summit deal rise." *Financial Times* 5-6 December 1987: 1.

Dickson, Tim and William Dawkins. "EC welcomes German farm compromise." *Financial Times* 25 January 1988: 1.

Dickson, Tim. "Brussels starts to take Strasbourg more seriously." *Financial Times* 18 January 1988: 4.

Dickson, Tim. "European poll finds backing for CAP." *Financial Times* 3 February 1988: 2.

Dickson, Tim. "Genscher confirms Bonn farm policy line." *Financial Times* 1 February 1988: 2.

Dickson, Tim. "Genscher warns over UK stand on EC rebate." *Financial Times* 26 January 1988: 2.

Dickson, Tim. "High expectations recede as ministers bow out of talks." *Financial Times* 27 November 1987: 2.

Dickson, Tim. "Stabilizers herald CAP reform." *Financial Times* 23 February 1988: 32.

Doherty, Michael. "Prime-Ministerial Power and Ministerial Responsibility in the Thatcher Era." *Parliamentary Affairs* 41 (January 1988): 49-67.

Earle, John. "Open-purse policy suits Italy." *The Times* 17 March 1984: 6.

Eban, Abba. "The West Bank: why have Europe's diplomats played such an unimpressive role?" *The Times* 13 June 1980: 14.

Eder, Richard. "Common Market Warns Russians Not to Take Action Against Poland." *New York Times* 3 December 1980: A8.

_____. "EEC summit: No Danegeld for Europe." *The Economist* 12 December 1987: 56.

_____. "Europe's hidden leaders: West Germany Ja, Minister." *The Economist* 5 December 1987: 56.

_____. "Europe's top club of frequent flyers." *The Economist* 2 May 1992: 64.

_____. "Farmers: EC Too Powerful, Family Farm Threatened." *The Week in Germany* 14 July 1989: 6.

Fitzmaurice, John. "An Analysis of the European Community's cooperation procedure." *Journal of Common Market Studies* 26 (June 1988): 389-400.

_____. "France's hostages: A deal, a bribe, or a neat solution." *The Economist* 5 December 1987: 54-5.

Gack, Thomas. "Bent gherkin and other tales of the red tape." Reprinted in *The German Tribune* 23 October 1992.

Geddes, Diana. "Peace brings joy for French leader." *The Times* 28 June 1984: 5.

_____. "Gonzalez backs closer EC ties on defence." *Financial Times* 20 October 1987: 2.

Graham, George. "France urges progress on EC budget deadlock." *Financial Times* 10 February 1988: 2.

Haas, Ernst. "International Integration: The European and the Universal Process." *International Organization* 15 (Summer 1961): 366-92.

Haas, Ernst. "Technocracy, Pluralism and the New Europe" in Graubard, S.A., ed. *A New Europe* Boston: Beacon, 1967, 62-88.

Haas, Ernst. "Words can hurt you: or who said what to whom about regimes." *International Organization* 36 Spring (1982): 207-44.

Hadler, Wilhelm. "Gesture value in farmland reduction plan." Reprinted in *The German Tribune* 17 January 1988: 3.

Hagel-Sørenson, Karsten and Hjalte Rasmussen. "The Danish Administration and Its Interaction with the Community Administration." *Common Market Law Review* 22 (June 1985): 273-300.

Harvey, D.R. and K. J. Thomson. "Costs, Benefits and the Future of the Common Agricultural Policy." *Journal of Common Market Studies* 24 (September 1985): 1-20.

Haviland, Julian. "A Summit perspective from London, Paris, Rome and Bonn: British war on waste." *The Times* 17 March 1984.

Haviland, Julian and Ian Murray. "Britain stands firm on principles at EEC summit." *The Times* 20 March 1984: 1.

Haviland, Julian and Ian Murray. "Europe's leaders gather in new mood of hope." *The Times* 25 June 1984: 1.

Heath, Edward. "European unity over the next ten years: from Community to union." *International Affairs* 64 (Spring 1988): 199-207.

Hendriks, Gisela. "Germany and the CAP: national interests and the European Community." *International Affairs* 65 (Winter 1988-1989): 75-83.

Henig, Stanley. "The Institutional Structure of the European Communities." *Journal of Common Market Studies* 12 (1974): 373-409.

Hoffmann, Stanley. "Obstinate or Obsolete? The fate of the nation state and the case of Western Europe." *Daedalus* 95 (1966): 862-915.

Hornsby, Michael. "Europe says PLO must have voice in peace quest." *The Times* 14 June 1980: 1.

Hornsby, Michael. "Mrs. Thatcher ready for crisis action after rebuff by EEC." *The Times* 1 December 1979: 1.

Howe, Sir Geoffrey. "The European Pillar." *Foreign Affairs* 63 (Winter 1984-85): 330-43.

Hrbek, Rudolph. "The German Länder and the European Community." *Aussen Politik* 38 (1987): 120-33.

Ierodiaconou, Andriana. "Greek president to replace defeated PM at EC summit." *Financial Times* 22 June 1989: 2.

Jannuzzi, Giovanni. "Europe and a security dimension." *NATO Review* April 1991: 3.

Jonquieres, Guy. "Challenge to the post-war world order." *Financial Times Survey* 17 November 1988: 4.

_____. "Kinkel Appeals to Serbian Leadership to 'Stop Murder and Destruction.'" *The Week in Germany* 12 June 1992: 1.

Krisel, William and Christopher Wolf. "Unity in doubt: Maastricth Vote Jolts E.C. Bar." *The National Law Journal* 19 October 1992: 31-33.

LaFranchi, Howard. "The World From Brussels." *The Christian Science Monitor* 2 April 1991: 4.

_____. "Le Sommet De La Haye: Vers une aide aux Noirs sud-africains." *Le Monde* 28 June 1986: 1.

Lewis, Paul. "Common Market Showdown Today." *The New York Times* 19 March 1984: A3.

Leon N. Lindberg and Stuart A. Scheingold, eds. Special Issue "Regional Integration: Theory and Research." *International Organization* 24 (1970).

Lindberg, Leon. "The European Community as a Political System." *Journal of Common Market Studies* 5 (June 1967): 344-87.

Lodge, Juliet. "The role of EEC Summit Conferences." *Journal of Common Market Studies* 12 (December 1974): 337-45.

MacDonald, Susan. "Spirits lifted on EEC summit." *The Times* 23 November 1987: 24.

_____. "Major discovers that everybody loves a winner." *The Times* 10 June 1992: 8.

Malanczuk, Peter. "European Affairs and the 'Länder' (States) of the Federal Republic of Germany." *Common Market Law Review* 22 (1985): 23772.

Markham, James M. "For Europe, Talks Fizzle: Community's Summit Seen As Disappointing." *The New York Times* 7 December 1987: 5.

Marsh, David and Andrew Fisher. "Karl Otto Pohl: Sceptical champion of EC monetary integration." *Financial Times* 1 July 1989: 7.

Marsh, David and Andrew Fisher. "Pohl doubts need for EC bank." *Financial Times* 1-2 July 1989: 2.

Marsh, David. "Bonn soothes fears on French defence link." *Financial Times* 22 January 1988: 2.

Marsh, David. "Dr. Schmidt prescribes strong medicine for his successor." *Financial Times* 18 April 1989: 2.

Marsh, David. "Stoltenberg calls for EC to end all capital controls." *Financial Times* 18 March 1988: 2.

May, Simon. "The European Community and the task for the British Presidency in 1986." London: Centre for Policy Studies, 1986.

McEwen, Andrew and Nicholas Wood. "Divisions remain on EEC crisis." *The Times* 30 January 1988: 24.

McEwen, Andrew. "EEC backing for Britain's crusade." *The Times* 6 December 1986: 1.

Murray, Ian. "Mitterrand's London Mission." *The Times* 5 March 1984: 4.

Murray, Ian. "Mitterrand takes summit guests on tour of his European dream world." *The Times* 25-26 June 1985: 6.

Murray, Ian. "Papandreou demand puts damper on EEC summit." *The Times* 5 December 1984: 1.

Murray, Ian. "Summit deal has bought time but Thorn sees tough bargaining ahead." *The Times* 28 June 1984: 5.

Murray, Ian. "Thatcher claims good EEC deal for Britain." *The Times* 27 June 1984: 1.

Murray, Ian. "Thatcher determined not to give way at summit: 24 hours that can settle EEC future." *The Times* 19 March 1984: 6.

Nau, Henry R. "From integration to interdependence: gains, losses and continuing gaps." *International Organization* 33 (Winter 1979): 119-47.

Nicoll, W. "EEC budgetary strains and constraints." *International Affairs* 64 (Winter 1987-88): 27-42.

Nicoll, W. "The Long March of the EC's 1988 Budget." *Journal of Common Market Studies* 27 (December 1988): 161-69.

Nicoll, W. "The Luxembourg Compromise." *Journal of Common Market Studies* 23 (September 1984): 35-43.

Norman, Peter and Simon Holberton. "Papering over the exchange rate difference." *Financial Times* 14 June 1989: 24.

Nuttall, Simon. "European Political Co-operation and the Single European Act." *Yearbook of European Law* 5 (1985): 203-32.

Oakley, Robin and George Brock. "Thatcher warns of growing German power." *The Times* 16 May 1992: 1.

Osborn, Alan. "Belgium." *Europe: Magazine of the European Community* October 1989: 46.

Owen, Richard. "Britain offers 'clean slate' scheme to end EEC food surpluses." *The Times* 24 November 1987: 10.

Owen, Richard. "Britain puts brakes on radical EEC reforms." *The Times* 2 December 1986: 1.

Owen, Richard. "Brussels budget hopes fade." *The Times* 27 November 1987: 10.

Owen, Richard. "Cohesion equals division." *The Times* 20 November 1987: 12.

Owen, Richard. "Dispute over freed hostages could wreck EEC summit." *The Times* 2 December 1987: 8.

Owen, Richard. "EEC agrees on reform deal after marathon." *The Times* 4 December 1985: 1.

Owen, Richard. "EEC farm crisis: Thatcher showdown is looming." *The Times* 25 November 1987: 9.

Owen, Richard. "EEC summit deadlock on sanctions." *The Times* 27 June 1986: 1.

Owen, Richard. "Howe plans EEC Pretoria 'troika.'" *The Times* 25 June 1986: 1.

Owen, Richard. "Howe sticks to his guns on farm plan." *The Times* 26 January 1988: 6.

Owen, Richard. "Praying for a European farm reform miracle." *The Times* 30 November 1987: 7.

Owen, Richard. "South African Crisis: Caution in Europe despite growing clamor for action: EEC shies away from complete embargo." *The Times* 16 June 1986: 7.

Owen, Richard. "Thatcher averts immediate EEC sanctions at summit: Howe in solo mission to Pretoria." *The Times* 28 June 1986: 1.

_____. "Parliament June 27, 1984: Kinnock invites Tories to join fight against deal." *The Times* 28 June 1984: 4.

Peel, Quentin. "An explosive cocktail of national interests." *Financial Times* 2 December 1987: 26.

Peel, Quentin. "Belgian attempt to clear way for summit accord." *Financial Times* 29 June 1987: 1.

Peel, Quentin. "Bonn hardens position on farm demands." *Financial Times* 30 November 1987: 24.

Peel, Quentin. "Bonn plans compromise on EC finance." *Financial Times* 8 December 1987: 2.

Peel, Quentin. "Civil Servant." *Financial Times* 19 October 1987: 19.

Peel, Quentin. "Danes present EC reform deal." *Financial Times* 28 November 1987: 2.

Peel, Quentin. "Delors call for firm guidelines on European Community finance." *Financial Times* 25 June 1987: 1.

Peel, Quentin. "EC spending talks collapse." *Financial Times* 16 June 1987: 1.

Peel, Quentin. "Kohl's explosion dooms passionless summit." *Financial Times* 7 December 1987: 2.

Peel, Quentin. "Martens launches bid to avert EC summit crisis." *Financial Times* 22 June 1987: 1.

Peel, Quentin. "Plea for summit flexibility." *Financial Times* 4 December 1987: 28.

Peel, Quentin. "Surprising degree of accord at the EC Summit." *Financial Times* 2 July 1987: 3.

Peel, Quentin. "Thatcher rejects deal on EC rebate." *Financial Times* 3 December 1987: 1.

Pendergast, William R. "Roles and attitudes of French and Italian delegates to the European Community." *International Organization* 30 (Autumn 1976): 669-77.

Policy Statement. Published by The British Information Services.

_____. "Progress Made At EC Copenhagen Summit, Kohl Asserts." *The Week in Germany* 11 December 1987: 1-2.

Raun, Laura. "Consensus on Europe means domestic issues prevail." *Financial Times* 31 May 1989: 4.

_____. "Report on the German Presidency of the European Community." *Statements and Speeches* German Information Center 17 June 1988: 6.

_____. "Return fire," *The Economist* 19 October 1991: 54.

Rosenthal, A.M. "The Grim Lesson of Yugoslavia." *The Miami Herald*, 26 May 1992: 11A.

_____. "Seatless Minister." *The Times* 6 December 1986: 5.

Shell, Donald. "The British Constitution in 1988." *Parliamentary Affairs* 42 (July 1989): 287-301.

Sherwood, Frank P. "Maggie the Manager: Administrative Reform in Britain." *The Bureaucrat*. 20 (Summer 1991): 39-44.

Smith, Diana. "Cavaco Silva expects an Es500bn bonanza." *Financial Times* 16 February 1988: 2.

Stephens, Philip and David Buchan. "Thatcher faces party split over European elections." *Financial Times* 19 June 1989: 1.

Stephens, Philip and David Buchan. "The battle for a market-led Europe." *Financial Times* 23 May 1989: 22.

Stephens, Philip. "Britain put under new pressure to join EMS." *Financial Times* 14 September 1987: 18.

Stephens, Philip. "Britain to offer no timetable." *Financial Times* 26 June 1989: 1.

Stephens, Philip. "Thatcher faces pressure from ministers over Europe." *Financial Times* 21 June 1989: 1.

_____. "Stoltenberg Resigns, Ruhe Is New Defense Minister." *The Week In Germany* 3 April 1992: 1.

Swinbank, A. "The Common Agricultural Policy and the Politics of European Decision-Making." *Journal of Common Market Studies* 27 (June 1989): 303-22.

_____. "Thatcher stands by position on budget controls." *Financial Times* 2 July 1987: 1.

_____. "That gloriously uncertain feeling." *Financial Times* 26 June 1989: 14.

The Europa Year Book. London: Europa Publications Limited.

Tindemans, Leo. "Le Conseil Européen." *European Yearbook* 28 (1980): 3-12.

Tomkys, Roger. "European Political Cooperation and the Middle East: A personal perspective." *International Affairs* 63 (Summer 1987): 425-36.

_____. "Vegetables deal may go to pot." *Financial Times* 5 June 1987: 22.

Walker, Jenonne. "Fact and Fiction about a European Security Identity and American Interests." *Occasional Paper of the Atlantic Council of the United States* April 1992.

Wallace, Helen. "Negotiations and Coalition Formation in the European Community." *Government and Opposition* 20 (Autumn 1985): 453-72.

Welsh, Michael. "Labour Market Policy in the European Community: The British Presidency of 1986." London: Royal Institute of International Affairs, Chatham House, discussion paper no. 4, 1988.

_____. "West Germany's precision-engineered policy machine." *Economist* 5 December 1987: 76.

_____. "What's European for justice?" *The Economist* 3 December 1988: 52.

_____. "Who's afraid of Europe, now?" *The Economist* 16 September 1989: 22.

Wood, David. "Dublin feels impact of feminine tactics." *The Times* 1 December 1979: 4.

Wyles, John. "France and Italy divided over budget." *Financial Times* 28 November 1987: 2.

Wyles, John. "Summit Setbacks Hide Real Progress." *Europe, Magazine of the European Community* May-June 1984: 27.

Documents and Unpublished Papers

Bieber, Roland. "The Institutions and the Decision-Making Process in the Draft Treaty Establishing the European Union." European University Institute. Working paper no. 164, 1985.

Bonvicini, Gianni and Elfriede Regelsberger. "The Organizational and Political Implications of the Establishment of the European Council on Both European Community and EPC Decision Making." Paper presented to Kerkrade Colloquium on the European Council, 26-27 October 1984.

_____. "Conclusions of the European Council, Brussels, 11-13 February 1988." *European Community News*. Washington, D.C.: EC Office of Press and Public Affairs, 18 February 1988.

Dondelinger, Jean. "Le Conseil Européen." Paper available from the library of the Council of Ministers of the European Community, 20 November 1975.

Dondelinger, Jean. "Les Origines du Conseil Européen: Historique et Motivations." Paper presented to Colloque sur "le Conseil européen," Louvain-la-Neuve, 6-7 October 1977.

_____. "Draft Treaty establishing the European Union." European Parliament Directorate-General for Information and Public Relations Publications and Briefings Division, 1984.

_____. "Europe — the Future." Paper presented by the British PM to the Fontainebleau European Council, June 1984. *Journal of Common Market Studies* 23 (September 1984): 73-81.

_____. "European Union." Fourteenth Report from the House of Lords' Select Committee on the European Communities, Session 1985-86, Her Majesty's Stationery Office, H L 226.

_____. "Federalism and European Union: Past, Present and Future in the European Community." Paper presented to The European Community Studies Association Inaugural Conference, Washington, D.C., May 1989.

Holt, Stephen and Jean-Marc Hoscheit. "The European Council and Domestic Policy-Making." Paper presented to Kerkrade Colloquium on the European Council, 26-27 October 1984.

Lemaitre, Philippe. "Les Réalisations du Conseil Européen." Paper presented to Kerkrade Colloquium on the European Council, 26-27 October, 1984.

_____. "Maastricht Treaty establishing the European Union." *Europe Documents* 1750/1751.

_____. "Report drawn up on behalf of the Political Affairs Committee on the role of the European Parliament in its relations with the European Council." Working paper no. 1-739, 1981.

_____. "Report on European Institutions." Presented by the Committee of Three to the European Council, October 1979.

_____. "The Single Act: A new frontier for Europe." *Bulletin of the EC*, Supplement 1, 1987.

_____. "The Single European Act: A Government Information Booklet." Dublin: The Stationery Office, May 1987.

Wessels, Wolfgang. "The European Council A Denaturing of the Community or Indispensable Decision-Making Body?" Paper presented to Kerkrade Colloquium on the European Council, 26-27 October 1984.

Index

Afghanistan, 108
Agricultural Council, 31-32, 45-46,
   53(nn 52, 58), 91
Agriculture
   CAP, iv. *See also* Common
      Agricultural Policy
   Delors Plan on, 31-32, 45-46
   EC negotiations concerning,
      50(n20)
   milk quotas, 22
   U.S.-EC controversy over policy,
      139-140
Ambassadors. *See* Committee of
   Permanent Representatives
Andriessen, Frans, 91
Antici Group, ii, 28-29, 33-34
   role at European Council
      sessions, 57, 59, 61
Arab states, 11-12, 106
Athens European Council session,
   1983, 41, 107
Attali, Jacques, v
Austria, vi

Baker, James, 109
Belgium, 85, 121
Benelux countries, 3, 4, 9, 14, 69
Birmingham European Council
   session, 1992, 139
Bonn summit, 1961, 3-4
British budget dispute, xi, 21, 34, 42,
   46, 48(n2), 67
   details of, 76-82
British Trade Union Congress
   (TUC), 35
Brussels
   European Council session of
      1984, 42, 67, 78

European Council session of
   1987, 52(n45), 57, 58, 68, 69, 85-
   87
European Council session of
   1988, 25, 68, 90-94
Brussels Treaty of 1948, ix
Budget, EC
   Budget Council, 46
   resources, 76, 83-84, 92-93,
      98(n32), 140
   spending, 80-81, 84-85, 85-86, 92.
      See also Common Agricultural
      Policy
   See also British budget dispute
Budgetary discipline, 80-81, 84-85,
   92
   British insistence on, 85-86
   See also Common Agricultural
      Policy
Bulmer, Simon, i
Bureaucratization, European
   Council, 60-61, 71-72. *See also*
   Institutionalization
Bush, George, 109, 116-117, 122, 138
Butler, Sir Michael, 30, 64, 80-81

Callaghan, James, 77
Camp David process, 106
CAP. *See* Common Agricultural
   Policy
Carrington, Lord, 105-106
Carter, Jimmy, 106, 126(n24)
Chile, 115
China, 113, 114
Chirac, Jacques, 58, 74(n26), 88, 90
Coalition governments, 55, 57-58
Cocor. *See* Co-ordinating
   Commission

Commission, xii-xiii
  accountability to European
    Parliament, 38-39, 40-41,
    51(n32)
  and budget disputes, 77, 80, 82-96
  cooperation with presidency, 34-
    36
  effect of European Council on, 23,
    42-43
  and formation of European
    Council, 2, 15, 17(n12)
  institutional weakness in, 13
  integration and role of, 130-133,
    135-136
  membership, 51(n33)
  and political cooperation/foreign
    affairs, 101-102, 114-115, 119,
    125(n17)
  public views of, 21-22, 140
  representation on European
    Council, 11, 18(n32), 55
Committee of Permanent
    Representatives (COREPER),
    iv, xii, 16(n3)
  role of, 13, 27-31, 47, 131
  shaping European Council
    agendas, 62
Common Agricultural Policy
    (CAP), iv, 4, 5-6, 76, 134
  British budget dispute and
    reforming, 78, 80-81
  Delors Plan and reforming, 82-83,
    84-85, 86, 87, 88, 90, 92, 93,
    99(n65)
Common Customs Tariff, 76
Communication
  between EC and U.S., 108-109,
    126(n32)
  during European Council
    sessions, 58-60, 61, 72(n9)
  informal contacts, 65-72, 73(n25)
  "troika" arrangement, 127(n47)
Conclave, 34

Conference on Security and Co-
    operation in Europe (CSCE), iv-
    v, 70, 101, 113, 115
  Measures and Conference on
    Disarmament in Europe, 118
Cooperation procedure, 40
Co-ordinating Commission (Cocor),
    49(n18)
Copenhagen
  European Council session of
    1987, i, 25, 28, 31-32, 87-90
  summit, 1973, 11-12, 18(n32)
COREPER. *See* Committee of
    Permanent Representatives
Correction mechanism, 77, 79-81,
    89, 91, 93
Council of Ministers, xi-xii, 2, 16(n3)
  advisory teams for, 55
  and Delors Plan, 86
  effect of European Council on, 23,
    24, 44-47, 82
  implementing European Council
    decisions, 11, 59-60
  majority voting in, 4-5, 138
  role of, 6, 13, 37
  secretariat, 26-27
  See also Agricultural Council;
    General Affairs Council
CSCE. *See* Conference on Security
    and Co-operation in Europe
Cyprus, 113

Decisionmaking
  Council of Ministers, xi-xii
  crisis in EC, 13-14
  effectiveness and preparation for
    European Council sessions, 20-
    23
  EPC and, 119-120
  European Council role in, ii, xi, 1,
    16, 23-24, 54, 71, 82, 146(n9)
  by European Parliament, 40

integration and process of, 130-145

smaller EC countries on, 124(n10)

De Gaulle, Charles
monetary policy, 8
on political cooperation, 101, 102
summits and European integration, 2-5, 17(n5), 139

Delegations, 133
to European Council sessions, 57-61, 71

Delors, Jacques, vi, 35, 42, 55
asessment of EPC, 100, 101
and Delors Plan negotiations, 82, 85, 88, 91, 96
effectiveness of, 132-133, 145
on foreign affairs, 67
view of European Council, 135-136

Delors II, 140

Delors Plan
agricultural ministers and, 31-32, 45-46
Commission proposal of, 37, 82-85
European Council role, xi, 45, 75, 99(n69)
European Parliament's role in, 40-41
as example of EC decisionmaking, 132, 133
negotiations on, 25, 28, 52(n40), 68, 85-96
technical complexity of, i-ii, 27

Denmark
on foreign affairs, 106, 118
on integrationist issues, 10, 14
parliament and EC matters, 32-33, 72(n10)
presidency, 88
public opinion in, 60, 139

De Ruyt, Jean, 108

d'Estaing, Giscard, 50(n20), 103, 133
and EMS, vi
relationship with Schmidt, 70
role in founding European Council, 1, 2, 14, 54, 55, 60

Development, 83, 98(n29), 137. See also Structural Funds

Directorates-general (DGs), xii, xiii

Discussion papers, 63-64, 73(n20)

Dondelinger, Jean, 3

Draft Treaty of European Union, 129

Dublin
European Council session of 1979, 77
European Council session of 1984, 36

Dumas, Roland, 70, 133

EAGGF Guidance Section, 83

Eastern and Central Europe, 100-101, 112, 114-115, 143-144

East-West relations, 66-67, 110-111, 113, 126(n39)

Eban, Abba, 106

EBRD. See European Bank for Reconstruction and Development

EC. See European Community

Ecofin, xi

Economic relations, 124(n7)
adjusting international, 8-9, 18(n21)
EC goals for, 136-137, 139
European Council effectiveness in, 13
German unification and effect on, 141-142
interdependence and, 7-9, 17(n17), 18(n37)
U.S.-European, 109
See also Monetary policy; Trade policy

ECSC. *See* European Coal and Steel
Community
ECU. *See* European Currency Unit
Edinburgh
European Council session of
1992, 140, 142
Summit, x
EEC. *See* European Economic
Community
EFTA. *See* European Free Trade
Association
Ellemann-Jensen, Uffe, 134, 139
EMS. *See* European Monetary
System
EMU. *See* European Economic and
Monetary Union
Energy policy, 18(n34), 137. *See also*
Oil crisis
Environment, 46
EPC. *See* European Political
Cooperation
ERDF. *See* European Regional
Development Fund
ERM. *See* Exchange Rate
Mechanism
Ersbøll, Niels, 26-27
ESF. *See* European Social Fund
Euratom. *See* European Atomic
Energy Community
European Agriculture Guidance
and Guarantee Fund (EAGGF),
76
European Atomic Energy
Community (Euratom), v, vii,
16(n4)
European Bank for Reconstruction
and Development (EBRD), v
European Coal and Steel
Community (ECSC), v, 16(n4)
European Community (EC)
European Council effects on, 21,
23-24. *See also* Integration

European Council involvement in
internal matters of, 75, 82
institutions of, xi-xii
membership, 6-7
on political cooperation, 100-104
and preparing for European
Council sessions, 24-36
scholarship on, i
See also Commission; Council of
Ministers; European Council;
European Parliament
European Council
and British budget dispute, 78-82
Delors Plan negotiations, 85-96
effects on EC institutions of, 23-
24, 36-37, 41-48. *See also*
European Community
extraordinary meetings and
formal sessions of, 48(n7), 54-
65. *See also cities of specific
meetings*
formation of, x, 2-15
informal contacts, 65-72
integration and, 130-145. *See also*
Integration
involvement in internal EC
matters, 75, 82
legitimacy of, 1-2, 15-16, 99(n69)
link with European Parliament,
39-41
membership, xii, 55-56
political cooperation/security
issues, 101-102, 104-123
preparing for sessions, 20-23, 24-
36, 47-48
role of, x-xi, 54, 146(n9)
scholarship on, i
staff, 56. *See also* Delegations
See also Presidency
European Council, The (Werts), i
*European Council: Decision-Making in
European Politics, The* (Bulmer
and Wessels), i

European Court of Justice, xii
European Currency Unit (ECU), v
European Defense Community, 102, 124(n10)
European Economic and Monetary Union (EMU), vi
  Commission and, 37
  European Council support for, 6, 9, 12
  Maastricht treaty on, 137
European Economic Area, vi
European Economic Community (EEC), i, v, 3, 16(n4). *See also* European Community
European Free Trade Association (EFTA), v-vi, 5, 132
European Monetary System (EMS), vi, 32, 99(n69), 133, 141
European Parliament
  budgetary powers, 4, 6, 52(n40)
  direct elections, 14, 23-24
  effect of European Council on, 2, 23-24, 44, 47
  on human rights, 116, 143
  integration issues and, 129, 145
  motions to censure Commission in, 51(n32)
  and political cooperation, 101-102, 125(n16)
  role of, xiii, 38-41, 135
European Political Cooperation (EPC), vii, viii-ix, xii
  and Eastern and Central Europe, 112
  European Council and defining role of, 118-120
  European Parliament on, 125(n16)
  formation of, 100-101, 103-104, 125(n15), 128(n57)
  and Gulf War, 120-121
  independence from U.S. of, 108-109
  and Middle East, 105-106

and Yugoslavia, 121-123
  See also Foreign Policy; Political cooperation; Security
European Political Union, 102-103
European Regional Development Fund (ERDF), 83
European Social Fund (ESF), 83
Exchange Rate Mechanism (ERM), vii, 8, 18(n21), 32, 141

Falklands, 106
Farm Ministers. *See* Agricultural Council
Federalism, 2, 129-130, 142. *See also* Integration
Financing. *See* Budget, EC
Finland, vi
FitzGerald, Garret, 69
Folketing Market Relations Committee (MRC), 32-33
Fontainebleau European Council session, 1984, 27, 42, 67, 79, 110
Foreign ministries
  COREPER member connections to, 27-28
  and developing political cooperation, 103, 104. *See also* Political cooperation
  EC involvement by, 49(n13), 70
  participation in European Council by, 55
  See also General Affairs Council
Foreign policy
  Commission's role in, 132
  Eastern and Central Europe, 100-101, 112, 114-115, 143-144
  EPC role in, vii, viii-ix, 118-120. *See also* European Political Cooperation
  expansion of European Council involvement in, 112-123
  and Gulf War, 109, 120-121

and Middle East, 11-12, 18(n34),
105-106, 113-114, 128(n64)
non-interference, 116. *See also*
Human rights
post-Cold War, 111-112. *See also*
East-West relations
and South Africa, 67, 104, 105,
106-107
and Yugoslavia, 109, 121-123,
125(n17), 144
See also Political cooperation;
Security
Fouchet, Christian, 3
Fouchet Plan, 3-4, 102-103, 124(n10)
France
and CAP, 5-6
and Delors Plan negotiations, 87,
89-90, 91
ideology and integration in, 2-5,
137
internal politics, 138, 140
political cooperation and foreign
affairs, 102, 103, 106, 109, 114-
115, 122
presidency, 114-115, 133
relations with Germany, 68-69,
141, 146(n18)
representatives for European
Council, 55-56, 58

G-7. *See* Group of Seven
GATT. *See* General Agreement on
Tariffs and Trade
General Affairs Council, 27
effect of European Council on, 44,
46
role of, 28, 31, 32-34
shaping European Council
agendas, 62
See also Foreign ministries
General Agreement on Tariffs and
Trade (GATT), vii, 10, 109, 140

Genscher, Hans-Dietrich, 50(n22),
70, 91, 134
Germany
and Delors Plan negotiations, 87,
88, 89-93
on foreign affairs, 106, 112, 115,
116, 122
on instituting GATT, 10
internal political considerations,
33, 50(n22), 90, 93, 137
monetary policy, 9
presidency, 91
relations with France, 68-69,
146(n18)
unification and effect on EC, 140-
142
Gonzalez, Felipe, 86, 92, 112, 137
Gorbachev, Mikhail, 66-67, 115
Goria, Giovanni, 89
Great Britain
Community membership for, 5,
6-7
and currency controversies, vi,
32, 141
and Delors Plan negotiations, 85-
86, 87, 88-93
ideologies and integration issues,
9, 10, 14, 16(n4), 51(n28), 132,
137
informal talks with Ireland, 69
internal political considerations,
30, 35-36, 73(n13), 124(n8)
on political cooperation and
foreign affairs, 106, 107, 109-
111, 118, 121, 122
Greece, 67, 106, 118
Group of 24, 114-115
Group of Seven (G-7), viii, 111, 114,
117, 127(n41)
Guillaume, Françoise, 91
Gulf War, 109, 120-121

Hague, The
  European Council session of
    1986, 58, 65, 67, 73(n20), 105,
    106-107
  summit, 1969, 5-6, 17(n14), 103
Hannay, Sir David, 68
Hanover European Council session,
    1988, 25
Haughey, Charles, 69
Heath, Edward, 10
Heeremann, Constantin, 90
Helsinki Final Act, iv, 115-116
Howe, Sir Geoffrey, 32, 34, 70, 86,
    110, 123
Human rights, iv, 112, 113, 115-116,
    117, 143-144
Hungary, 115
Hurd, Douglas, 120

Iceland, vi
Ideology
  EC integration and national, 136-
    137. See also Integration
IGCs. See Intergovernmental
    conferences
Informal contacts, 65-72, 73(n25)
  and British budget dispute, 78
Ingham, Bernard, 110
Institutionalization
  of European Council, x
  of political cooperation, 101, 103-
    104
  See also Bureaucratization,
    European Council
Integration
  and CAP, 78
  Delors Plan and, 94
  European disagreements over, 2-
    5, 6-7, 9, 10, 14-15
  future prospect of, 136-145
  intergovernmentalism and effect
    on, 24, 41-48, 129-136

  political cooperation/security
    issues, 102, 120
Interdependence, economic, 17(n17)
  effect on government policy, 7-9,
    18(n37)
  See also Economic relations
Intergovernmental conferences
    (IGCs), viii, 70, 118
"International Role of the European
    Community," 112, 127(n45)
Iran-Contra scandal, 66
Ireland, 10, 69, 93
  on foreign affairs, 106, 118,
    128(n57)
Israel, 106, 125(n23)
Italy, vi, 4, 29-30
  and Delors Plan negotiations, 87,
    93
  on foreign affairs, 106

Jannuzzi, Giovanni, 112
Jenkins, Roy, 133
Jumbo Councils, 41-42, 52(n45)

Kiesinger, Kurt, 5
Kinkel, Klaus, 121, 141
Kohl, Helmut, 68, 141, 142
  and Delors Plan negotiations, 25,
    89, 90, 91, 92, 133
  on foreign affairs, 106
  relations with British ministers,
    70, 71
Kurds, 117

Lawson, Sir Nigel, 32
Legitimacy
  of Commission, 22
  of Delors Plan, 95
  EC integration and, 143
  of European Council, 1-2, 15-16,
    99(n69)
  for military action, 123
Liechtenstein, vi

London Declaration, 66
London European Council session, 1986, 62-63, 64, 66-67, 82, 108, 111
Lubbers, Ruud, 89, 106-107
Luns, Joseph, 7
Luxembourg, 30, 93
  European Council session of 1980, 50(n20)
  European Council session of 1985, 67
  European Council session of 1991, 116, 117
  European Council session of 1992, 140
Luxembourg Compromise, 4

Maastricht European Council session, 1991, ii, 117-120
Maastricht Treaty on European Union, x, xiii, 60, 118-120, 128(n64), 130, 136-140
  provisions on EMU, vi
  provisions on foreign policy and security, xvii, 117-120
Madrid European Council session, 1989, 32, 113-114
Major, John, 32, 70, 116-117, 133
  ideology and integration issues, 137, 146(n13)
  and political cooperation, 111
MCAs. *See* Monetary Compensatory Accounts
Merger Treaty (1965), iv, 16(nn 3, 4), 47
Middle East, 11-12, 18(n34), 105-106, 113-114, 128(n64)
Mitterrand, François, 79, 133
  and British budget dispute, 42
  and Delors Plan negotiations, 68, 89
  and French political considerations, 58, 137, 138, 140

Mondale, Walter, 106
Monetary Compensatory Accounts (MCAs), 68, 69, 74(n37)
Monetary policy
  currency policy, v, 6
  EMS and EMU, vi
  ERM, vii
  G-7 role in, viii
  German unification and 1992 currency crisis, 141-142
  interdependence and international monetary crisis, 7-9, 17(n17)
Monnet, Jean, v, 11, 13-14
MRC. *See* Folketing Market Relations Committee

Natali, Lorenzo, 55
NATO. *See* North Atlantic Treaty Organization
Neo-functionalism, 130
Netherlands, 15, 55, 72(n2)
  on British EC membership, 7
  and Delors Plan negotiations, 89, 90
  on foreign affairs, 106
Nixon, Richard, 7, 10
Noël, Emile, 57
Non-interference, 116
North Atlantic Treaty Organization (NATO), viii, 109, 118
Norway, vi
Nuclear weapons, 111-112, 116-117
Nuttall, Simon, 125(n15)

Oil crisis, 11-12, 105
Ordóñez, Francisco Fernández, 112

Papandreou, George, 65, 107
Paris
  summit, 1961, 2-3
  summit, 1972, 7, 9-11
  summit, September 1974, 14

summit, December 1974, 1, 14-16
Paris Treaty of 1951, v, 3
Peacekeeping, 112
Petersburg Declaration, 119
PoCo. *See* Political Committee
Poland, 112, 115
Political Committee (PoCo), viii-ix, 103, 104
Political cooperation, 16(n1)
    European Community on, 100-101, 102-104
    European Council as organ for, 15-16, 101-102, 104-123, 128(n64)
    summits and arguments over, 3-4, 5, 6-7, 9, 11-13
    See also European Political Cooperation; Foreign policy; Security
Political Directors, 68, 103
Politics
    and CAP reform, 90, 93
    EC governments and internal, 33, 35-36, 50(n22), 73(n13), 108, 122, 140. *See also specific countries*
Pompidou, Georges, 2, 5, 6, 9, 11, 12-13
Portugal, 93-94, 95, 118
Presidency
    cooperation with Commission, 34-36, 37-38
    in Delors Plan negotiations, 85, 88, 91, 96
    role of, 24-26, 42, 43-44
    setting agendas, 61-63
    staff for, 56
    "troika" arrangement, 114, 127(n47)
Public relations
    EC and British, 124(n8)
    European Council concerns with, x, 21-22

heads of government and, 60
Maastricht referenda, 138-140
military actions and, 123
See also Politics

Question time, 39

Reagan, Ronald, 66, 73(n25), 110
Redistributive policies, 132
Regional Fund, 52(n40)
Rejkjavík Summit, 66, 74(n26), 110
Report of the Three Wise Men, 71
Resources, EC, 76, 83-84, 92-93, 98(n32), 140
Rhodes European Council session, 1988, 112, 127(n45)
Rocard, Michel, 53(n52)

Schlüter, Poul, 72(n10), 88
Schmidt, Helmut, vi, 53(n52), 73(n25), 133, 141
    relationship with d'Estaing, 70
    role in founding European Council, 54, 55, 60
Scope enlargement, 95, 130
SDI. *See* Strategic Defense Initiative
SEA. *See* Single European Act
Security
    Commission's role in, 132
    EC cooperation on, 101, 110-112, 113, 116-117, 118, 128(n57), 142
    supranational organizations concerned with, iv-v, vii, viii, ix, xii
Set-aside program, 87, 89, 90, 91, 132
Single European Act (SEA), ix, xiii
    budgetary difficulties in enacting, 84
    effect on European Parliament, 40
    and European Council, 1, 67, 130
    on majority voting, 5, 15

on political cooperation, 103-104, 118, 128(n57)
"Single Group of Preparation," 41
Solemn Declaration, 118
South Africa, 67, 104, 105, 106-107
Spain, 95
  and Delors Plan negotiations, 91-92, 99(n61)
  on foreign affairs, 106, 112-114
  presidency, 112-114
  and WEU, 118
Spending controls. *See* Budgetary discipline
Spillover, 130
Spinelli, Altiero, 129
Stoltenberg, Gerhard, 50(n22), 116
Strasbourg European Council session, 1989, 115-116
Strategic Defense Initiative (SDI), 110
Structural Funds, 83, 85, 89-90, 92, 99(n61), 140
Stuttgart European Council session, 1983, 64, 79
Subsidiarity, 143
Summitry, 2-16, 17(n12), 102
Sweden, vi
Switzerland, xi

Technical Councils, 31-32, 46. *See also* Council of Ministers
Thatcher, Margaret
  anti-integrationism, 2, 17(n5), 134, 137
  and British budget dispute, 76, 77-81, 145
  and British politics, 60, 73(n13)
  and Delors Plan negotiations, 85-86, 88, 89, 92-93, 133
  in European Council, 21, 22, 32, 48(n2), 67, 68, 135, 138
  on foreign affairs, 106, 107, 109-111

informal contacts with Ireland, 69
  presidency of, 62-63
  relationship with Delors, 35-36, 133
  relationship with Kohl, 71
Thorn, Gaston, 79
Tindemans, Leo, 71
Trade policy
  in agriculture, iv. *See also* Agriculture
  EFTA, v-vi
  G-7 role, viii
  GATT, vii, 10, 109, 140
  See also Economic relations
Trans-Atlantic Declaration, 126(n32)
Treaty of Rome, iv, xiii, 1-2, 3, 15
TUC. *See* British Trade Union Congress
Tugendhat, Sir Christopher, 34, 78
Turkey, 67, 116

UN. *See* United Nations
United Nations (UN), ix
  Europeans and Security Council, 121
  foreign affairs and, 101, 114
  human rights and peacekeeping, 112, 122
United States
  controversy over agricultural policy with, 139-140
  foreign policy and EC relations, 105, 106, 108-111, 114, 117, 120-121, 122, 142-143
  and GATT talks, 10
  monetary/economic policy and, 7, 8-9, 18(n21)
  reaction to European integration, 138

Value added tax (VAT), 76, 79, 98(n32), 99(n63), 134

Van den Broek, Hans, 104, 125(n17), 134

Van Miet, Karel, 131

VAT. *See* Value added tax

Venice Declaration on the Middle East, 18(n34), 105-106, 125(n23)

Venice European Council session, 1980, 105-106

Wallace, Helen, 131

Webb, Carole, 45

Werts, Jan, i

Wessels, Wolfgang, i

Western European Union (WEU), ix, 70, 110-111, 118, 119, 121 working groups, 126(n37)

West German Farmers' Association, 90, 99(n65)

WEU. *See* Western European Union

Williamson, David, 68

Wilson, Harold, 13, 14, 77

Yeltsin, Boris, 124(n7)

Yugoslavia, 109, 121-123, 125(n17), 144

17 55